Homer's Iliad

BOOKS I–VI

A Commentary on Homer's Iliad

BOOKS I–VI

M. M. WILLCOCK

*Professor of Classics in the University of Lancaster
and formerly Fellow of Sidney Sussex College, Cambridge*

MACMILLAN

ST MARTIN'S PRESS

First published 1970 *by*
MACMILLAN AND CO LTD

London and Basingstoke
Associated companies in New York Toronto
Dublin Melbourne Johannesburg and Madras

Library of Congress catalog card no. 74–108403

SBN (boards) 333 11307 1
(paper) 333 11319 5

Printed in Great Britain by
RICHARD CLAY (THE CHAUCER PRESS), LTD
Bungay, Suffolk

CONTENTS

List of Maps   vii

Preface   ix

INTRODUCTION

  I   Homer and the Mycenaean Age. History and Language   xi
 II   Mythology   xiv
III   Formulas and Themes   xvii
 IV   Scansion   xxi
  V   Bibliography   xxvi

COMMENTARIES ON BOOKS I–VI

  I   *The Quarrel between Achilleus and Agamemnon*   I
 II   *The Dream of Agamemnon; the Testing of*
     the Morale of the Army; the Catalogue of Ships;
     the Trojan Catalogue   35
III   *Preparations for the Single Combat between*
     Paris and Menelaos; the View from the Wall;
     the Single Combat; Paris and Helen   91
 IV   *The Breaking of the Truce; Agamemnon's*
     Review; the Beginning of the Battle   117
  V   *The Great Deeds of Diomedes*   147
 VI   *Continued Fighting; Meeting of Glaukos*
     and Diomedes; Hektor in Troy   187

INDEXES

  I   Greek   223
 II   English   227

LIST OF MAPS

1 Homeric geography: northern and central Greece   67
2 Homeric geography: the Peloponnese   72
3 Homeric geography: Asia Minor, etc.   86

PREFACE

THERE is a need for a new English-language commentary on the
Iliad, suitable for school and university students. The existing ones, by
D. B. Monro (Oxford U.P., 1884) and Leaf and Bayfield (Macmillan,
1895–8), have both given good service; but Homeric studies have
hardly stood still in the intervening seventy years, and there is much
that a present-day student ought to be told which is not to be found in
them. The present volume is the first of four, the rest of which should
appear in the next few years. The notes have been based on T. W.
Allen's Oxford Classical Text, but I have attempted to point out the
few occasions where a student using another text may meet a different
reading.

This edition differs from its predecessors in one or two respects,
apart from the fact that it is being published on its own, without the
Greek text. There is no grammatical introduction. Unfamiliar forms
and features of Homeric Greek are noted when they first occur in each
book. Moreover, references are kept to a minimum outside the con-
fines of the individual books. The effect of this is that each book is self-
contained, and each would be equally suitable for the beginner to start
on. It is true that this has involved a certain amount of repetition in the
notes, e.g. an exactly similar note on a common feature such as *tmesis*
will be found at the point of first occurrence in each book. This
duplication seemed more desirable than an elaborate system of cross-
references which few follow up, or the compilation of a grammatical
introduction which few consult.

I have deliberately made the notes as full as possible for the first
sixty lines or so of each book. The reason for this is the same, that each
book may be a student's introduction to Homer, in which case he
needs the completest assistance with the initially strange forms and
particles. I strongly recommend to such a student the use of Autenrieth's *Homeric Dictionary* in preference to a general Greek lexicon.
The fact that the vocabulary is limited to Homer more than com-
pensates for any awkwardness caused by the slightly old-fashioned

presentation (first edition 1877, but still in print). Finally, if, in spite of my intention to explain all unfamiliar forms and endings as they first occur in each book, a particle or other small word is not understood, and recourse to the dictionary is of no avail, the Greek Index at the end of this volume should be consulted; in it I have tried to include all those forms which would have appeared in a grammatical introduction as variants on common words.

My debts to others are naturally immense. I have been most helped by the commentaries of Pierron, Faesi, Leaf and Ameis–Hentze–Cauer; and by P. von der Mühll's *Kritisches Hypomnema zur Ilias*, by P. Chantraine's *Grammaire Homérique* and (on questions of arms and armour) Miss H. L. Lorimer's *Homer and the Monuments*. In addition I wish to record my gratitude to Mr E. C. Kennedy, who gave most helpful advice about the form of the commentary, and to Mr J. L. Creed, Mr M. J. Osborne, Mr J. G. Randall, Professor B. R. Rees, Dr D. C. A. Shotter and Mr M. A. Thorpe, each of whom kindly read part of this volume in typescript and made valuable suggestions. The maps, on pp. 67, 72 and 86, are reprinted from *A Companion to Homer* with the kind permission of Dr Stubbings and the publishers.

On the difficult question of the spelling of Greek proper and place-names, it does not seem possible to be wholly consistent. My general practice has been to avoid the Latinised forms. If there is an English form which is in common use, such as Helen, Priam or Corinth, I have used it; otherwise I have normally transliterated the Greek name. Thus the notes refer to Aias, Achilleus, Patroklos and not to Ajax, Achilles, Patroclus.

M. M. W.

Lancaster, 1969

INTRODUCTION

I. HOMER AND THE MYCENAEAN AGE. HISTORY AND LANGUAGE

THE *Iliad*, composed probably about 750 B.C., purports to describe a brief episode in the war against Troy, which according to Greek tradition took place shortly after 1200. The poet was thus dealing with events some four and a half centuries before his own time.

From about 1600 B.C. a rich and powerful civilisation had flourished in the southern part of Greece, centred on the city of Mycenae (Greek *Mykenai*) near the east coast of the Peloponnese. We call that civilisation, unearthed for us during the last hundred years by the archaeologists, the Mycenaean age. One of its last exploits, if we may assume that the heroic traditions of later Greece had a basis in historical fact, was the sending of an expedition to the city of Troy at the entrance to the narrows that lead to the Black Sea, and the eventual destruction of Troy.

By that time it appears that the empire of Mycenae was already beginning to weaken, and in the following century waves of more barbarous invaders from the north destroyed the Mycenaean citadels one after another. These were (or included) the Dorians. Their invasion had two important results: in the first place it drove some of the Greeks who had occupied the country before to leave their homes and emigrate to the islands in the Aegean Sea and cities on the coast of Asia Minor; secondly, it ushered in a dark age of several centuries, in which life was hard, communities were separate and the glories of the Mycenaean past became a heroic legend. Their memory was preserved, not in writing because the knowledge of writing was lost in this period but orally, and particularly in verse. The *Iliad* was composed when Greece was emerging from the dark age, in the eighth century; of its poet, Homer, next to nothing is known or can be surmised, except that he was an Ionian Greek from across the Aegean Sea, where the memory of the Mycenaeans may be presumed to have survived most strongly among their descendants.

DATES

c. 1600–1100	The Mycenaean age
c. 1200	Supposed date of the Trojan War
c. 1100	Dorian invasion
c. 750	Composition of the *Iliad*

The reconstruction of the time relationship between the *Iliad* and the society it describes is based on (*a*) the evidence of history and archaeology for the whole period,[1] (*b*) the mythological background to the *Iliad* (section II of the Introduction) and (*c*) the internal atmosphere of the poem, which makes it clear that the poet is looking back to a heroic past, while himself living in an unheroic present. Moreover, (*d*) the *language* of the Homeric poems is strong evidence for a considerable antiquity of this literary form. This is shown by two features: first, it is a composite language, made up of words and forms from several different dialects, and must have taken a long time to develop; secondly, there are preserved like fossils in certain *fixed phrases* in this poetic language very ancient words no longer current in eighth-century Greek. These, often titles of the gods, such as

ἀργειφόντης	II 103	(Hermes)
Ἀτρυτώνη	II 157	(Athene)

had their origins in the remote past.

The fixed phrases, which were the medium of the preservation of these words, will be further discussed in section III of this Introduction; the composite dialect may be briefly described here. Of the three main divisions of the Greek language, Ionic, Aeolic and West Greek (including Doric), the Homeric dialect is both predominantly and in appearance Ionic, but contains a large number of Aeolic forms and case-endings, often acting as metrically useful alternatives to their Ionic equivalents. Behind the mixture of these two dialects there is a substratum (mostly of alternative vocabulary) which is called Arcado-Cyprian, because these words found in Homer have parallels only in those two remote and easily by-passed areas of the Greek world, Arcadia and Cyprus, where they were no doubt as much survivals from the distant past as they are in the Homeric dialect.

Whatever the true original relationship between the three dialects

---

[1] Knowledge of the Mycenaean age has been greatly expanded during the last hundred years, since the first excavations at Troy by the German H. Schliemann in 1870. For the resulting picture, see (among the works cited in the bibliography at the end of this section) Kirk, pt i, Nilsson, chap. ii, and Severyns, vol. i.

Ionic, Aeolic and Arcado-Cyprian, and between them and the presumed 'Achaean' spoken by the Mycenaeans (and now once again
partially extant through the decipherment by Ventris and Chadwick
of the Linear B tablets from Knossos and Pylos), it is clear that heroic
verse had had a long history before the *Iliad*, during which it had
gathered to itself relics of its passage through different linguistic areas,
whether of space or time. Scholars are agreed that this development
had gone on for centuries.

It is then a composite language, but mainly Ionic. Ionic itself, however, was still developing, and Homeric Greek is archaic compared
with that of the Attic–Ionic authors of the classical period. In fact it is
helpful, as a way of describing the state of the language, to mention
two changes that were taking place around the time of the composition
of the *Iliad*. The first is the loss of the digamma. This letter (written *F*
and pronounced *w*) disappeared from most Greek dialects, including
Ionic, and is not found in the text of Homer. But the influence of the
lost consonant is still discernible in the scansion of the lines; it can still
have an effect in situations of *lengthening by position, correption* and
hiatus (for the meaning of these terms, see pp. xxiv ff.) just as if it was
still there, as no doubt it partially was in pronunciation. Even in the
same word the digamma is sometimes respected in scansion and sometimes disregarded. For example, 'honey-sweet wine' occurs from time
to time at the end of the line in both the accusative and the genitive
case – μελιηδέα οἶνον, μελιηδέος οἴνου. In the accusative the *hiatus*
is only apparent, as οἶνος originally began with a digamma (cp. Latin
vinum); in the genitive the digamma has been forgotten. (A selection
of words that normally have the digamma could also include (*F*)ἄναξ,
(*F*)ἰδεῖν, (*F*)ἑ, (*F*)οἱ, (*F*)οἶκος. It occurred, moreover, in the interior
of words as well as initially, and in this case is sometimes represented
for us by υ, e.g. δεύομαι = δέομαι; ἀπούρας (e.g. I 356), aorist participle, for ἀπό(*F*)ρας.)

The second change taking place about the time of the composition
of the *Iliad* is a specifically Ionic feature – what is called *metathesis of
vowels*, whereby -āo changed (by way of a presumed -ηo) to -εω
through a sort of reversal of the strength of the two vowels. In Homer
-āo and -εω forms are found interchangeably. For example, the genitive
singular of first-declension masculine nouns in Greek was originally
in -āo, and we get Ἀτρείδαο ('of the son of Atreus') in II 9, but
Ἀτρείδεω in II 185; and Πηληιάδεω, genitive of Πηληιάδης ('son of
Peleus'), occurs in the first line of the *Iliad*. The same thing happens

with first-declension genitive plurals, which are normal in -ᾱων but common also in -εων.

BIBLIOGRAPHY[1]

General

Bowra, *Tradition and Design in the Iliad.*
Kirk, *The Songs of Homer.*
Nilsson, *Homer and Mycenae.*
Page, *History and the Homeric Iliad.*
Severyns, *Homère.*

Linguistic

Chadwick, 'The Greek Dialects and Greek Pre-history'.
Chantraine, *Grammaire Homérique.*
Hoekstra, *Homeric Modifications of Formulaic Prototypes.*

II. MYTHOLOGY

The word *myth* probably suggests to a modern reader simply that a thing is untrue. It would be a mistake, however, to insist on this aspect when dealing with Greek mythology. The myths, for the Greeks, were a great body of tales or stories (μῦθος = 'story'), offering a broad picture of the remote and heroic past, which was treated as historical in the absence of any more accurate information. Under the heading of mythology, we may distinguish three types of story: (*a*) saga (based on something like historical fact); (*b*) imaginatively created stories, often with a psychological, anthropological or religious basis; (*c*) folk-tales and fairy-tales. As examples, we may take (*a*) the background legend of the war against Troy and the names of many of the characters; (*b*) the story in II 594–600 of how Thamyris the poet challenged the Muses at singing, and was punished for his presumption; (*c*) the detail in the Bellerophontes story in VI 179–95, of how he was set three tasks to perform, and on successful completion of them was given the hand of the princess and half the kingdom. (In fact, Homer makes little use of folk-tale and fairy-tale motifs in the *Iliad*, although they abound in the *Odyssey*.)

However, all types of myth tended to coalesce into a great body of information about the past. And this was Greek mythology. The stories contained in it were sung by bards like Homer, no doubt

[1] For details of the references, see the consolidated bibliography in section v.

normally in short lays very different from the *Iliad*, but in the same style and language; and judging by the allusiveness with which a non-Trojan myth may be introduced tangentially in the *Iliad*, the Homeric audience had a wide familiarity with mythology.

There were four main cycles of myths, and generally speaking the characters were kept separate. The four were the Trojan cycle, the Theban cycle, the stories of the Argonauts and the tales of Herakles.

The Trojan cycle ran from the preliminaries of the war, with the abduction of Helen by Paris, through the events of the war itself and the sack of Troy to the misfortunes which befell the individual heroes on their return home to Greece. The *Iliad* describes the events of a few days in the last year of the war. In it we can see that the Trojan cycle had developed to a point where the *personalities* of the leaders were as important as the incidents of the story. In reading the *Iliad* one finds the Greek leaders so strongly and clearly characterised by their actions that by the end of the epic they seem familiar and predictable. This is true of Aias son of Telamon, Agamemnon, Diomedes, Menelaos, Nestor, Odysseus, and even such relatively less significant figures as Aias son of Oileus and Idomeneus. These may be said to be the saga figures – the characters of the *narrative Iliad*, which tells the story of the war against Troy. The *Iliad* has, however, in addition to the narrative element, a *dramatic* plot – the beginning, consequences and conclusion of the wrath of Achilleus. Characterisation in drama is achieved by speech, not action, and situation matters as much as personality; Achilleus himself, whose speeches are the finest in the *Iliad*, is a dramatic figure, and so to a large extent are those others who are caught up in his tragedy – Hektor, Patroklos, and the three women of Troy, Andromache, Helen and Hekabe. Although the *Iliad* is in itself a unity, it is nevertheless some help to our understanding to distinguish the narrative from the dramatic in this way. The narrative characters came from the saga, at least in their main outlines; the dramatic characters, and particularly Achilleus, may indeed have had a place in the saga, but their particular problems are derived from their situation in the *Iliad*, and thus the intensity of their portrayal is the work of the *Iliad*'s poet, Homer.

The epics of the Theban cycle, had they been preserved, would have been very relevant to Homer, and we can only regret the loss of the *Thebaid*, which might have provided the best of all parallels to the *Iliad*. The comparison would lie in the fact that at Thebes, as at Troy, the myth told of an attack on a walled city by the main Greek force, against the desperate defence of the inhabitants. To be accurate, there were in the Theban myth two attacks; for the earlier and more famous expedition, that of the Seven against Thebes, was unsuccessful, and it was left to the Sons of the Seven, the Epigonoi, in the next generation, to succeed where their fathers had failed, and destroy Thebes. This is a case where there is some overlap of personnel between the myths, and three of the Epigonoi take part in the *Iliad* (see note on IV 405), in particular the magnificent Diomedes, who is a leading figure in books IV to VI. As a result, these books have several allusions to the attack on Thebes, and the exploits of Diomedes' father Tydeus. The legends of Herakles, and to a much lesser extent the Argonautic stories, are referred to haphazardly in the *Iliad*, but hardly at all in the first six books.

Apart from the four main cycles there were also countless local legends, which were more or less familiar outside their parochial circle, depending on chance or the fame of their heroes; there are, for example, detailed allusions in the *Iliad* to the war of the Lapiths against the centaurs, and the hunt of the Calydonian boar. In addition the *Iliad* is full of minor characters, often with a local habitation and the name of a father given; in some of these cases it may be that the person is part of the heroic tradition, and information about him may derive from the past, and eventually perhaps even from a real person in Mycenaean times. More often one has the impression that Homer is simply selecting from a stock of epic names and attributes, although he has a great art in infusing reality and life into these minor figures.

The myths are almost exclusively located in the Mycenaean age. This is shown by internal evidence, and particularly the geographical location of the myths and their heroes, which fits the distribution of Mycenaean citadels as shown by the findings of archaeology. We can take it, therefore, that the world of mythology was an idealised memory of the remote past, of a time of action and danger and heightened awareness, in fact a heroic age. Such heroic ages have been part of the retrospective vision of other peoples also; their distinguishing features have been a concentration on the military virtues of personal honour and absolute loyalty to one's immediate superior, accompanied by political instability and eventual disaster.

Another essential feature of the Greek mythological world is the closeness of men to the gods. The greater gods are represented as a family living on Mount Olympos, and mostly taking sides in the struggles going on down on earth, some (particularly Athene and Hera) favouring the Greeks, and some (Apollo, Ares and Aphrodite) the Trojans. Zeus, the king of the gods, is impartial, but knows that Troy is doomed. The influence of the gods on men is subtle and various, ranging from apparently straightforward physical action to psychological encouragement (see, for examples, the passages cited in the English Index under 'Gods'). A much noted and unexpected effect of the divine–human interplay in the *Iliad* is that the gods often appear frivolous by comparison. Life, for human beings, is real and earnest; for the gods, the absence of death takes away the seriousness of life. They are thus quite often used by the poet as light relief from the sombre actions down below – as for example at the end of book 1, where the bickering of Zeus and Hera on Olympos reflects the quarrel of Achilleus and Agamemnon; and the book, which began with the plague and bitter feelings on earth, ends with laughter and festivity in heaven.

BIBLIOGRAPHY[1]

Chadwick, *The Heroic Age.*
Nilsson, *The Mycenaean Origin of Greek Mythology.*
Rose, *Gods and Heroes of the Greeks.*

III. FORMULAS AND THEMES

The conventional character of Homeric language and diction was referred to in section 1 of this Introduction. In the last half-century there has been a great deal of discussion of this aspect, concentrating particularly on the consequences for the poet of *oral composition*. To take an obvious feature of Homeric poetry, few who have read even a small part of either of the two epics can have failed to notice the frequent repetition of a large number of apparently particularised descriptive epithets (the *wine-dark* sea, Hektor *of the shining helmet*, Poseidon the *earth-shaker*) – in fact, the so-called stock epithets. It is only in recent years that it has been clearly realised that the reason for these epithets is that they form, together with the noun they qualify, a metrical unit for the construction of the hexameter verse; and that the desirability of having such units is strictly related to the fact that this sort of verse was composed orally by illiterate bards. These metrical units, of two or more words, are called *formulas*. The bard, singing his lays extempore at the request of his audience, relied on his memory in two respects – for the story he wanted to tell, and for a stock of

---

[1] For details of the references, see the consolidated bibliography in section v.

metrically useful phrases or formulas which he had assimilated when he learned his trade from other bards as a boy, or from his own practice in later years. Without this stock it would have been impossible for him to keep up the flow of hexameter lines in front of an audience, unless he had in fact memorised whole songs; and it has been shown that exact memorisation is not a characteristic of oral poetry – indeed it cannot be, for without writing there is no fixed text.

The impulse to the study of the stock of formulas possessed by the poet or poets of the *Iliad* and *Odyssey* was given by the work of the American scholar Milman Parry. He took as his starting point the pervasive system of noun–epithet formulas for proper names. Consider the following examples of five of the Greek leaders in the nominative case:

τὸν δ' αὖτε ⎤ προσέειπε(ν) ἄναξ ἀνδρῶν 'Αγαμέμνων	IX 114
πρότερος ⎦ ποδάρκης δῖος 'Αχιλλεύς	XX 177
βοὴν ἀγαθὸς Διομήδης	VI 122
βοὴν ἀγαθὸς Μενέλαος	X 36
πολύτλας δῖος 'Οδυσσεύς	IX 676
τὸν ⎤ δ' ἀπαμειβόμενος προσέφη κρείων 'Αγαμέμνων	I 130
τὴν ⎦ πόδας ὠκὺς 'Αχιλλεύς	I 84
κρατερὸς Διομήδης	V 814
ξανθὸς Μενέλαος	*Od.* IV 147
πολύμητις 'Οδυσσεύς	X 382

The lists could easily be extended to show that the poet had a more or less complete system of noun–epithet phrases for his characters when they are the subject of a sentence, to fit the two most useful sections of the second half of the line: $\cup - \overline{\cup\cup} - \overline{\cup\cup} - \cup$ and $\overline{\cup\cup} - \overline{\cup\cup} - \cup$. The epithets are not of course completely otiose, or irrelevant to the characters. But nor are they particular to the sentence in which they find themselves; they describe either a general heroic quality (βοὴν ἀγαθός, κρατερός), or a general characteristic of that hero (ἄναξ ἀνδρῶν, πολύμητις). With their nouns, they are exactly what is meant by formulas – fixed word-groups filling (at least in these cases) a given part of the hexameter line. The poet does not in practice bother with other possibilities; having such a phrase, he uses it whenever the need arises.

The system of noun–epithet formulas for proper names in the nominative case is, of course, only a small part of Homeric diction. But when we take a broader view, we find a similar situation. To a

large extent the poetry is composed not in individual words but in
groups of two or more words, the closeness of the connection between
which is shown by their repeated occurrence together; the groups may
be noun–epithet, adverb–verb, conjunction–verb or other collocations.
These word-groups are not always so metrically fixed as those quoted
above, and may appear at various points in the line, and in some cases
be declined, conjugated or otherwise modified as the poet finds
necessary for his composition, while still retaining their basic group
identity. As an example of such modification, consider 'a gold cup' –
χρύσεον δέπας:

Βελλεροφόντης δὲ χρύσεον δέπας ἀμφικύπελλον   VI 220
(the basic formula)

Ἥρη δὲ χρύσεον καλὸν δέπας ἐν χερὶ θῆκε   XXIV 101
(separated)

πολλὰ δὲ καὶ σπένδων χρυσέῳ δέπαι λιτάνευεν   XXIII 196
(dative singular)

χρυσέῳ ἐν δέπαι, ὄφρα λείψαντε κιοίτην   XXIV 285
(in different form)

νέκταρ ἐῳνοχόει· τοὶ δὲ χρυσέοις δεπάεσσι   IV 3
(dative plural)

There is another aspect of repetitive phraseology in the Homeric
poems, like, but not quite the same as, the formulas. This is the
apparent creation of phrases *by analogy*, on the pattern of existing
phrases. For example, the following half-lines obviously conform to
a pattern which could accommodate a very large number of verbs,
following the wishes of the poet:

αὐτὰρ ἐπεί ῥ᾽ ἵκοντο   I 484
αὐτὰρ ἐπεί ῥ᾽ ἤγερθεν   XXIV 790
αὐτὰρ ἐπεὶ δὴ σπεῦσε   *Od.* IX 250

Such half-lines show a fixed group (αὐτὰρ ἐπεί) followed by a variable
(a particle and a verb). One can go even further, and argue that
phrases in which each word is variable may nevertheless exemplify
patterns; for although there is no common vocabulary between, for
example,

τὸν δ᾽ ἀπαμειβόμενος προσέφη κρείων Ἀγαμέμνων   I 130

and

ὣς ἄρα φωνήσας ἀπέβη Τελαμώνιος Αἴας   XII 370

the lines are very similar. After a couple of pronouns/adverbs/conjunctions the main part of the first half is taken by a participle in the nominative, agreeing with the subject of the verb; the verb then comes immediately after the third-foot caesura (see p. xxii), and the line is completed by a nominative proper-name formula. The lines have the same rhythmical and word pattern, although none of the words is the same. This may be called a *phrase-pattern*. Such patterns were just as much part of the poet's linguistic repertoire as the formulas. Taken together, they show that most of the lines and parts of lines in the *Iliad* had a pre-existence either actually (as formulas) or potentially (as patterns) in the poetical experience of Homer, whether in his own compositions or those of his predecessors. It is important to realise this, and to be very careful about ascribing particular significance to the placing of individual words in the lines.

The formalisation of the poet's technique involved not only the elements of his diction but also the incidents in the stories he told. The same subjects would be found in different poems, or (if it was a long one) in the same poem. These are called *themes*. Obvious examples are the beaching of a ship, or the holding of a sacrifice followed by a feast, or the arming of a hero. The poet used these themes as elements in his composition just as he used the formulas. That is, he had a regular way of describing that particular topic, and when he came to it in the story he would describe it in that way, without any search for originality or variety. The only change he would make in regular cases like these would be either to lengthen the version by adding ornamental material, or to shorten it by cutting out such material. A ready example of this procedure is provided by the arming scenes, of Alexandros in III 330–8, Agamemnon in XI 17–43, Patroklos in XVI 131–9 and Achilleus in XIX 369–91.

Less obvious examples of themes are what might better be called *recurrent motifs*. Greek heroic poetry has certain story patterns which, no doubt because they appeared in a number of songs known to the poet, also formed part of his technique, and were available to him when he needed them. We see them, for example, in the various stories which show the dire consequences attendant on a human being who challenges a god (see note on II 594–600). They are also to be recognised in many passing incidents in the story, and in much of the action characterising the heroes. For particular examples, see the passages cited in the English Index under 'Themes, recurrent motifs, etc.'.

Themes and recurrent motifs are, in the contents of the poems, exactly parallel to the formulas and phrase-patterns of the diction. All four classes of phenomena arise from the repetition of heroic verse in an illiterate age. They are a necessary part of *oral composition*.

Whether the *Iliad* itself[1] was orally composed is another question. Although it clearly came at the end of a long tradition of heroic poetry, it can hardly have been typical of the poems in that tradition. It is reasonable to suppose that it differed from them in length and sophistication, as well as in the obvious fact that it has survived while they have not. The *Iliad* dates from the eighth century, the time when the borrowing of the Phoenician alphabet had made writing once more possible in Greece; and we may surmise that the coming of writing, which soon destroyed the old art of oral poetry, also provided the conditions for both the composition and the survival of the *Iliad*. We may surmise this, but we cannot know, and scholars are deeply divided on the question. What we *can* say is that the poet of the *Iliad* *uses the techniques of the oral poet*, and that they came to him from his predecessors. Nor would we be right in thinking that these techniques were restrictive, or inhibiting to the genius of the poet. His skill lay in handling the material, and operating freely (as clearly he does) within a broad, but nevertheless limited, set of expressions and concepts.

BIBLIOGRAPHY[2]

Parry, *L'Épithète Traditionnelle dans Homère*.
——, 'Studies in the Epic Technique of Oral Verse Making'.
Lord, 'Composition by Theme in Homer and Southslavic Epos'.
——, *The Singer of Tales*.
Hainsworth, *The Flexibility of the Homeric Formula*.

IV. SCANSION

Questions of scansion may be divided between *metre* (the rules governing the structure of the verse) and *prosody* (the rules governing the way the individual words fit into the metre). We take these two main sections in turn, and then define four technical terms relating to prosody: *elision, hiatus, correption* and *synizesis*.

---

[1] The arguments of this paragraph apply with equal force to the *Odyssey*. It appears that it was composed later than the *Iliad;* whether by the same poet or another is uncertain.

[2] For details of the references, see the consolidated bibliography in section v.

Metre

The verse of Greek epic is the dactylic hexameter, consisting of six successive feet each scanned – ‿ ‿, except that

(*a*) the sixth dactyl is reduced to two syllables;
(*b*) each pair of short syllables may be replaced by a single long;
(*c*) the final syllable in the line may be either long or short.

The scheme is therefore

$$ \overset{1}{|-\smile\smile|}\overset{2}{-\smile\smile|}\overset{3}{-\smile\smile|}\overset{4}{-\smile\smile|}\overset{5}{-\smile\smile|}\overset{6}{-\smile|} $$

This line, with from twelve to seventeen syllables, was invariable in epic, occurring some 28,000 times in the *Iliad* and *Odyssey* alone.

It is reasonable that there should be conventional places for regular breaks between words to divide up such a long line. *Caesura* (Latin, 'cut') is the name for a break that falls within a foot. Although obviously this may happen in any foot, in discussing metre we deal mainly with caesuras in the third foot. Almost all lines in Homer have a break between words there. If it is after the long syllable, it is called a *strong caesura*; if after the first of the two shorts (and this is in fact commoner), it is called a *weak caesura*. The first line in the *Iliad* has a strong caesura:

1 1 | – ‿ ‿|– ‿ ‿|–// –|–‿‿| – ‿‿| –‿|
     Μῆνιν ἄειδε, θεά, Πηληϊάδεω Ἀχιλῆος

The second has a weak caesura:

1 2 |– ‿ ‿|– –| – ‿// ‿| – –| – ‿ ‿|– ‿|
     οὐλομένην, ἣ μυρί᾽ Ἀχαιοῖς ἄλγε᾽ ἔθηκε

A break between words which coincides with the end of a foot is called a *diaeresis* (διαίρεσις, 'separating'). Particularly favoured in the hexameter is the diaeresis at the end of the fourth foot, called the *bucolic diaeresis* (because it was so frequent in the later bucolic, i.e. pastoral, poets such as Theocritus). If there is a bucolic diaeresis, the fourth foot is normally trisyllabic (although this is not the case in 1 2 quoted above). 1 4 has a weak caesura and a bucolic diaeresis:

1 4 |– –|– – | – ‿//‿|– ‿‿| – ‿ ‿|– ‿|
     ἡρώων, αὐτοὺς δὲ ἑλώρια τεῦχε κύνεσσιν

Many monosyllabic words are treated from the metrical point of view as belonging either to the word that precedes them or to the word that follows. Clear understanding of this will often be necessary for the correct appreciation of a caesura or diaeresis. Monosyllables which are treated as belonging to the preceding word (sometimes called *postpositives*) are:

all enclitics, such as τε, γε, νυ(ν), τοι, κε(ν), με, σε, μιν, τις, που, ποι;

connecting and other particles which cannot come as the first word in the sentence, such as γάρ, μέν, δέ, οὖν, ἄν, δή.

As these words are taken closely with the word that precedes, there can be no caesura or diaeresis *before* them. Thus in 1 4 quoted above, the caesura is a weak one after δέ, not a strong one after αὐτούς.

Monosyllables which are treated as belonging to the following word (sometimes called *prepositives*) are:

the definite article (when so used; see 1 9 n.);

prepositions;

conjunctions which come first, such as καί, εἰ, ἤ, ὡς, ὅς;

interrogatives – τίς, ποῦ, ποῖ, etc.

As these words are taken closely with the word that follows, there can be no caesura or diaeresis *after* them. Thus in

$$|- \cup \cup| \ - -|- \ // \ \ \cup \ \ \cup|- \ \ \cup \ \ \cup|- \ \cup \cup| - -|$$

1 33 ὡς ἔφατ᾽, ἔδεισεν δ᾽ ὁ γέρων καὶ ἐπείθετο μύθῳ

there is a strong caesura after ἔδεισεν δ᾽, and not a weak caesura after ὁ.

The learner will probably find it easier to practise scanning lines by dividing them into their six constituent feet. Experienced readers of Homer are more likely to notice the subtle differences of rhythm caused by the word-breaks (i.e. the caesuras and diaereses). 1 1 above would fall naturally into two halves:

$$- \cup \cup - \cup \cup - // - - \cup \cup - \cup \cup - \cup$$

1 2 and 1 4 share a more complicated rhythm, with a major pause in the sense at the strong caesura in the *second* foot, and breaks at the weak caesura and the bucolic diaeresis:

$$- \overline{\cup \cup} - // - - \cup // \cup - \overline{\cup \cup} // - \cup \cup - \cup$$

Prosody

To scan the individual words, it is necessary to know which syllables are 'short' and which 'long', for the measurement of Greek verse is *by length of syllables*. Briefly, a short syllable is one in which there is a single short vowel (ε, ο, and short ᾰ, ῐ, ῠ) followed by not more than one consonant; a long syllable is one containing *either* a long vowel (η, ω, and long ᾱ, ῑ, ῡ), *or* a diphthong, *or* a short vowel followed by two or more consonants (ζ, ξ, ψ count as double consonants; so does ρ at the beginning of a word). The consonants in question may be in the same word as the short vowel, or in the following word, or split between them. This procedure, called *lengthening by position*, is exemplified in the following two lines:

$$| - \ - \ | \ \ - \ \ -| - \ // - |- \ \ \cup\cup|- \ \ \cup\cup|- \cup \ |$$

13   πολλὰς δ᾽ ἰφθίμους ψυχὰς ῎Αιδι προίαψεν

$$|- \ -|- \cup \cup \ | \ - \ \cup// \ \cup|- \ \ \ \cup \ \cup|-\cup \cup \ | \ - \ \ -|$$

15   οἰωνοῖσί τε πᾶσι, Διὸς δ᾽ ἐτελείετο βουλή

An exception to the practice of lengthening by position is that occasionally a short vowel remains short[1] before two consonants, if they fall into the pattern called 'mute and liquid' (πρ, τρ, πλ and others); e.g. ᾿Αφροδῑ́τη, whose name could not in fact enter the verse if it were not possible to scan her first syllable as short. More rarely still, and only from strict metrical necessity, a short vowel is left short before two consonants other than 'mute and liquid', before Σκάμανδρος necessarily whenever it occurs (e.g. v 774), and other such names (Ζάκυνθον, II 634; Ζέλειαν, II 824).

Contrariwise, a short vowel is sometimes lengthened before what is in our texts a single consonant (usually δ, λ, μ, ν, σ), whether because a second consonant (often digamma, cp. p. xiii) has dropped out, *or* because the single consonant was in some way 'rolled' in pronunciation, *or* merely for metrical utility. Thus in I 33 (quoted above):

ὣς ἔφατ᾽, ἔδεισεν δ᾽ ὁ γέρων καὶ ἐπείθετο μύθῳ

the first syllable of ἔδεισεν is long because the word originally contained a digamma – ἔδ(Ϝ)εισεν. On occasion a short vowel is lengthened before no consonant at all, in which case the explanation always includes the loss of a digamma and perhaps another letter as well. In

$$|- \ \ -|- \ \ \cup \ \ \cup \ |- \ \ \cup// \ \cup|- \cup \ \cup \ |- \ \ - \ |- \ \ \ \cup|$$

III 172   αἰδοῖός τέ μοί ἐσσι, φίλε ἑκυρέ, δεινός τε

---

[1] This is technically incorrect, in that it is the *syllable*, not the short vowel in it, which is lengthened or not as the case may be by following consonants. It is, however, conventionally acceptable to speak of a short vowel 'lengthened by position'.

two successive final short epsilons are lengthened, one before no visible consonant, the other before a single consonant. The explanation is that ἑκυρός ('father-in-law') certainly had a digamma, and may have kept the traces of having at one time begun with σϜ- (cp. German *Schwieger*); and δεινός derives from an earlier δ(Ϝ)εινός.

Elision (Latin, 'striking out')

A short open vowel (i.e. one not followed by a consonant) at the end of a word is normally elided before a vowel beginning the following word; examples in the lines quoted above are 1 2 μυρί(α), ἄλγε(α), 1 3 δ(έ), 1 5 δ(έ), 1 33 ἔφατ(ο), δ(έ). In addition to most short vowels, the -αι of certain verbal forms is regularly elided.

Hiatus (Latin, 'gaping')

Hiatus is the non-occurrence of elision, where a vowel (long or short) is left unaffected at the end of a word before a vowel beginning the next word. Hiatus is very common in the text of Homer; sometimes a long vowel is left in hiatus at the point of metrical stress, the first syllable of the foot; sometimes a pause in the sense, or even one of the main caesuras or diaereses in the line, seems to justify hiatus; often the hiatus is only apparent, being due to the loss of an original digamma at the beginning of the following word; sometimes none of these explanations applies. Examples in the lines quoted have been Πηληιάδεω | Ἀχιλῆος in 1 1 (under the metrical stress at the beginning of the fifth foot); δὲ | ἑλώρια in 1 4 (at the caesura); φίλε | ἑκυρέ in III 172 (loss of digamma).

Correption (Latin, 'shortening')

A long vowel or diphthong, standing in hiatus, may be scanned as short. This is very common, for example, καὶ ἐπείθετο in 1 33, μοί ἔσσι in III 172.

Synizesis (συνίζησις, 'settling down together')

Two vowels either within a word or in successive words may under certain circumstances be treated as coalescing into a single long syllable, for example Πηληιάδεω in 1 1. In 1 15, which begins

| – ◡ ◡|– –| –//

χρυσέῳ ἀνὰ σκήπτρῳ, the final two letters of χρυσέῳ have first formed one long syllable by *synizesis*, and then been shortened by *correption*.

An example of synizesis involving two words is to be found in v 466,

$$|- \quad \cup \cup |- \quad \cup \cup |-//$$

which begins ἦ εἰς ὅ κεν ἀμφὶ πύλης.

BIBLIOGRAPHY[1]

Introductory

Halporn, Ostwald, Rosenmeyer, *The Metres of Greek and Latin Poetry*.
Raven, *Greek Metre*.

More advanced

Maas, *Greek Metre*.
Porter, 'The Early Greek Hexameter'.

V. BIBLIOGRAPHY

Texts, Commentaries, etc.

Allen, T. W., *Homeri Opera: Ilias*, 3rd ed. (Oxford, 1920).
——, *Homeri Ilias* (Prolegomena and text) (Oxford, 1931).
Ameis, K. F., Hentze, C., and Cauer, P., *Homers Ilias*, various eds (Leipzig, 1868–1932; repr. Amsterdam, 1965).
Bothe, F. H., *Homeri Ilias* (Leipzig, 1832).
Dindorf, G., and Maass, E., *Scholia Graeca in Homeri Iliadem* (Oxford, 1875–88).
Erbse, H., *Scholia Graeca in Homeri Iliadem* (Berlin, in progress).
Eustathius, *Commentarii ad Homeri Iliadem* (ed. Stallbaum, Leipzig, 1827–9; repr. Hildesheim, 1960).
Faesi, J. U., and Franke, F. R., *Homers Iliade* (Berlin, 1871–7).
Leaf, W., *The Iliad*, 2nd ed. (London, 1900–2; repr. Amsterdam, 1960).
—— and Bayfield, M. A., *The Iliad of Homer* (London, 1895–8).
Monro, D. B., *Homer, Iliad* (Oxford, 1884).
Pierron, A., *L'Iliade d'Homère* (Paris, 1869).
van Leeuwen, J., *Ilias* (Leiden, 1912–13).

Dictionaries, Grammars, etc.

Autenrieth, G., *Homeric Dictionary*, trans. R. P. Keep (London, 1886).
Chantraine, P., *Grammaire Homérique* (Paris, 1948–53).
Cunliffe, R. J., *Homeric Proper and Place Names* (London, 1931).

---

[1] For details of the references, see the consolidated bibliography in section v.

Ebeling, H., *Lexicon Homericum* (Leipzig, 1885; repr. Hildesheim, 1963).

Liddell, H. G., Scott, R., and Jones, H. S., *A Greek–English Lexicon*, 9th ed. (Oxford, 1940).

Monro, D. B., *Homeric Grammar*, 2nd ed. (Oxford, 1891).

Prendergast, G. L., *A Complete Concordance to the Iliad of Homer* (London 1875); revised and enlarged by B. Marzullo (Darmstadt, 1962).

Thesaurus Linguae Graecae, *Lexicon des frühgriechischen Epos* (Göttingen, in progress).

General

Allen, T. W., *Homer, the Origins and the Transmission* (Oxford, 1924).

Arnold, M., *On Translating Homer* (London, 1861).

Bolling, G. M., *The External Evidence for Interpolation in Homer* (Oxford, 1925; repr. 1968).

—— *The Athetized Lines of the Iliad* (Baltimore, 1944).

Bowra, C. M., *Tradition and Design in the Iliad* (Oxford, 1930).

Broccia, G., *Struttura e Spirito del Libro VI dell' Iliade*, parte prima (Sapri, 1963).

Chadwick, H. M., *The Heroic Age* (Cambridge, 1912; repr. 1967).

Chadwick, J., 'The Greek Dialects and Greek Pre-history' (from *Greece and Rome*, n.s., III (1956)), in *Language and Background of Homer*, ed. G. S. Kirk (Cambridge, 1964), pp. 106–18.

Dodds, E. R., Palmer, L. R., and Gray, D., 'Homer', in *Fifty Years (and Twelve) of Classical Scholarship* (Oxford, 1968), pp. 1–49.

Drerup, E., *Das fünfte Buch der Ilias* (Paderborn, 1913).

Fenik, B., *Typical Battle Scenes in the Iliad*, Hermes Einzelschriften 21 (Wiesbaden, 1968).

Friedrich, W.-H., *Verwundung und Tod in der Ilias* (Göttingen, 1956).

Hainsworth, J. B., *The Flexibility of the Homeric Formula* (Oxford, 1968).

Halporn, J., Ostwald, M., and Rosenmeyer, T., *The Metres of Greek and Latin Poetry* (London, 1963).

Hoekstra, A., *Homeric Modifications of Formulaic Prototypes* (Amsterdam, 1965).

Kakridis, J. T., *Homeric Researches* (Lund, 1949).

Kirk, G. S., *The Songs of Homer* (Cambridge, 1962).

—— (ed.), *Language and Background of Homer* (Cambridge, 1964).

Lesky, A., *Göttliche und menschliche Motivation im homerischen Epos* (Heidelberg, 1961).

Lesky, 'Homeros', in Pauly–Wissowa, *Realencyclopädie der Classischen Altertumswissenschaft*, suppl. xi (Stuttgart, 1968), pp. 687–846.

Leumann, M., *Homerische Wörter* (Basel, 1950).

Lord, A. B., 'Composition by Theme in Homer and Southslavic Epos', *Transactions of the American Philological Association*, LXXXII (1951), 71–80.

——, *The Singer of Tales* (Oxford, 1960).

Lorimer, H. L., *Homer and the Monuments* (London, 1950).

Maas, P., *Greek Metre*, trans. H. Lloyd-Jones (Oxford, 1962).

Mazon, P., *Introduction à l'Iliade* (Paris, 1948).

Nilsson, M. P., *Homer and Mycenae* (London, 1933).

——, *The Mycenaean Origin of Greek Mythology* (Berkeley, 1932).

Page, D. L., *History and the Homeric Iliad* (Berkeley, 1959).

Pagliaro, A., 'Il Proemio dell' Iliade', *Rendiconti Lincei*, ser. viii, X (1955), 369–96.

Parry, M., *L'Épithète Traditionnelle dans Homére* (Paris, 1928).

——, 'Studies in the Epic Technique of Oral Verse Making', *Harvard Studies in Classical Philology*, XLI (1930), 73–147; XLIII (1932), 1–50.

Porter, H. N., 'The Early Greek Hexameter', *Yale Classical Studies*, XII (1951), 3–63.

Raven, D. S., *Greek Metre* (London, 1962).

Reinhardt, K., *Die Ilias und ihr Dichter* (Göttingen, 1961).

Rose, H. J., *Gods and Heroes of the Greeks* (London, 1957).

Schadewaldt, W., 'Hektor und Andromache' (from *Die Antike*, XI (1935)), in *Von Homers Welt und Werk*, 3rd ed. (Stuttgart, 1959), pp. 207–33.

——, *Iliasstudien*, 2nd ed. (Leipzig, 1943; repr. Darmstadt, 1966).

Severyns, A., *Homère*: I. *Le Cadre Historique*; II. *Le Poète et son Œuvre*; III. *L'Artiste* (Brussels, 1944–8).

——, *Grèce et Proche-Orient avant Homère* (Brussels, 1960).

Snodgrass, A. M., *Early Greek Armour and Weapons* (Edinburgh, 1964).

Strasburger, G., *Die kleinen Kämpfer der Ilias* (Frankfurt, 1954).

von der Mühll, P., *Kritisches Hypomnema zur Ilias* (Basel, 1952).

Wace, A. J. B., and Stubbings, F. H., *A Companion to Homer* (London, 1962).

Wilamowitz-Moellendorff, U. von, *Die Ilias und Homer* (Berlin, 1916; repr. 1966).

BOOK I

The Quarrel between Achilleus and Agamemnon

1–7. These lines form the introduction to the *Iliad*. They stress the fact that the subject of the whole poem, and its starting point, are found in the 'anger' of Achilleus, resulting from his quarrel with Agamemnon.

1. μῆνιν: The first word ('wrath', 'anger') shows that the plot of the *Iliad* is to be primarily psychological, and that at any rate we do not have here a simple chronicle of the fighting at Troy. Similarly the *Odyssey* begins with the key word ἄνδρα, 'the man'.

ἄειδε: 'sing', because the hexameter verse was not spoken verse, but intoned to a musical accompaniment. What was a reality for Homer became a convention for later poets (*arma virumque cano*, 'I sing of arms and the man' (Virgil); 'Sing, heavenly Muse' (Milton)).

θεά: 'goddess', that is, the muse. The muse was a personification of the poet's inspiration. He sang what came into his mind to sing, and it was the muse who put it there.

Πηληιάδεω: genitive of a first-declension nominative Πηληιάδης, 'son of Peleus'. The commonest form of patronymic was in -ιδης, and Πηλείδης is frequently found for Achilleus in the *Iliad*; the form here is a longer alternative, useful for metrical purposes. The ending -εω is a form of the genitive ending of first-declension masculine nouns; cp. l. 75 n.

Peleus, who had in his youth married the sea-goddess Thetis, was the father of Achilleus.

Ἀχιλῆος: genitive of Ἀχιλεύς, alternative form of Ἀχιλλεύς.

Πηληιάδεω Ἀχιλῆος: The last two letters of Πηληιάδεω are to be pronounced as one long syllable -εω by *synizesis*, and there is *hiatus* between the two words (for synizesis and hiatus, see Introduction, p. xxv).

2. οὐλομένην: 'accursed'; this is the aorist participle middle, ὀλομένην (ὄλλυμι), with the first syllable lengthened to allow it to

fit into hexameter verse. The usage is exactly parallel (though on a more dignified plane) to the English slang epithet 'perishing'.

μυρία: 'countless'; the more specific meaning 'ten thousand', found in later Greek authors than Homer, is conventionally accented on the first syllable – μύρια.

Ἀχαιοῖς: The Greeks in Homer are called by three names, without distinction of meaning: Achaians (as here), Argives (e.g. l. 79) and Danaans (e.g. l. 42).

3. ἰφθίμους ψυχάς: 'mighty souls'; an awkward expression, because the 'soul' in Homeric belief survives after death only as a strengthless shadow of the living man. Here ἰφθίμους must be a sort of transferred epithet, 'many mighty souls of heroes' meaning 'many souls of mighty heroes'.

Ἄιδι: dative of *Ἄις, an alternative, third-declension, form of the usual first-declension Ἀΐδης, Hades, the god of the underworld.

4. αὐτοὺς δέ: i.e. 'their bodies'.

τεῦχε: for ἔτευχε; the augment is very often omitted in Homer. Cp. διαστήτην (l. 6), ὀλέκοντο (l. 10), λίσσετο (l. 15).

κύνεσσιν: Aeolic (see Introduction, p. xii) dative plural of κύων (Attic κυσίν).

'It made their corpses a prey for the dogs.' In early Greek thinking, to be left unburied was a great misfortune, and a handicap to proper entry to the underworld. For this reason it is a common threat in the *Iliad* that one will give one's enemy's body to the dogs and birds to eat, and not allow his friends to bury it. In practice, however, this remains a threat only, and no corpses are specifically described as being eaten by the dogs and birds.

5. οἰωνοῖσί τε πᾶσι: 'and for all the birds'; the word πᾶσι is flat and inaccurate, seeing that only certain birds, such as vultures, would be interested. An alternative reading δαῖτα ('and a feast for the birds') is quoted as having been preferred by Zenodotus, the early Alexandrian editor of Homer, and is believed to be much older than Zenodotus, because Aeschylus seems to copy it in *Suppl.* 801. πᾶσι was the reading of Aristarchus, the great textual critic of Alexandria.

Διὸς δ' ἐτελείετο βουλή: The plan of Zeus, fulfilled eventually in the *Iliad*, was the agreement he made with Thetis in the scene starting in l. 498 of this book, that he would honour Achilleus by helping the Trojans until the Greeks realised Agamemnon's mistake.

ἐτελείετο: imperfect; the plan of Zeus was moving towards fulfilment while the disasters of ll. 2–5 were being suffered.

6. ἐξ οὗ: '(beginning) from the time when'. Many scholars connect these words with ἄειδε in l. 1, thus making the poet instruct his muse to start singing at this particular point in the long saga of the Trojan War; for this there are good parallels in *Odyssey* I 10 and VIII 500. But the distance from ἄειδε, and the choice of the relative ἐξ οὗ, which is temporal, not spatial, make this interpretation very difficult, if not impossible. It is better to continue the sense naturally from the previous line: the disasters of the Achaians began, and the design of Zeus started to be achieved, from the time when Agamemnon and Achilleus quarrelled.

τὰ πρῶτα: adverbial neuter plural = πρῶτον.

διαστήτην: dual of the aorist, without augment (cp. τεῦχε, l. 4).

ἐρίσαντε: dual of the aorist participle.

7. Ἀτρείδης: The poet does not need to explain that the son of Atreus is Agamemnon, any more than he needs to explain (l. 9) that the son of Leto and Zeus is Apollo.

8. τίς τ᾽ ἄρ: Homeric verse uses all three forms ἄρα, ἄρ and the enclitic ῥα, merely as required by the metre; the particle has a mild inferential force. τε is found occasionally in this particular combination with ἄρα after an interrogative word; it has no effect on the sense that is recognisable to us.

σφωέ: dual of the third-person pronoun, 'those two'.

θεῶν: partitive genitive with τίς.

ἔριδι ξυνέηκε μάχεσθαι: 'brought them into conflict'; lit. 'brought them together (from συνίημι) in strife, to fight'.

9. Λητοῦς καὶ Διὸς υἱός: cp. l. 7 n.

ὁ: 'he'; what later Greek knew as the definite article is still primarily a demonstrative pronoun in Homeric Greek.

10. νοῦσον = νόσον, the plague described in ll. 50–2.

ὦρσε: from ὄρνυμι.

11. τὸν Χρύσην: τόν has caused great difficulty here, because Homeric Greek does not really use the definite article (l. 9 n. above). τόν must mean 'that man', 'him', although Chryses has not previously been mentioned in the poem. Scholars explain by the assumption that either Chryses was a well-known figure in the saga or else the poet wishes to give the impression that he was. Taken this way, Χρύσην and ἀρητῆρα

are in apposition to τόν. Others have replaced τόν by a more amenable monosyllable (τοῦ, Nauck; οἵ (cp. l. 72 n.), Wackernagel).

ἠτίμασεν: from ἀτιμάζω, not ἀτιμάω.

12. θοάς: 'swift', a common epithet of ships, even when they are, as here, drawn up on the beach.

νῆας: The ships form the background of the Achaians' camp.

13. λυσόμενος: 'to request the release of'; middle.

θύγατρα: Chryseis; we learn the details of the story later (ll. 366 ff.).

14. στέμματα: These were wreaths of wool wrapped round the top of the staff that the priest carried by virtue of his sacred office.

ἑκηβόλου: a stock epithet of Apollo, 'he who strikes from afar'; Apollo was the archer-god who sent the plague (l. 48).

15. χρυσέῳ ἀνά: For this to scan, the two vowels -εῳ have to be united by synizesis (cp. Πηληιάδεω, l. 1), and then shortened before the a- of the following word by correption (Introduction, p. xxv).

16. Ἀτρείδα: dual of the first declension. The two sons of Atreus were Agamemnon and Menelaos; in l. 7 the singular Ἀτρείδης was used of Agamemnon alone, as the more important.

17. ἐυκνήμιδες: The greaves were shin-guards, worn particularly as a protection against stones and arrows.

18. ὑμῖν μέν: The two lines of the μέν clause are an attempt to get the goodwill of his audience, in preparation for the responding παῖδα δ'ἐμοί, etc., of l. 20. 'May the gods help you to sack Troy, if only you will give me back my daughter.'

δοῖεν: optative for a wish.

19. Πριάμοιο: The genitive singular of -ος declension nouns and adjectives may be in -οιο as well as -ου.

οἴκαδε: The suffix -δε shows motion towards.

20. λύσαιτε: optative of a wish that is really a prayer.

τὰ δ'ἄποινα: lit. 'these things, the ransom'; cp. l. 9 n.

δέχεσθαι: infinitive for imperative.

23. αἰδεῖσθαι: dependent on ἐπευφήμησαν of the previous line, 'to respect'.

δέχθαι: This is thought to be a present infinitive, from *δέγμαι, an alternative form of δέχομαι.

24. θυμῷ: 'in his heart'.

25. ἀφίει: imperfect (ἀφίημι).

ἐπί ... ἔτελλε: ἐπέτελλε, 'laid upon him'; the elements which later constituted a compound verb are still separable in Homer, with the preposition able to stand by itself as an adverb. The phenomenon is called *tmesis* (from τέμνω, 'cut'). In practice one may treat this as if a verb has been divided into its two parts, although the true situation is that the two parts have not yet coalesced. 'Sent him away roughly, and laid a stern command upon him.'

26. μή ... κιχείω: 'let me not find'; a prohibition.

κοίλῃσιν = κοίλαις.

νηυσί = ναυσί.

κιχείω: subjunctive as if from a verb in -μι (*κίχημι), which provides tenses serving as the aorist system of κιχάνω, 'find'.

28. μή: 'lest'; the clause is then negatived by οὐ.

νυ: the same as the enclitic νυν.

τοι: the same as the enclitic σοι, the unstressed dative of σύ.

χραίσμῃ: second aorist subjunctive of χραισμέω, the present of which does not seem to occur in Homer.

θεοῖο: cp. Πριάμοιο (l. 19).

29. πρίν: adverb.

μιν: the epic form of νιν, accusative third-person pronoun, 'her'.

καί: stresses the statement that is being made; 'before that, old age itself will come on her'.

30. ἐνί = ἐν.

ἐν Ἄργει: Argos may be Agamemnon's own kingdom, or the whole Peloponnese, or simply Greece.

πάτρης = πάτρας; the η for α even after ε, ι, ρ is the most obvious Ionic feature of the Homeric dialect.

31. ἱστὸν ἐποιχομένην: 'walking back and forwards at the loom'; 'weaving'.

ἐμὸν λέχος ἀντιόωσαν: 'coming to my bed'.

ἀντιόωσαν: This, from the verb ἀντιάω, would if uncontracted be ἀντιάουσαν, if contracted ἀντιῶσαν. By a peculiarity of Homeric Greek (caused no doubt by the opposed pressures of contraction of vowels and the requirements of the metre), the contracted form has suffered a sort of expansion or distension. This, technically called *diektasis*, is found particularly with verbs in -αω.

It is cruel and insensitive of Agamemnon to speak in these terms to the girl's father. Already here at the beginning the poet has given a little touch towards the delineation of the king's character. We may remember what did happen when Agamemnon went home, taking with him Kassandra, a girl who had been allotted to him as part of the booty of Troy.

32. ἴθι: imperative of εἶμι.

σαώτερος: 'safer', i.e. than if you *do* annoy me.

κε: κε (κεν) is the alternative form of the modal particle ἄν, and is used in the same way.

νέηαι: second person, subjunctive; Attic νέῃ.

33. ὥς: Accented in this way, or with the circumflex ὧς, this is an adverb = οὕτως, 'so'; the conjunction ὡς is unaccented.

ἔφατο: imperfect middle of φημί; there is no distinction of meaning from the active.

ὁ γέρων: This, and ὁ γεραιός (l. 35), are closer to the later use of ὁ as the definite article, and more acceptable than τὸν Χρύσην (l. 11) because they refer to somebody already mentioned.

36. τόν: for ὅν, the later article being occasionally used as a relative.

37. κλῦθι: second aorist imperative.

μευ = μου.

Χρύσην: Chryse, a town near Troy, where Chryses was priest of Apollo.

ἀμφιβέβηκας: 'protect'; lit. 'bestride', a metaphor from the defence of a fallen friend in battle. For example, in v 299 Aineias took up this protective position over the body of Pandaros – ἀμφὶ δ' ἄρ' αὐτῷ βαῖνε.

38. Killa was a town near Troy, Tenedos a small island off the coast.

ἶφι: 'by force'; -φι is the old instrumental case-ending, here with the noun (F)ἴς (Latin *vis*).

39-41. A common prayer form: 'If I have ever pleased you by my worship in the past, help me now.'

39. Σμινθεῦ: lit. 'mouse-god'. σμίνθος was an ancient word for 'mouse', which survived (we are told) in Cretan in historical times. It is now generally agreed that this title of Apollo, which occurs only here, derives from a time when the god was worshipped in animal form, as Hera the cow and Athene the owl (see l. 206 n.). The mouse was perhaps associated with bubonic plague (which is carried by rats), so that the title Smintheus may be particularly fitting for the present appeal by Chryses. In 1 Samuel vi 4-5 the Philistines are instructed to make golden images of mice to help remove a plague.

τοι: cp. l. 28 n.

ἐπί ... ἔρεψα: *tmesis* (l. 25 n.); the roofing over of a holy place, perhaps with branches of trees, does not necessarily imply the 'building' of a temple.

νηόν: Ionic for normal Greek ναόν, Attic νεών.

40. κατά ... ἔκηα: *tmesis* (κατακαίω).

μηρία: The practice at sacrifices was to wrap the thigh-bones of the animal in a fold of fat (πίονα) and burn this portion as an offering to the gods; the more nutritious parts were eaten by the worshippers.

41. ἠδέ: an alternative word for 'and'.

κρήηνον: aorist imperative from κραιαίνω, a lengthened form of κραίνω.

42. βέλεσσιν = βέλεσιν; the 'arrows' of the archer-god bring death (ll. 48 ff.).

43. ὥς: cp. l. 33 n.

44. κατ' Οὐλύμποιο καρήνων: 'down from the peaks of Olympos'; Olympos in the *Iliad* is still the mountain in north Thessaly where the gods were thought to live.

κῆρ: accusative of respect, 'in his heart'.

45. ἀμφηρεφέα: This would be ἀμφηρεφῆ in later Greek; uncontracted forms are common in Homer.

46. χωομένοιο: lit. 'of him, being angry'.

47. αὐτοῦ κινηθέντος: genitive absolute. αὐτοῦ is very emphatic; Apollo himself is on the move. Trans. 'at the movement of the god'.

ἤιε: imperfect of εἶμι.

νυκτὶ ἐοικώς: 'dark as night'; the same phrase is used in *Odyssey* XI 606 to describe the appearance of Herakles in the underworld.

46 and 47 are awkward lines, and were considered spurious by Zenodotus among ancient, and Bentley among modern scholars. 47 is the weaker, and could be removed with advantage.

48. ἀπάνευθε νεῶν: 'apart from the ships', i.e. the camp of the Greeks.

μετά ... ἕηκε: *tmesis* (μεθίημι); 'let fly'.

51. αὐτοῖσι: 'the men', as opposed to the animals.

54. τῇ δεκάτῃ: understand ἡμέρᾳ.

ἀγορήνδε: cp. οἴκαδε (l. 19).

καλέσσατο: middle; 'had the people summoned to assembly'. Achilleus takes the initiative. It appears that any of the chiefs could summon a meeting of the army, but in doing so he claimed a certain authority. Compare the reactions when Telemachos summons an assembly of the Ithakans in *Odyssey* II.

55. Ἥρη: Hera; for the second η, cp. 1. 30 n. Hera, the wife of Zeus, king of the gods, is, with Athene, the most constant divine supporter of the Greeks and enemy of the Trojans.

57. ἐπεὶ οὖν: This is a particular Homeric use of οὖν, in a subordinate clause with ἐπεί or ὡς, stressing the completion of an action.

ἤγερθεν: a shorter form of the third-person plural = ἠγέρθησαν.

58. τοῖσι δέ: This is the so-called *apodotic* δέ, introducing the main sentence after a subordinate clause. One can see how the τοῖσι δέ picks up the οἱ δέ at the beginning of the sentence.

πόδας ὠκύς: the common Greek accusative of respect, most regularly used with reference to parts of the body.

59. ἄμμε = ἡμᾶς.

60. εἴ κεν (l. 32 n.) . . . φύγοιμεν: The optative in the condition is more remote than the subjunctive, which would be invariable with ἐάν in later Greek.

61. δαμᾷ: future.

62. ἄγε: Though certainly the imperative of ἄγω, this is used as an indeclinable exclamation, being here and elsewhere associated with a plural verb; 'come now'.

ἐρείομεν: a form of present subjunctive from ἐρέω. For the short vowel in the ending, cp. 1. 67 n.

63. ὀνειροπόλον: 'interpreter of dreams'.

καὶ γάρ τε, etc.: The second half of the line is a gnomic explanatory phrase. τε is often found in such proverbial or general statements. It is not to be translated.

64. ὅς κ' εἴποι: 'who could tell us'.

ὅ τι: 'why', lit. 'with respect to what'.

65. εὐχωλῆς, ἑκατόμβης: genitives of cause; 'because of (failure to fulfil) a vow or a sacrifice'.

ἑκατόμβης: supposedly of 'a hundred' animal victims, but used of any large sacrifice.

66. αἰ: the Aeolic form of εἰ.

αἴ κέν πως: 'if by any chance', 'in the hope that',

κνίσης, etc.: dependent on ἀντιάσας.

τελείων: 'without blemish'.

67. βούλεται: Subjunctives with short vowels are found commonly in Homer, but normally in *athematic* tenses such as the first aorist; this example is therefore irregular.

69. Kalchas was the famous seer in the Greek army.

ὄχα: 'by far'; the word only occurs in the phrase ὄχ' ἄριστος.

70. ἤδη: past tense of οἶδα.

πρό τ' ἐόντα: i.e. τά τε προόντα.

71. 'And guided the fleet of the Achaians to Ilion.'

ἡγέομαι with the dative is 'to lead' in the sense of showing the way. εἴσω is an adverb, but here used with the accusative Ἴλιον it has the same effect as if it was the preposition εἰς.

72. ἥν: possessive pronoun, 'his'.

οἱ: dative of the third-person pronoun, 'to him'. Exceptional skill at anything is likely to be described by the Homeric poet as the personal gift of a god.

73. ἐυφρονέων: uncontracted; cp. l. 45 n.

74. κέλεαι: Attic κέλει, second-person present indicative.

75. ἑκατηβελέταο: The old form of the genitive of -α declension masculine nouns was in -αο. (This sometimes becomes, by Ionic metathesis of vowels (see Introduction, p. xiii), -εω (l. 1).) The word is merely a longer equivalent of ἑκηβόλου (l. 14).

76. σύνθεο: σύνθου, aorist middle imperative.

77. ἦ μέν: the regular formula to begin an oath; Attic ἦ μήν.

πρόφρων: predicatively with ἀρήξειν; 'that you will exert all your efforts to help me'.

78. χολωσέμεν: an alternative form for the infinitive χολώσειν; the word is transitive, ἄνδρα its object.

μέγα: adverb, 'greatly'.

79. οἱ: cp. l. 72 n.

Strictly speaking this ought to be another relative clause, parallel to ὅς ... κρατέει; but a second relative clause with change of case of the relative word (καὶ ᾧ) is stylistically unpleasing, and Greek naturally slips into an independent main sentence.

80. ὅτε χώσεται: Later Greek would have ὅταν χώσηται; χώσεται here is aorist subjunctive with short vowel (l. 67), not future. ἄν is often omitted in this sort of indefinite clause in Homeric Greek; so also εἰ ... καταπέψῃ in l. 81, and ὄφρα τελέσσῃ in l. 82.

χέρηι: 'less important'; a shorter form of χερείονι (cp. l. 114).

81. For the *proverbial* τε is this line and the next, see l. 63 n.

καταπέψῃ: 'swallows'.

82. ἀλλά: This use of ἀλλά at the beginning of the main sentence after the conditional clause is somewhat like the *apodotic* δέ (l. 58 n.); 'all the same'.

ὄφρα: 'until'.

83. φράσαι: aorist middle imperative, 'consider'.

85. μάλα: with εἰπέ, 'as much as you like'; cp. l. 173 φεῦγε μάλα, 'run away if you want to'.

86. οὐ μὰ 'Απόλλωνα: 'no, by Apollo'.

89. κοίλης: κοίλαις (cp. κοίλῃσιν, l. 26).

90. συμπάντων Δαναῶν: depends on τις, l. 88.

οὐδέ 'not even'.

91. πολλόν = πολύ, adverbial.

εὔχεται: Neither 'boasts' nor 'claims' produces the right effect in English. Agamemnon is ἄριστος 'Αχαιῶν and his claim to be so is legitimate and accepted by others. On the other hand, the form of expression in the line (including the words νῦν and πολλόν) is not conciliatory towards Agamemnon, who was obviously the person Kalchas referred to in ll. 78 ff.

93. cp. l. 65.

97. πρίν ... πρίν: The first πρίν is an adverb, the second a conjunction.

In place of Δαναοῖσιν ἀεικέα λοιγὸν ἀπώσει, which comes to us from the scholia as the reading of Aristarchus, the manuscript tradition (i.e. the vulgate from the ancient world) has λοιμοῖο βαρείας χεῖρας ἀφέξει. This can be taken in two ways ('he will not remove his heavy hands from the plague', or 'he will not withdraw the heavy hands of the plague'); neither is acceptable. Editors therefore prefer Aristarchus' reading; but they cannot explain the state of the text.

98. ἀπό ... δόμεναι: *tmesis*; an alternative form of ἀποδοῦναι; the subject is the Danaans (l. 97).

99. ἀπριάτην ἀνάποινον: adverbs, not adjectives, according to our ancient authorities.

100. πεπίθοιμεν: This is the optative of a *reduplicated aorist*, an old tense-formation of which numerous examples are found in Homer.

103. μένεος δέ, etc.: 'and his dark heart was filled full (μέγα) all round with anger'. This is a difficult expression, in which the most awkward word is μέλαιναι. The φρένες were treated as the seat of emotion and thus can be properly translated 'heart'; most commentators take μέλαιναι figuratively, explaining that Agamemnon's heart was 'darkened' with anger. Such a *particular* use of a descriptive epithet is, however, contrary to Homer's normal practice. It is therefore rather more likely that μέλαιναι is a stock epithet of φρένες (dark, as hidden in the body), and is no more significant than the same word applied to ships (l. 141).

104. ὄσσε: dual, 'eyes'.
λαμπετόωντι: *diektasis*; cp. l. 31 n.
εἴκτην: dual of pluperfect of ἔοικα.

105. κάκ' ὀσσόμενος: 'with a threatening look'.

107. μαντεύεσθαι: an explanatory infinitive attached to the sentence.

110. δή: ironical; 'how – if we are to believe you – it is for this reason that, etc.'

111. Χρυσηΐδος: This is the first time the girl has been named; to be accurate it is more a description than a name – 'the daughter of Chryses'.

112. πολὺ βούλομαι: 'I much prefer'.
αὐτήν: 'her herself', as opposed to the ransom.

113. οἴκοι: locative, 'at home'.
προβέβουλα: an active-form perfect from προβούλομαι.
This overt comparison of a slave-girl with his 'wedded wife' portrays the same sort of insensitivity in Agamemnon as he showed in his words to Chryses; cp. l. 31 n.

114. ἕθεν: genitive of the third-person pronoun.

115. δέμας is outward appearance, i.e. 'figure'; φυή is growth, i.e. 'stature'. These and the following two nouns are further examples of accusatives of respect (cp. l. 58 n.).

116. ὥς: cp. l. 33 n.

117. βούλομαι: 'prefer'; cp. l. 112.
ἔμμεναι: εἶναι.

118. γέρας: 'gift of honour', due to the king as a mark of distinction.
ὄφρα: final, 'in order that'.

119. ἔω: ὦ.
οὐδὲ ἔοικε: 'it is not at all proper'.

120. λεύσσετε, etc.: 'for you all see that my prize is going elsewhere'.
ὅ = ὅτι.

122. It is instructive to see the stages by which Achilleus and Agamemnon lose their tempers. Here Achilleus is still polite, apart from
the one word φιλοκτεανώτατε. Later he becomes much ruder.

124. 'We do not know of quantities of public property stored anywhere.'

125. τὰ μέν: relative.
πολίων: i.e. the little towns near Troy; Achilleus refers to plunder-
ing expeditions such as that in which Chryseis had been captured
(ll. 366 ff.).
ἐξεπράθομεν: ἐκπέρθω.
δέδασται: δατέομαι.

126. 'It is not fair that the people should collect these things together
again.'

127. θεῷ πρόες: 'give her up to the god'.

128. ποθί: που.

129. δῷσι: lengthened form of the subjunctive, δῷ (cp. l. 324 n.).

131. ἀγαθός: 'good' in the sense of a good fighter; 'brave'.
περ: This enclitic particle lays a slight stress on the previous word;
the result is often concessive, as here and in the regular later use of
καίπερ.

132. κλέπτε νόῳ: 'try to deceive me with a trick'.
παρελεύσεαι: second-person singular, future of παρέρχομαι; 'you
will not get past me'.

133–4. 'Do you wish, in order to keep your own prize, that I on the
other hand should sit by on my own without one; is this why you are
telling me to give back the girl?' This is an awkward sentence, and
other possible interpretations have been suggested. The above is the

most simple. ὄφρα introduces a purpose clause with the verb in the subjunctive; αὐτάρ is like ἀλλά in l. 82, placed with adversative effect at the beginning of the main sentence after a subordinate clause.

δευόμενον: δεόμενον.

135–6. ἀλλ᾽ εἰ μέν, etc.: There is no apodosis to this conditional sentence; one must understand 'all right', 'I will accept that'.

136. ἄρσαντες (ἀραρίσκω): 'making it (the γέρας) conform'.

κατὰ θυμόν: understand ἐμόν; 'to my wishes'.

137. εἰ δέ κε ... ἐγὼ δέ κεν: The two parts of the line take the form of two parallel statements, as if the εἰ clause is not yet treated as subordinate. From the point of view of later Greek, this is another example of apodotic δέ (l. 58).

κεν ἕλωμαι: The subjunctive is more direct than the optative, and differs little in sense from a future; 'I will take her myself'. Contrast εἴ κεν φύγοιμεν (l. 60) and the note there.

138. τεόν: 'yours'.

ἢ Αἴαντος ... ἢ Ὀδυσῆος: Aias, when mentioned without further means of identification, is always the greater Aias, the son of Telamon. He and Odysseus are named here as the two most important leaders of the Greeks apart from Agamemnon and Achilleus himself.

139. κεχολώσεται: future perfect; κεν with the future is rare, but not unknown.

140. μεταφρασόμεσθα: The ending is a metrically useful alternative to -ομεθα.

141. ἄγε: cp. l. 62 n.

ἐρύσσομεν: aorist subjunctive (l. 67 n.); also ἀγείρομεν (l. 142) and βήσομεν (l. 144).

142. ἐν δέ: 'and in it'; ἐν is here adverbial.

ἐπιτηδές: 'for the purpose'.

ἐς (εἰς) ... θείομεν: εἰστίθημι. This also is aorist subjunctive, with short vowel.

143. ἄν: The preposition ἀνά, shortened by apocope (the cutting-off of the last syllable); it is separated from its verb βήσομεν by tmesis.

144. βήσομεν: active future (βήσω) and first aorist (ἔβησα) of βαίνω are transitive; 'make to go', 'embark'.

εἷς δέ τις, etc.: ἀνὴρ βουληφόρος go with εἷς as the subject of the verb ἔστω; ἀρχός is predicate.

145. Ἰδομενεύς: the powerful leader of the Cretan contingent.

146. ἐκπαγλότατε: 'most terrible'. The word is not in itself abusive, but has some offensiveness in that it appears to be a rejoinder to Achilleus' insulting φιλοκτεανώτατε.

147. ἑκάεργον: an old title of Apollo, like ἑκηβόλου in l. 14, and perhaps with the same meaning, 'archer'.

ἱλάσσεαι: second-person singular, aorist middle subjunctive.

148. ὑπόδρα ἰδών: 'frowning'.

Achilleus seems hardly to have heard the second half of Agamemnon's speech, from l. 140, in which the king suggested that they postpone the present dispute and see to the return of the girl.

149. ἀναιδείην ἐπιειμένε: 'clothed in shamelessness' (ἐφέννυμι).

150. πείθηται: deliberative subjunctive; 'how is anyone to obey?'

152. ἤλυθον: ἦλθον.

αἰχμητάων: Notice the normal genitive plural of the -α declension in Homer, in -αων (cp. Latin -arum).

154. ἤλασαν: ἐλαύνω.

μέν: μήν.

155. ἐν Φθίῃ: Phthia, part of Thessaly, was Achilleus' home.

159. τιμήν: not 'honour', but 'compensation' in a material sense.

Μενελάῳ: because the expedition was intended to avenge the carrying-off of Menelaos' wife Helen.

κυνῶπα: vocative.

160. πρός with the genitive: 'from'.

τῶν: relative, referring not to the just-mentioned Trojans, but to the loyal service of the Greek army described by Achilleus in ll. 158–9.

162. ᾧ ἔπι: ἐφ᾽ ᾧ.

164. εὖ ναιόμενον: 'prosperous'.

The reference here is not to Troy itself, but (as in l. 125) to the small towns near Troy against which the Greeks had made expeditions.

170. ἴμεν: ἰέναι.

οὐδέ σ᾽ ὀίω, etc.: 'it is not my intention to stay dishonoured here and amass wealth for you'. The elision of σοι in l. 170 is unique in Homer, although μοι is elided more than once (e.g. VI 165). ἀφύξειν is a metaphor from drawing water from a well; Achilleus refuses to stay as Agamemnon's servant.

This final sentence is strained in expression and metaphor; the effect is of an emotional climax to the speech (cp. l. 291).

173. φεῦγε μάλα: 'run away if you want to'.
ἐπέσσυται: ἐπισεύω; 'is eager to'.

174. ἐμεῖο: ἐμοῦ.
πάρα: πάρεισι.

175. κε + future: cp. l. 139 n.
μητίετα: nominative, first-declension masculine.

176. ἐσσί: εἶ.

180. Μυρμιδόνεσσιν: The Myrmidons were the subjects of Achilleus, and lived in Thessaly.

182. Double accusative with a verb of taking away. The thought of this and the following lines is 'As Apollo takes Chryseis away from me, so I will take Briseis from you'; but the second clause is divided into two statements, correlated by μέν and δέ.

184. κ' ἄγω: equivalent to ἄξω. For the construction, cp. l. 137 n.
Βρισηΐδα: the daughter of Briseis (l. 392). Homer gives her, as he gave Chryseis (l. 111), only this descriptive name. Achilleus had captured Briseis after killing her husband and brothers when the town of Lyrnessos was taken (II 690, XIX 291 ff.); it was on the same expedition (II 691) on which he had taken Hypoplakian Thebe, made numerous captives including Chryseis (I 366), and killed the father and brothers of Andromache (VI 416 ff.). (On the similarity between the fates of Briseis and Andromache, and on other obscurities in the details given in the *Iliad* of Briseis' past, see Reinhardt, *Die Ilias und ihr Dichter*, pp. 50–7.)

186. ὅσσον (ὅσον): 'how much'.

187. ἶσον (adverb) ἐμοὶ φάσθαι: 'to speak on equal terms with me'.

188. Πηλείωνι: 'the son of Peleus'; as well as the common Greek patronymic in -ιδης, Homer uses also forms in -ιος (adjectival) and -ιων, as here.
ἐν: with στήθεσσιν.
οἱ: dative of the pronoun; trans. 'his'.
ἦτορ: subject of μερμήριξεν.

190. ἤ ... ἦε (l. 192): 'whether ... or'; these are the two alternatives considered by Achilleus. The optatives ἀναστήσειεν, etc., represent what would be deliberative subjunctives in primary sequence.

ὅ γε: not necessary to the sense, but a natural insistence on the hero about to act; so also ὁ δέ in the next line.

193. ἦος: ἔως.

194. ἕλκετο: imperfect, as ὥρμαινε in the previous line; while Achilleus was thinking, and slowly drawing his sword, Athene appeared.

ἦλθε δ' 'Αθήνη: This is the main sentence after the two subordinate verbs in the ἦος clause; the δέ is *apodotic* (l. 58).

195. οὐρανόθεν: 'from heaven'.

πρό . . . ἧκε: προίημι.

196. ὁμῶς = ὁμοίως, 'equally'.

197. ξανθῆς κόμης: partitive genitive, common with verbs of grasping and touching.

198. The gods are visible only to those by whom they wish to be seen.

200. δεινὼ δέ οἱ ὄσσε φάανθεν: This is the reason why Achilleus recognised that it was Athene. So the δέ is to be translated 'for'; and οἱ refers to Athene. 'For her eyes gleamed terribly.'

φάανθεν: ἐφάνθησαν (l. 57).

201. ἔπεα πτερόεντα: 'winged words', in that they fly from mouth to ear; an ancient poetic phrase.

202. τίπτε: τί ποτε, 'why?'

αὖτε: not so much 'again' as 'in addition'; it is, as Leaf says, an expression of impatience, not a reference to a previous appearance of Athene.

αἰγιόχοιο: The *aigis* is a supernatural weapon of the gods, carried by Zeus, but used from time to time by Athene and Apollo. It is normally defensive, like a shield (the popular etymology suggested a goat-skin), but can be used offensively, because when shaken in the face of the enemy it strikes terror in their hearts.

203. 'Ατρεΐδαο: for the ending, cp. l. 75 n.

204. ἔκ τοι ἐρέω: ἐξερῶ σοι.

τελέεσθαι: future middle infinitive with passive meaning; 'and I think that it will be accomplished'.

205. τάχα: 'soon'.

ἂν θυμὸν ὀλέσσῃ: 'he will die'; cp. l. 137 n.

206. γλαυκῶπις: The word doubtless meant 'bright-eyed' or 'grey-eyed' to Homer, but this is not inconsistent with the possibility that it originally meant 'owl-faced', Athene having once been worshipped in

the form of an owl; cp. l. 39 n. for Apollo the mouse-god, and l. 551 for βοῶπις πότνια Ἥρη.

207. αἴ κε πίθηαι: 'if you will obey'. Notice how Homer preserves the human dignity of his characters. The goddess can advise, but she does not compel; the decision and the responsibility remain with Achilleus.

211. ὡς ἔσσεταί περ: 'how it will be', i.e. 'what will happen'.

213. καί: with τρὶς τόσσα.

214. ἴσχεο: imperative middle of ἴσχω, a by-form of ἔχω; 'restrain yourself'.

ἡμῖν: i.e. 'Hera and me'.

216. σφωίτερον: pronominal adjective of the second-person dual, 'of you two'.

εἰρύσσασθαι: 'respect'; see ἐρύω (B) in Liddell – Scott – Jones.

218. An obviously proverbial line; features common in such general statements are the τε (cp. l. 63 n.) and the *gnomic aorist* ἔκλυον; this is the aorist found in proverbs, of things which happen now and have always happened.

219. ἦ: 'he spoke'; past tense of ἠμί, which survived in Attic (particularly Plato) in the common phrases ἦ δ' ὅς, ἦν δ' ἐγώ.

σχέθε: 'restrained', 'held back' his hand.

221. βεβήκει: pluperfect, but simply means 'went'.

222. ἐς: with δώματα.

μετά + accusative: 'to the company of'.

225. Blistering abuse. 'Drunkard, with the eyes of a dog and the heart of a deer.'

228. κήρ: 'death'; 'you avoid *that* like the plague'. Cp. III 454 (the Trojan attitude to Paris) ἶσον γάρ σφιν πᾶσιν ἀπήχθετο κηρὶ μελαίνῃ, 'they all hated him like black death'.

230. ἀποαιρεῖσθαι ὅς τις: i.e. 'from the man who'.

232. ἦ γὰρ ἄν: 'for otherwise', 'or else'.

234. ναὶ μά: 'yes, by . . .' (cp. l. 86).

τόδε σκῆπτρον: i.e. the sceptre Achilleus is holding, for we learn elsewhere in the *Iliad* that a speaker in the assembly holds a sceptre which has been handed to him by one of the heralds (e.g. XXIII 568).

235. πρῶτα = πρῶτον, adverb; cp. τὰ πρῶτα (l. 6).

236. ἑ: accusative pronoun, 'it'. περιλέπω, like other verbs of taking away (l. 182), takes two objects in the accusative.

238. θέμιστας: 'the traditions'; the accepted standards and judgements handed down from one's ancestors.

239. εἰρύαται: It is a feature of the Ionic dialect that the ν of the third-person plural is sometimes vocalised as an α; εἴρυνται (cp. l. 216).

244. ὅ τε: accusative neuter of the relative used adverbially; 'with respect to the fact that', 'because'. It is not distinguishable in meaning from ὅτι, which, however, is never elided.

ἔτεισας: better ἔτισας, from τίω 'honour'.

245. ποτί: πρός; tmesis.

247. Nestor now intervenes in the quarrel. He is the oldest by far of the Achaian leaders, and thus a figure to whom respect is due. Nestor is one of Homer's favourite characters; in his actions, and more especially in his speeches, the poet dwells lovingly on the characteristics of the old man.

248. λιγύς: 'clear-voiced', a complimentary term for an orator.

Πυλίων: Pylos, Nestor's kingdom, was on the west coast of the Peloponnese, in an area unimportant in later Greece, but one of the two or three strongest kingdoms in Mycenaean times (see II 591 n.).

250. Nestor is represented as having lived through two generations and now being king in the third, i.e. he was approximately in his seventies.

μερόπων: an epithet whose meaning was almost certainly lost even for Homer; it is used only in formulas with cases of ἄνθρωποι, apart from II 285 with βροτοί.

251. ἐφθίατο: for ἔφθιντο; cp. εἰρύαται (l. 239). Third-person plural, pluperfect.

τράφεν: ἐτράφησαν.

256. κεχαροίατο: third-person plural, optative, of a reduplicated aorist middle of χαίρω; cp. πεπίθοιμεν (l. 100).

257. εἰ σφῶιν τάδε πάντα πυθοίατο: πυνθάνομαι is construed with the accusative of the thing and the genitive of the person; 'if they heard all this about you two fighting'. σφῶιν and μαρναμένοιιν are dual genitives.

258. περί, which is repeated in the μέν and δέ clauses, is in tmesis with ἐστέ; περιεῖναι means 'to be superior'.

βουλήν: accusative of respect, parallel here to the infinitive μάχεσθαι.

259–74. A mythological example adduced to increase the persuasive-
ness of Nestor's intervention. The passage has the common 'ring-
form': (1) Accept my advice. (2) I once associated with better men
than you. (3) They accepted my advice. (4) You should accept it.

It is probable enough that the association of Nestor with the
Lapiths in their war against the centaurs is an *ad hoc* invention of the
poet for the purpose of this passage. For more about the war, see
II 742–4 and the note on l. 742. The centaurs were wild creatures, half
man, half beast, who were associated with Mount Pelion in Thessaly;
the Lapiths were a human tribe, not much less wild than their
opponents.

262. οὐδὲ ἴδωμαι: 'nor shall I see'; subjunctive with future sense.

263. οἷον Πειρίθοον, etc.: Instead of a subordinate clause introduced
by οἷος ἦν, the relative word has been attracted into the accusative of
its antecedent τοίους, and Πειρίθοον and the others are in apposition to it.

Πειρίθοον: the king of the Lapiths, friend of Theseus.

265. This line, not found in the best manuscripts nor referred to in the
ancient scholia (see l. 343 n.), seems to have been an early addition to
the text. (It occurs in the same context, a list of those who led the
Lapiths against the centaurs, in the pseudo-Hesiodic *Shield of Herakles*,
182.)

It is a strange fact that Theseus, the traditional hero of Athens,
about whom so many legends were told, has no mention (apart from
the doubtful presence of this line) in the *Iliad*, the Athenian contingent being led by the unimportant Menestheus. If l. 265 is an interpolation, however, there is no need to assume an Athenian hand at
work; Theseus, the friend of Peirithoos, is a natural figure in this story,
as he was the most important supporter of the Lapiths in their war
against the centaurs.

268. φηρσίν: the Aeolic form for Aeolic creatures; cp. II 743, where
φῆρας occurs, also of the centaurs; elsewhere Ionic θήρ, θῆρες.

270. ἀπίης: 'distant', adjective from ἀπό, as ἀντίος from ἀντί. Later
the dramatists used the word of the Peloponnese, with a long α
(ᾱπία γῆ).

271. κατ' ἔμ' αὐτόν: 'on my own'.

273. βουλέων: for βουλάων by Ionic *metathesis* of vowels (Introduction,
p. xiii), by the same process as genitive masculine singular -εω for -αο

(l. 75 n.). There is a contraction, or *syniζesis*, of the second syllable -εων.

ξύνιεν: συνίεσαν.

275-6 are an appeal to Agamemnon; 277-81 to Achilleus; 282-4 to Agamemnon again. Nestor is doing his best.

275. ἀγαθός: 'strong'; cp. l. 131.

277. Πηλείδη ἔθελ᾽: printed as in the Oxford text, this involves the *syniζesis* of the two vowels η-ε into one syllable; alternatively editors print either 'θελ᾽ (with *prodelision*) or θέλ᾽ from the shorter form of the verb.

278-9. A proverbial statement; 'no ordinary honour is the lot of a sceptre-bearing king, to whom Zeus has given glory'.

οὐχ ὁμοίης: 'not the same', i.e. much greater.

ἔμμορε: probably perfect, from μείρομαι.

279. σκηπτοῦχος βασιλεύς: Achilleus himself is of course a βασιλεύς; but Agamemnon is perhaps particularly entitled to be called a σκηπτοῦχος βασιλεύς, as ruling the whole army; and he has his own personal and hereditary sceptre (II 101 ff.).

ᾧ τε: relative, referring to βασιλεύς; the τε does not mean 'and', but is the generic, proverbial τε (cp. l. 63 n.).

280-1. καρτερός and φέρτερος are put antithetically in the same position in the two lines, and sound as if they are comparable words, although in fact the one is a positive adjective, meaning 'strong', and the other a comparative meaning 'stronger'.

280. θεά: Thetis.

281. ἀλλά: cp. l. 82 n.

283. Ἀχιλλῆι: 'in favour of Achilleus'.

286. κατὰ μοῖραν: 'properly'.

287. περὶ πάντων ἔμμεναι: cp. l. 258 n. ἔμμεναι = εἶναι.

289. τινα: subject of πείσεσθαι; Agamemnon is thinking particularly of himself.

291. The difficulty here lies in προθέουσιν. The most straightforward sense would be obtained by a word meaning 'permit' or 'encourage' with the gods as subject; and some have viewed προθέουσιν as a by-form of προτιθέασιν from προτίθημι, which could give this sense. But the form is unparalleled and the explanation therefore unacceptable. The alternative (unless indeed, as I suspect, the word is

corrupt) is to take προθέουσιν as third-person plural of προθέω 'run forward', with ὀνείδεα as its subject; 'is it for that reason that his abusive remarks burst out to be spoken?' This is decidedly uncomfortable, but the parallel of ll. 170–1 may support a violent and obscure metaphor as the climax of a strongly felt speech.

292. ὑποβλήδην: 'abruptly'; it is noticed that Achilleus does not in this speech begin with any form of address to Agamemnon.

299. τῳ: τινί.

301. οὐκ ἂν φέροις: a firm negative; 'you cannot take'.

302. εἰ δ' ἄγε: In this phrase εἰ is an exclamatory particle, and with ἄγε (cp. l. 62 n.) may be translated 'come on now'.

305. ἀνστήτην: for ἀναστήτην, by apocope of the preposition (l. 143).

306. ἐίσας: 'well proportioned'; epic form of ἴσας.

307. ἤιε: cp. l. 47.

Μενοιτιάδῃ: the son of Menoitios, Patroklos, who was Achilleus' friend. It is significant that Patroklos can be referred to by his patronymic name alone, on the first occasion when he appears in the *Iliad* (just as Agamemnon was in l. 7), and strongly suggests that he was a familiar figure in the legend to Homer's audience.

309. ἐν: adverbial; 'therein'.

ἔκρινε: 'chose'.

310. ἀνά . . . εἶσεν: ἀνέζω.

311. Ὀδυσσεύς: Odysseus is the most capable of the Greeks for any sort of activity, and is the natural choice to see that Chryseis is properly handed back to her father.

313–14. The army engages in a ritual purification after the plague.

317. ἐλισσομένη περὶ καπνῷ: 'eddying round in the smoke'; περί seems to be used here of something going round *inside* something else, as in XXII 95, where a snake is described as ἐλισσομένος περὶ χειῇ, 'twisting round in its hole'.

321. κήρυκε: The functions of the heralds included the taking of messages, arranging of sacrifices, and general assistance to the kings.

322. κλισίην: accusative of the goal of motion.

Πηληιάδεω: cp. l. 1 n.

323. χειρὸς ἑλόντε: 'taking her by the hand'.

ἀγέμεν: infinitive for imperative.

324 = 137 (with a slight change in the first verb).

δώῃσιν: The epic dialect possessed, for the three singular persons of the subjunctive, alternative endings in -ωμι, -ησθα, -ησι. These forms are regularly used to produce a third-foot caesura, as here.

326. Cp. l. 25.

330. An effective understatement.

336. σφῶι: dual of the second-person pronoun; the enclitic σφωίν (l. 338) is the dual of the third-person pronoun.

337. Πατρόκλεες: vocative of a variant form Πατροκλέης.

339. πρός: 'in the presence of'.

340. τοῦ βασιλῆος ἀπηνέος: 'him, the ruthless king'; the word-order would be impossible in later Greek, with τοῦ as the article (cp. l. 11 n.).

343. ἅμα πρόσσω καὶ ὀπίσσω: 'the immediate future, and the more distant future'. The A scholia (scholia are marginal and other notes derived from ancient commentaries on Homer and preserved alongside the text in some of our manuscripts; the A scholia are those in the important manuscript 'Venetus A') say among other things καὶ νῦν καὶ ὕστερον.

344. μαχέοιντο: The optative is difficult to explain grammatically; several editors change to μαχέονται (future). If correct, the optative must simply make the clause more hypothetical and remote.

349. ἑτάρων: with νόσφι.

350. θῖνα: with ἔπι.

ἐπ' ἀπείρονα πόντον: The manuscripts and the majority of editors read ἐπὶ οἴνοπα ποντον. The text is that of Aristarchus.

In general, and certainly in this line, ἅλς is the sea near the shore, πόντος or θάλασσα the open sea.

351. μητρί: the sea-goddess Thetis.

353. ὄφελλεν: ὀφέλλω is the epic form of ὀφείλω; 'ought'.

354. ὑψιβρεμέτης: as the god of thunder.

οὐδὲ τυτθόν: 'not even a little'.

ἔτεισεν: cp. l. 244 n.

356. ἀπούρας: aorist participle, an interesting form in which the original digamma (ἀπο-Ϝρας) has been vocalised as a υ.

358. πατρὶ γέροντι: Nereus, the old man of the sea, father of the Nereids.

362. σε φρένας: double accusative, of 'the whole and the part'.

363. εἴδομεν: subjunctive, from οἶδα.

365. τίη: often printed τί ἦ, 'why'.

ταῦτα πάντα: object primarily of ἀγορεύω, but also of ἰδυίῃ.
ἰδυίῃ: εἰδυίᾳ.

366. ᾠχόμεθα: i.e. on one of the expeditions referred to in l. 125.

Θήβην: This is the so-called Hypoplakian Thebe, near Troy, the home of Andromache, whose father Eetion was king (VI 395–7). Chryseis had apparently been taken among the captives there, not in her own home town of Chryse; cp. l. 184 n.

371–5 = 12–16; 376–9 = 22–5. The repetition of lines and even passages like this is a natural feature of oral poetry.

371. χαλκοχιτώνων: This is a common formulaic epithet of the Achaians, and must refer to defensive armour worn in the Mycenaean age. Miss Lorimer (*Homer and the Monuments*, pp. 201, 209) refers to figures on the Warrior Vase from Mykenai, who seem to be wearing both *chitons* and jerkins strengthened by metal disks. Trans. 'bronze-clad'.

382. ἧκε: ἵημι.

385. ἑκάτοιο: This is the fourth title of Apollo beginning with the syllable ἑκ- that has appeared in this book: ἑκηβόλου (l. 14); ἑκατηβελέταο (l. 75); ἑκάεργον (l. 147); and ἑκάτοιο in this line. ἕκατος appears to be a masculine form of the much commoner Hekate, the name of Artemis as an underworld goddess.

387. Ἀτρείωνα: For the form, cp. Πηλείωνι (l. 188).

390. ἐς Χρύσην: 'to (the town) Chryse'.
ἄνακτι: Apollo.

391. νέον: adverb, 'just now'.

392. Βρισῆος: 'of Briseus'.

393. περίσχεο: imperative of the aorist middle of περιέχω, 'protect'; cp. ἀμφιβέβηκας (l. 37).
ἑῆος: genitive of the adjective ἐύς, corresponding to the adverb εὖ. The rough breathing is an accident of the transmission.

394. λῖσαι: imperative of ἐλισάμην, first aorist of λίσσομαι.
εἴ ποτε δή τι: cp. ll. 39–41 n.

395. ὤνησας: ὀνίνημι.

396–406. This story of a revolt on Olympos, which Thetis helped to prevent by bringing Briareos–Aigaion to defend Zeus, is not attested anywhere else. Every consideration makes it probable that we have here the free invention of the poet, not an allusion to pre-existing myth. Homer required a reason for Zeus to be under obligation to Thetis, and therefore created one. Cp. ll. 259–74 n.

The introductory statement, 'many times have I heard you boasting in my father's house', is used in the same way in XXI 475, where the verisimilitude of the alleged recollection is no greater than here (cp. also v 832).

396. σεο: with ἄκουσα.

πατρός: Peleus, Achilleus' father.

397. Κρονίωνι: the son of Kronos, Zeus.

400. These three deities are in the *Iliad* the allies of the Greeks. Thetis is now to be asked to ask Zeus to help the Trojans; so these gods would try to oppose her request. By a strange sort of reflex effect, it seems that the real circumstances at Troy have conditioned the choice of detail in the invented myth.

402. ἑκατόγχειρον: The hekatoncheirs Kottos, Briareos and Gyas (with a hundred arms each, fifty pairs of shoulders and fifty heads) were a distinct group of monstrous creatures from the early dawn of the world. Hesiod tells how they supported Zeus and the Olympian gods in the war against the Titans (*Theogony*, 617 ff.). Briareos' appearance as a supporter of Zeus here, therefore, is probably a characteristic use of a known theme (cp. Introduction, p. xx).

403–4. On four occasions in the *Iliad* different names are quoted from the languages of gods and men. They are

I 403 (a giant)	Βριαρέως/Αἰγαίων
II 813 (a hill)	σῆμα Μυρίνης/Βατίεια
XIV 291 (a bird)	χαλκίς/κύμινδις
XX 74 (the river)	Ξάνθος/Σκάμανδρος

(gods' names first). The accepted explanation is that the gods' language is the transmitted poetical language from the past, while the language of men is the common and everyday terminology known to the poet.

The name Aigaion suggests an emanation from the Aegean Sea. Contradictory information about this figure is given in our ancient sources. Homer's identification of him with the hekatoncheir is un-explained, and adds to the impression that these lines are sheer in-vention.

404. ὁ γὰρ αὖτε, etc.: 'for he in his turn is stronger than his father'. The point of this comment remains obscure, in spite of the efforts of the scholia (see l. 343 n.) and modern commentators. It is possible that there is a submerged connection with the quite different story linking Thetis with Zeus (found in Pindar's *Eighth Isthmian* and Aeschylus' *Prometheus Vinctus*), namely that the sea-goddess, if mated with Zeus or Poseidon, was fated to bear a son *stronger than his father*. At least the motif is the same.

βίην: accusative of respect; the manuscript tradition gives βίη.

405. κύδεϊ γαίων: 'glorying in his superiority'.

406. οὐδ᾽ ἔτι: καὶ οὐκέτι.

407. λαβὲ γούνων: The attitude of a suppliant was to clasp the knees of the person appealed to with one hand and reach for his chin with the other; cp. ll. 500–1.

408. αἴ κέν πως: cp. l. 66 n.

ἐθέλῃσιν: ἐθέλῃ (cp. l. 324 n.).

We should not fail to notice that Achilleus is now asking Zeus to help the Trojans, his enemies, to kill his friends the Greeks; his personal honour weighs more with him than the lives of his friends.

409. πρύμνας: because the ships were drawn up on the beach with their prows to the water.

ἔλσαι: εἴλω.

410. ἐπαύρωνται: 'may get the benefit of their king', i.e. learn what it is to have such a king.

412. ἄτην: The Homeric concept of ἄτη is of an infatuation which temporarily destroys a person's judgement, so that he behaves as he would not normally behave.

ὅ τε: cp. l. 244 n.

414. αἰνά: adverb; 'unhappy in being a mother'.

416. ἐπεί νύ τοι, etc.: The verb ἐστί can be used with adverbs, and is here to be understood both with μίνυνθα and with δήν.

417. περί: 'beyond'; cp. l. 258.

418. ἔπλεο: πέλομαι.

τῶ: 'therefore'.

423-4. The absence of the gods at a feast given by the Aithiopes makes a pause in the story during which Chryseis may be given back to her father and the Greeks may begin to learn what it is like to be without Achilleus on the battlefield (ll. 488-92). The same device is used at the beginning of the *Odyssey*, where Poseidon's absence visiting these same Aithiopes enables the other gods to start Odysseus on his homeward voyage.

Ὠκεανόν: The earth was thought of as a flat disk, bordered by the river Okeanos.

Αἰθιοπῆας: a god-loving people, far to the south-east.

425. δωδεκάτη: The interval of twelve days is used for the activities mentioned in the note on ll. 423-4, but it also has the strange effect of isolating the action of the *Iliad* from the continuity of the Trojan War, especially as there is a similar interval of twelve days at the end of the *Iliad*, for such is the length of the truce which Achilleus agrees with Priam for the Trojans to mourn and bury Hektor (XXIV 667).

426. ποτί: πρός.

δῶ: δῶμα.

428. ἀπεβήσετο: This is an example of the *sigmatic second aorist*, in which the σ is added to the stem to form the aorist, as in the usual first aorist, but the endings are those of the second aorist.

429. γυναικός: causal genitive.

430. ἀέκοντος: genitive with ἀπηύρων, which would normally (as a verb of taking away) take a double accusative.

ἀπηύρων: a development of the verb whose aorist participle appeared as ἀπούρας in l. 356 (see note there). The aorist indicative form ἀπηύρα was misunderstood by Ionian bards as the imperfect of a contracted verb *ἀπαυράω, and other imperfect forms such as the one found in this line were created.

434. The ἱστοδόκη was a crutch, a forked piece of wood at the stern of the ship, into which the mast was lowered by slackening the forestays (προτόνοισιν ὑφέντες) (Leaf).

436-9. Note four successive lines beginning with the word ἐκ (in each case in *tmesis* with the verb) to describe the disembarkation.

εὐνάς: heavy stones used as anchors. The ship was moored facing out to sea; the εὐναί were thrown out at the front, while the stern was tied to the shore by πρυμνήσια.

444. ἱλασόμεσθα: subjunctive.

447. τοί: an alternative form of the nominative plural οἱ.

449. οὐλοχύτας: Barley grains were sprinkled between the horns of the sacrificial victim.

ἀνέλοντο: 'took up with their hands' from a basket.

450. τοῖσι: 'in their presence'.

451–2 = 37–8.

453. ἠμέν ... 455. ἠδέ: The particles correlate the two sentences; 'both ... and', 'as ... so'.

454. τίμησας: With this accent it is the second-person singular of the aorist indicative, a new verb without connection with the previous line; if this is correct, l. 454 is an explanation of ἔκλυες in l. 453. Trans. 'As you heard my prayer before, honoured me, but greatly afflicted the people of the Achaians, so now, etc.' But τιμήσας participle may be preferable.

ἴψαο: ἴπτομαι.

458–66. This is a complete description of the procedure at a sacrifice. After a prayer, and the scattering of the grains of barley between the horns of the victim (l. 458), they pulled the head back to expose the neck, cut its throat, and skinned it (l. 459); then they cut out the thigh-bones, covered them with a layer of fat above and below, and laid on top of them pieces of flesh, to symbolise the offering of the whole animal (ll. 460–1). These pieces were then burnt as an offering to the god, while libations of wine were poured; the young men stood by the priest holding five-pronged forks on which they quickly roasted the entrails (heart, liver, lungs, kidney, stomach) (ll. 462–3). These were eaten, or perhaps just ritually tasted, as a first course, and then they cut all the meat up small, pierced it on the spits, and roasted it (ll. 464–6). II 421–9 describe a sacrifice in exactly the same terms apart from two lines in the middle.

459. αὐέρυσαν: from ἀν-Ϝερυσαν, 'they pulled up'.

460. μηρούς: cp. l. 40 n.

463. νέοι δὲ παρ' αὐτόν, etc.: It is not clear from the Greek whether the young men were standing there waiting to take part in the main roasting that starts in l. 465, or whether they were engaged in roasting the σπλάγχνα (l. 464). The latter is more logical, and is strongly supported by the line that comes at this point in the description in book II:

II 426 σπλάγχνα δ' ἄρ' ἀμπείραντες ὑπείρεχον Ἡφαίστοιο ('They spitted the entrails and held them over the fire.')

464. κατὰ μῆρε κάη: better, with the manuscript tradition, to read κατὰ μῆρ' ἐκάη; the dual μῆρε is odd, and is not even the normal dual of the -ος declension, which is μῆρω. μῆρ' would be μῆρα, a neuter plural.

467. τετύκοντο: reduplicated aorist middle of τεύχω.

468. ἐίσης: 'equally apportioned', the same for all (cp. l. 306 n.).

469. ἐξ ἔρον ἔντο: 'put away from themselves (ἐξίεμαι) their desire', i.e. had satisfied it. The whole line is a recurring formula meaning 'when the meal was over'; it is hypercritical to see an inconsistency between πόσιος here and the arrangements for serving wine in ll. 470–1.

470. κρητῆρας: It was very rare in the ancient world to drink wine neat; it was usually diluted with water, and that was the purpose of the 'mixing-bowl'.

471. ἐπαρξάμενοι δεπάεσσι: Before the company drank the wine, a small amount was put into each man's cup and poured out by him on the ground as a libation. This ritual is denoted here by ἐπαρξάμενοι.

472. μολπῇ: song and dance.

473. καλόν: adverbial with ἀείδοντες.
παιήονα: a hymn to Apollo, asking for release from the plague.

477. This line occurs twenty times in the *Odyssey*, but only twice in the *Iliad* (here and XXIV 788).

478. ἀνάγοντο: 'sailed out of the harbour'.

481. ἐν ... πρῆσεν (ἐμπρήθω): 'blew into'.
ἀμφί: 'on both sides'.

482. στείρῃ: locative, 'at the stem', i.e. the front part of the keel.

488–92. These lines show the passing of time (the twelve days until the gods should return from the Aithiopes), and certainly imply that fighting was going on, but without Achilleus.

490. πωλέσκετο: Forms in -εσκον, etc., formed from either present or aorist of the verb, are very common in Homer as *frequentatives*; 'he never used to go'. Cp. the verbs in the next two lines.

491. φίλον: 'his'; φίλος with parts of the body, possessions, or close relatives, is approximately the same as the personal pronoun.
φίλον κῆρ: accusative of respect.

493. ἐκ τοῖο: from the time when Thetis told Achilleus that the gods would return in twelve days (l. 425); any awkwardness caused by the intervening description of the voyage to Chryse is minimised by ll. 488–92, which clearly take us back to the beginning of the wrath.

496. ἀνεδύσετο: cp. ἀπεβήσετο (l. 428).

497. ἠερίη: 'early'.

500–1. The suppliant's attitude; cp. l. 407 n.

503. εἴ ποτε δή: cp. ll. 39–41 n. It may be noticed that Thetis does not mention the supposed story of her saving Zeus when the gods wished to bind him (ll. 396–406).

505. ὠκυμορώτατος ἄλλων: By a common Greek idiom, she describes her son as 'most short-lived of (i.e. in comparison with) all others.'

508. τεῖσον: τίω.

μητίετα (= 175) and 511. νεφεληγερέτα: These first-declension masculine nominatives belong to a largish group of ancient forms in -ᾰ found in Homer, almost all of them being formulaic adjectives of gods or heroes.

509. ἐπί ... τίθει: tmesis.

510. ὀφέλλωσίν ἑ τιμῇ: not so much 'increase him in honour', as 'improve his standing by paying him compensation'.

513. ἔχετο: 'held on'.
ἐμπεφυυῖα: 'clinging to him'.

515. ἔπι: ἔπεστι.

517. μέγ' ὀχθήσας: 'much disturbed'.

518. λοίγια ἔργα: an exclamation, like our 'a bad business'.
ὅ τε: cp. l. 244 n.; 'in that you will cause me to quarrel with Hera'.

520. καὶ αὔτως: 'even as it is'.

523. κε ... μελήσεται: for κε with the future, cp. l. 139.

524. εἰ δ' ἄγε: cp. l. 302 n.

526. ἐμόν: There is no noun for this word; its place is supplied by the phrase in the next line ὅτι κεν κεφαλῇ κατανεύσω. Trans. 'Nothing from me is reversible'.

528–30. This powerful description combines Zeus the anthropomorphic king of the gods with the sky and weather god from whom he originated – the dark brows being the underside of the storm cloud, the flowing hair the 'anvil' of cirrus spreading from the top of the cloud, and the thunder shaking Mount Olympos.

528. ἐπί ... νεῦσε: *tmesis.*

529. ἐπερρώσαντο: ἐπιρρώομαι. Here, 'flowed out'.

531. διέτμαγεν: διέτμαγησαν (from διατμήγω, in prose διατέμνω), 'separated'.

532. ἆλτο: old aorist of ἄλλομαι.

533. Ζεὺς δέ: understand ἔβη, by a sort of zeugma from ἆλτο.

536. μιν: probably object of ἠγνοίησεν as well as of ἰδοῦσα; this is an example of the common Greek idiom whereby the person involved in a subordinate clause after a verb of perception is made the object of the verb in the main clause (e.g. I know *thee* who thou art, οἶδά σε ὅστις εἶ). 'Nor was Hera unaware, when she saw him, that, etc.'

539. κερτομίοισι: understand ἐπέεσσι.

541. ἐόντα: accusative, in spite of τοι dative, because the participle's main syntactical relationship is as subject of the infinitive δικαζέμεν.

542. κρυπτάδια: with φρονέοντα.
δικαζέμεν: 'to take decisions'.
οὐδέ πω ... τέτληκας: 'you have never liked to'.

547. ἀλλ' ὃν μὲν (μῦθόν) κ' ἐπιεικὲς (ᾗ σοι) ἀκουέμεν.

551. βοῶπις: cp. the note on γλαυκῶπις (l. 206).

Zeus and Hera are now engaged in an unseemly family quarrel, so much less dignified and less 'heroic' than the quarrel of Achilleus and Agamemnon which to a large extent is the cause of it. It is a strange fact that the gods in the *Iliad* have particularly human failings.

554. ἄσσα: ἅτινα (Attic ἄττα).

555. παρείπῃ: In later Greek a fear that something has already happened is put into the indicative; here and elsewhere in Homer, however, the aorist subjunctive is used: 'I am very much afraid that Thetis has persuaded you.'

558–9. ὡς τιμήσῃς, ὀλέσῃς δέ: ὡς with the subjunctive may with difficulty be interpreted here as a kind of purpose clause, or the subjunctive may be treated as the equivalent of a future. Most editors, however, prefer the very slight change to τιμήσεις, ὀλέσεις.

559. Ἀχαιῶν: with πολέας (πολλούς).

561. δαιμονίη: 'This word, always found in the vocative, seems to mean properly one who is under the influence of a δαίμων or un- favourable divine intelligence; that is, one whose actions are either unaccountable or ill-omened' (Leaf). It is used by a person re- monstrating with another. Trans. 'my dear'.

αἰεὶ μὲν ὀίεαι: a reference to her use of the word ὀίω in l. 558; 'you are always *fancying*'. The ending -εαι of the second-person singular is found again in the next two lines.

562. πρῆξαι: πράσσω is πρήσσω in Ionic.

ἀπὸ θυμοῦ, etc.: 'you will be the more disliked by me'.

566-7. As on other occasions when Zeus faces opposition from the other gods, he becomes a bully and threatens physical violence.

566. χραίσμωσιν: The verb really means 'to be of use', but here by a sort of extension of meaning it takes an object of what the gods are not going to be of use *against* – ἄσσον ἰόντα (με).

571. Hephaistos, the divine smith and god of fire, lame from birth, was the son of Hera and Zeus.

572. ἐπὶ ἦρα φέρων: 'doing a favour'; ἐπί ... φέρων is *tmesis* for ἐπιφέρων; ἦρα is an accusative singular.

577. καὶ αὐτῇ περ νοεούσῃ: 'though she realises it herself'.

578. ἐπὶ ἦρα φέρειν: cp. l. 572 n.

580. εἴ περ γάρ, etc.: No apodosis to this condition is expressed, although an explanation is given in the ὁ γάρ clause (l. 581); 'if he wishes, etc. (what can we do about it?); for he is far the strongest'.

582. καθάπτεσθαι: infinitive for imperative.

584. ἀμφικύπελλον: 'two-handled' is the most intelligible of the various interpretations which have been proposed for this word.

590 ff. A different version of the fall of the lame god from Olympos is given in xvIII 395 ff. Zeus throwing gods out of heaven is a re- peated motif; in xv 22-4 several gods are recorded as having been so thrown; and in xIX 130-1 the story is told of how he threw out Ate, the goddess of delusion.

μεμαῶτα: 'eager', a participle from the shorter stem of the perfect μέμονα.

591. τεταγών: reduplicated aorist, of which no present is found. The form is obviously the same as Latin *tetigi* from *tango*.

592. πᾶν δ' ἦμαρ, etc.: Milton adapted these lines as follows:

> from Morn
> To Noon he fell, from Noon to dewy Eve,
> A Summers day; and with the setting Sun
> Dropt from the Zenith like a falling Star
> On Lemnos th' Ægæan Ile.
>
> (*Paradise Lost*, 1 742–6)

593. κάππεσον (κατέπεσον): κατά, having been shortened to κατ by *apocope*, has its final consonant assimilated to the π at the beginning of the verb.

ἐν Λήμνῳ: The island of Lemnos, at the north of the Aegean Sea, was sacred to Hephaistos.

597. ἐνδέξια: 'from left to right'.

598. ἀπὸ κρητῆρος: The gods drink nectar as men drink wine, apparently, first mixing it with water in a mixing-bowl (l. 470).

599. γέλως: It was the sight of the clumsy movements of Hephaistos which drove the simple-minded and carefree gods to laughter, and so relieved the tension (l. 570), as Hephaistos no doubt intended.

600. ποιπνύοντα: The word seems originally to have signified 'to breathe heavily'; but it is used in the *Iliad* rather with the meaning 'to bustle about'.

603. μέν: μήν.

603–4. The Muses singing, with Apollo accompanying them on the lyre, were the usual musical entertainment at celestial occasions.

604. ἀμειβόμεναι: 'antiphonally', i.e. with alternating voices.

606. κακκείοντες: for κατακείοντες (cp. κάππεσον, l. 593). κείω is a *desiderative* verb formed from κεῖμαι. Trans. 'to go to bed'.

607. ἀμφιγυήεις: 'crooked in both feet', 'lame'.

610. ἔνθα: relative meaning 'where' in this line, but demonstrative 'there' in the next line.

611. παρά: adverb, 'by his side'.

BOOK II

*The Dream of Agamemnon;
the Testing of the Morale of the
Army; the Catalogue of Ships;
the Trojan Catalogue*

1. ῥα: Homeric verse uses all three forms ἄρα, ἄρ, and enclitic ῥα merely as required by the metre. The particle has a mild inferential force.

ἀνέρες = ἄνδρες.

ἱπποκορυσταί: 'fighting from chariots'. κορύσσειν is 'to arm' or 'equip'; ἵπποι in Homer regularly mean 'chariot'.

2. ἔχε = εἶχε. The augment is very often omitted in Homer; cp. μερμήριζε (l. 3), φαίνετο (l. 5).

νήδυμος: 'sweet'; always of sleep.

'All other gods and men slept through the night, but Zeus did not sleep'; this typically Greek antithesis makes an excellent start to the second book, and to the deceptive dream that Zeus sent to Agamemnon. There is, however, a slight inconsistency. At the end of book 1 we were told that all the gods went home to bed, and Zeus slept beside his wife Hera. Now we are informed that he did not sleep after all. This is only a small difficulty, and would not worry the ancient hearer or modern reader unduly; it is made less apparent and less significant by the fact that the book division here at least falls at a natural break in the story.

3. ὁ: 'he'; what later Greek knew as the definite article was still primarily a demonstrative pronoun in Homeric Greek.

μερμήριζε: cp. the note on ἔχε (l. 2).

Ἀχιλῆα: accusative of Ἀχιλεύς, alternative form of Ἀχιλλεύς.

Achilleus has withdrawn from the battle in anger at the slight done to him by the king, Agamemnon. At his request, his mother, the sea-goddess Thetis, persuaded Zeus to undertake to support the Trojans and let them defeat the Greeks until the latter realised how badly off they were without Achilleus. Zeus is now considering how to fulfil that promise.

4. τιμήσῃ, ὀλέσῃ: deliberative subjunctives.

πολέας = πολλούς.

νηυσίν = ναυσίν.

c

'Αχαιῶν: probably dependent on πολέας, not on νηυσίν. Notice that there are three names used by the poet indistinguishably for the Greeks – Achaians ('Αχαιοί), Argives ('Αργεῖοι) and Danaans (Δαναοί).

5. οἱ: dative of the third-person pronoun, 'to him'.

6. 'Ατρείδη: 'the son of Atreus'; the Homeric language is very fond of patronymics.

οὖλον = ὀλοόν, 'destructive'; exactly as the wrath of Achilleus is described in 1 2 as οὐλομένην.

7. μιν: the epic form of νιν, accusative third-person pronoun; 'him'.

ἔπεα πτερόεντα: 'winged words', in that they fly from mouth to ear; an ancient poetic phrase.

ἔπεα: Attic ἔπη; uncontracted forms are common in Homer.

προσηύδα: imperfect of προσαυδάω.

8. βάσκ' ἴθι: Both words are imperatives; 'off with you and go'.

θοάς: 'swift'; a common epithet of ships, even when they are as here drawn up on the beach.

9. 'Ατρείδαο: The old form of the genitive of -α declension masculine nouns was in -αο.

10. μάλα: may be taken either with πάντα or with ἀτρεκέως; 'absolutely'.

ἀγορευέμεν: an alternative form for the infinitive, = ἀγορεύειν; here it is used as an imperative.

11. ἑ: accusative of the third-person pronoun, 'him'.

κάρη κομόωντας: The phrase is taken to mean 'with hair growing over the whole head', as opposed to tribes such as the Thrakes, who are described (IV 533) as ἀκρόκομοι, i.e. 'with topknots'. Trans. 'long-haired'.

κάρη: a neuter noun; here accusative of respect with κομόωντας.

κομόωντας: This, from the verb κομάω, would if uncontracted be κομάοντας, if contracted κομῶντας. By a peculiarity of Homeric Greek (caused no doubt by the opposed pressures of contraction of vowels and the requirements of the metre), the contracted form has suffered a sort of expansion or distension. This, technically called *diektasis*, is found particularly with verbs in -αω.

12. κεν: κε (κεν) is the alternative form of the modal particle ἄν, and is used in the same way. Here, with the optative, it is potential; 'he can take', 'he may take'.

13. οὐ γὰρ ἔτι: οὐκέτι γάρ.

ἀμφίς: adverb, 'on two sides'; with φράζονται, 'think differently', 'are divided'.

14. φράζονται: middle, not passive.

ἐπέγναμψεν: 'has bent', 'has won over'.

15. Ἥρη: Hera, the queen of the gods, is an inveterate enemy of Troy. The second η in her name is an example of the most obvious Ionic feature of the Homeric dialect – η for α even after ε, ι, ρ; cp. κλισίην (l. 9).

κήδεα: 'cares', 'troubles'.

ἐφῆπται: perfect passive of ἐφάπτω; lit. 'have been fastened to'.

16. ὥς: Accented in this way, or with the circumflex ὧς, this word is an adverb, = οὕτως, 'so'; the conjunction ὡς is unaccented.

φάτο: imperfect middle of φημί; there is no distinction of meaning from the active.

18. τόν: cp. l. 3 n.

19. περί ... κέχυτο: περιεκέχυτο, pluperfect passive of περιχέω; the elements which later constituted a compound verb are still separable in Homer, with the preposition able to stand by itself as an adverb. The phenomenon is called *tmesis* (from τέμνω, 'cut'). In practice one may treat this as if a verb has been divided into its two parts, although the true situation is that the two parts have not yet coalesced.

ἀμβρόσιος: 'heavenly', an adjective formed from ἄμβροτος, 'immortal'.

20. υἷι: a third-declension form of the dative of υἱός.

Νηληΐῳ υἷι: 'Neleus' son'; Νηλήιος is simply an adjective formed from Νηλεύς. The adjective formed from the father's name is often used alone as a patronymic, e.g. Τελαμώνιος Αἴας (l. 528).

ἐοικώς: perfect participle of εἴκω, used with the dative to mean 'resembling', 'like'.

21. γερόντων: 'advisers', 'councillors'; the genitive is dependent on μάλιστα.

22. τῷ (see l. 3 n.) is to be taken with ἐεισάμενος, μιν (see l. 7 n.) with προσεφώνεε.

ἐεισάμενος: first aorist participle of εἴδομαι, 'to be like'. The first ε is not of course the augment (which would not be present on the participle) but a *prothetic* vowel, as in ἐθέλω (θέλω), ἐέργω (ἔργω).

προσεφώνεε: uncontracted; cp. ἔπεα (l. 7).

23. ἱπποδάμοιο: The genitive singular of -ος declension nouns and adjectives may be in -οιο as well as -ου.

24. παννύχιον: adjective agreeing with ἄνδρα, but used predicatively with εὔδειν; cp. l. 2.

25. ἐπιτετράφαται: third-person plural of the perfect passive of ἐπιτρέπω, for ἐπιτετραφ-νται. The ν (fourth letter from the end) has been vocalised as an α, such a collocation of consonants as -φντ- being quite impossible. τόσσα = τοσαῦτα.

μέμηλε: perfect of μέλω.

26. ἐμέθεν = ἐμοῦ, genitive with ξύνες.

ξύνες: aorist imperative of συνίημι.

τοι: the same as the enclitic σοι, the unstressed dative of σύ.

27. σεῦ = σοῦ, to be taken with κήδεται; the other verb, ἐλεαίρει, would take the accusative, and σέ can easily be understood from σεῦ.

ἐών = ὤν.

ἠδέ: an alternative word for 'and'.

28-32 = 11-15 (see the notes on those lines), apart from the necessary changes of σε for ἑ, κέλευσε for κέλευε, and ἕλοις for ἕλοι.

33. σῇσιν = σαῖς.

ἔχε: 'keep *this*'.

34. εὖτε: 'when'. It is followed here by a normal *indefinite* clause, with ἄν and the subjunctive.

35. ὧς: cp. l. 16 n.

ἀπεβήσετο: This is an example of a *sigmatic second aorist*, i.e. the σ is added to the stem to form the aorist, as in the usual first aorist, but the endings are those of the second aorist. This is a middle aorist of ἀποβαίνω.

αὐτοῦ: 'there'.

36. τά: cp. l. 3 n.; the antecedent of ἅ.

τελέεσθαι: future middle with passive meaning, 'to be accomplished'.

ἔμελλον: The neuter plural subject ἅ takes here a plural verb.

37. φῆ = ἔφη from φημί, but here meaning 'he thought', not 'he said'.

38. νήπιος: a fairly common comment by the poet on human short-sightedness; the reason for the criticism is given in the rest of the line.

τά ... ἅ: cp. l. 36.

ἤδη: past tense of οἶδα.

39. θήσειν ... ἐπί: i.e. ἐπιθήσειν (ἐπιτίθημι); another example of
tmesis (l. 19).

40. διά: 'in the course of'.

41. ἔγρετο: aorist middle of ἐγείρω; 'he woke up'.

ἀμφέχυτο: aorist middle of ἀμφιχέω; 'surrounded'.

ὀμφή: the voice of a god.

42. χιτών was a tunic worn next to the skin; φᾶρος (l. 43) was a
cloak.

43. νηγάτεον: a word of uncertain origin, probably meaning 'not
previously worn', 'new'.

περί ... βάλλετο: tmesis (l. 19). Middle voice, 'he put it on himself'; cp. the middle verbs in the next two lines.

44. ποσσί = ποσί.

ὑπό ... ἐδήσατο: tmesis (l. 19).

λιπαροῖσιν: 'bright', 'shining', 'well cared for'.

45. ἀμφί ... βάλετο: tmesis (l. 19).

ἀργυρόηλον: 'with rivets of silver' (for attaching the blade to the
handle).

The sword belt was hung over the right shoulder.

46. εἵλετο: aorist middle of αἱρέω; 'he took'.

σκῆπτρον: The staff showed the authority of the king; in the
assembly it was passed to the speaker, to show his right to speak. This
particular sceptre is described in ll. 101–8 of this book; it is hereditary
in Agamemnon's family (πατρώιον) and was made by a god, Hephaistos (ἄφθιτον αἰεί).

47. τῷ: cp. l. 3 n.

χαλκοχιτώνων: This is a common formulaic epithet of the Achaians,
and must refer to defensive armour worn in the Mycenaean age. Miss
Lorimer (*Homer and the Monuments*, pp. 201, 209) refers to figures on
the Warrior Vase from Mykenai, who seem to be wearing both
chitons and jerkins strengthened by metal disks. Trans. 'bronze-clad'.

48. προσεβήσετο: cp. ἀπεβήσετο (l. 35).

μακρόν: 'high'.

Ὄλυμπον: Olympos, the mountain, not heaven.

Commentators ancient and modern have pointed out the accuracy of Homer's observation here; the peaks of the mountain are first lit by the dawn.

49. φόως = φάος (Attic φῶς), 'light'.
ἐρέουσα: 'to announce'; future participle.

50. κηρύκεσσι: 'heralds', whose functions included the summoning of an assembly and the arrangements at sacrifices, as well as the taking of messages from the kings.

51. ἀγορήνδε: The suffix δε with an accusative shows motion towards; = εἰς ἀγορήν.
κάρη κομόωντας: cp. l. 11.

52. τοί: an alternative form of the nominative plural οἱ.

53. Agamemnon decides to hold a meeting of the council (βουλή) before the general assembly of the army.

54. βασιλῆος is in apposition to the genitive Νέστορος implied in the adjective Νεστορέη.
Πυλοιγενέος: Nestor was king of Pylos.

55. πυκινήν = πυκνήν; 'concentrated', 'carefully thought out'.

56. κλῦτε: aorist imperative.
ἐνύπνιον: adverb; = ἐν ὕπνῳ.

57. ἀμβροσίην: see l. 19 n.

58. εἶδος is 'appearance', μέγεθος 'size', φυή 'physique'. The words are accusative of respect, a common Greek accusative, most regularly used with parts of the body.
ἄγχιστα: 'most closely'; the word is tautologous after μάλιστα (l. 57).
ἐῴκει: pluperfect of εἴκω; cp. l. 20 n.

59. πρός ... ἔειπεν: tmesis; the compound verb here takes two objects.

60–70 (φρεσίν) = 23–33. See the notes on those verses. 65–9 appear now for the third time, as 28–32 repeated 11–15. The repetition of lines and even whole passages is a natural feature of oral poetry.

71. ἀποπτάμενος: participle from ἀπεπτάμην, aorist of ἀποπέτομαι.
ἀνῆκεν: from ἀνίημι.

72. ἄγετε: 'come!'
αἰ: the Aeolic form of εἰ.
αἴ κέν πως 'if by any chance', 'in the hope that'.

θωρήξομεν = θωρήξωμεν; aorist subjunctives with a short vowel are normal in Homer.

73. πρῶτα: adverb, = πρῶτον.

ἣ θέμις ἐστί: The phrase means 'as is customary'; no doubt it *was* customary to test the reaction of the army to a major policy decision. Agamemnon's method here, however, was probably not a commonly used one.

74. Agamemnon intends to suggest that the army should give up the war at Troy, and return home to Greece, in the hope that this proposal will result in a demand to continue the fighting. It is a perilous plan, and only too likely to lead to the actual result – a rush for the ships. Commentators suggest that the morale of the army was so low, after nine years' inconclusive fighting, then the plague and the withdrawal of Achilleus, that desperate measures were called for. This is not, however, clearly stated by the poet.

πολυκλήισι: 'with many benches for oarsmen'.

75. ἄλλοθεν ἄλλος: 'from all directions', 'on all sides'.
ἐρητεύειν: infinitive for imperative.

79. Nestor has intelligence enough to suspect the advice of the dream; but he is unquestioningly loyal to the supreme king.

80. ἔνισπε: aorist of ἐνέπω.

81. νοσφιζοίμεθα: 'we would turn our backs on it', 'disregard it'.

82. εὔχεται: neither 'boasts' nor 'claims' produces the right effect in English. Agamemnon *is* ἄριστος Ἀχαιῶν, and his claim to be so is legitimate and accepted by others.

83 = 72.

84. βουλῆς ἐξ: ἐκ βουλῆς.

86. ἐπεσσεύοντο: imperfect passive of ἐπισεύω, 'came up eagerly'.

87. This is the first full simile in the *Iliad*, and the first of many in this book. The swarming throng of Greek soldiers coming to the meeting-place from among the tents and ships is likened to a swarm of bees coming out of their nest in a hollow rock.

ἠύτε: 'just as'.
εἶσι: 'come forth', third-person singular of εἶμι ('go').

μελισσάων, etc.: notice the normal genitive plural of the -α declension in Homer, in -αων (cp. Latin -*arum*).

ἀδινάων: The adjective is used of things in quick, restless movement; trans. 'swarming'.

88. νέον: adverbial; 'freshly', 'newly', 'one after another'.

89. βοτρυδόν: 'in a cluster', like grapes; 'swarming'.

90. τε: The enclitic particle τε often accompanies a proverbial or general statement in Homer, and is very much at home in similes. So twice in this line. It is not to be translated.

ἔνθα ... ἔνθα: 'this way ... that way'.

ἅλις: 'in swarms'.

πεποτήαται: for πεπότηνται (cp. ἐπιτετράφαται, l. 25), 'have taken flight'.

91. νεῶν: from ναῦς.

92. βαθείης: 'deep' from the point of view of the onlooker from the land, i.e. 'wide'.

ἐστιχόωντο: ἐστιχῶντο (cp. l. 11 n.).

93. μετά + dative: 'among'.

Ὄσσα: 'Rumour' (personified).

δεδήει: intransitive pluperfect of δαίω, 'had spread like a flame'.

95. τετρήχει: intransitive pluperfect of ταράσσω, 'was in confusion'.

96. σφεας: third-person pronoun, 'them'.

97. βοόωντες: cp. l. 11 n.

ἐρήτυον: *conative* imperfect; 'were trying to restrain them'.

εἴ ποτ' αὐτῆς σχοίατο (σχοῖντο): indirect question; 'to see if they might stop shouting'.

99. σπουδῇ: 'with difficulty', 'at length'.

ἐρήτυθεν: an alternative shorter form for ἐρητύθησαν.

101–8. The history of Agamemnon's sceptre, with a genealogy of his family.

101. τό: for ὅ, the later article being occasionally used as a relative.

κάμε τεύχων: 'manufactured'.

102. Κρονίωνι: 'son of Kronos'; as well as the common Greek patronymic in -ιδης (e.g. Ἀτρείδη, l. 6), Homer also uses adjectival forms in -ιος (e.g. Νηληΐῳ, l. 20) and -ιων, as here.

103. Both titles of Hermes are obscure in meaning. Many explanations of διάκτορος have been given; the simplest is that it means 'guide'

(διάγω). ἀργειφόντης was traditionally supposed to mean 'the slayer of Argos' (the giant set to watch over the bovine Io), and it may have meant this to Homer. Its true origin, however, is probably not now recoverable.

105. αὖτε: 'in his turn'.

106. Thyestes, Atreus' brother, apparently held the kingship after Atreus, and then left it at his death to his nephew Agamemnon; Homer shows no knowledge of the violent hatred between Atreus and Thyestes which we find in tragedy.

107. Θυέστα = Θυέστης; cp. ἱππότα (nom.), l. 336.

φορῆναι: Aeolic infinitive, = φορεῖν.

108. Agamemnon's kingdom – 'many islands and all Argos' (i.e. the whole Peloponnese? or all Greece?). This is not consistent with the very restricted kingdom ascribed to Agamemnon in ll. 569–80: Jachmann (*Die homerische Schiffskatalog und die Ilias*, pp. 92 ff.) argues that the general overlordship of Agamemnon is a poetic exaggeration, brought out especially in statements such as this.

109. ἐρεισάμενος: 'leaning on'; a staff, therefore, rather than what we think of as a sceptre.

110–41. Agamemnon's speech is a mixture of arguments for and against departure.

111. μέγα: adverb.

ἄτη: The Homeric concept of ἄτη is of an infatuation which temporarily destroys a person's judgement, so that he behaves as he would not normally behave; trans. 'recklessness', 'folly'.

112. πρὶν μέν is answered by l. 114, νῦν δέ.

113. ἐκπέρσαντα: accusative, in spite of μοι, became the prime syntactical relationship of the participle is as subject of ἀπονέεσθαι.

ἀπονέεσθαι: present infinitive, with future meaning.

115. δυσκλέα: for δυσκλεέα (δυσκλεῆ).

116. μέλλει: 'it seems probable that'.

117. πολίων κάρηνα: lit. 'heads of cities', i.e. the crown of towers and walls of the citadel on the acropolis.

119. τόδε: explained by the accusative and infinitive construction in ll. 120 f.

πυθέσθαι: explanatory infinitive; 'even for future generations to hear of'.

122. πέφανται: φαίνω.

123. εἴ περ γάρ, etc.: a long hypothetical condition, the protasis going on till l. 127. The only difference from later Attic practice here is the κε (= ἄν) in the protasis as well as the apodosis.

124. The throats of the sacrificial victims (ὅρκια) were *cut* at the making of a truce. Trans. 'having made a solemn truce'.
ἀριθμηθήμεναι: infinitive; = ἀριθμηθῆναι.

125. ἐφέστιοι: i.e. οἳ ναίουσι κατὰ πτόλιν (l. 130).
ἔασιν: εἰσίν (also l. 131).

127. ἕκαστοι: i.e. each group of ten Greeks.

128. δευοίατο: δεύοιντο, δέοιντο; 'would lack'.
Agamemnon has chosen a graphic way of showing the great difference of numbers between the Trojans (minus their allies) and the Greeks.

129. τόσσον: adverbial accusative of extent, 'so much more numerous' (πλέας).
πλέας: πλέονας.

131. πολλέων: feminine genitive plural, = πολλάων, by Ionic metathesis of vowels (see Introduction, p. xiii).

132. πλάζουσι: 'distract', 'prevent'.
εἰῶσι: ἐῶσι.

134. βεβάασι: βαίνω.

135. 'The ships planks are rotten and the rigging decayed.' Neuter plural subjects may evidently take either a singular or a plural verb.

137. ἥαται: ἧνται (ἧμαι).
ποτιδέγμεναι: προσδεχόμεναι; ποτί = πρός; δέγμενος is thought to be present participle of *δέγμαι, an alternative form of δέχομαι; cp. δέκτο (l. 420).
ἄμμι: ἡμῖν.

138. αὔτως: strengthens ἀκράαντον, 'simply uncompleted'.
ἱκόμεσθα: a metrically useful variant of ἱκόμεθα (ἱκνέομαι).

139. ἄγετε: cp. l. 72 n.

140. Agamemnon makes his dangerous suggestion of flight.

143. μετά: 'among'; normally with the dative in this meaning, not the accusative.

144. φή = ὡς; a very ancient word, found only twice in the *Iliad*.

145. πόντου Ἰκαρίοιο: defining θαλάσσης; Ikaria was an island near Samos, by the eastern shore of the Aegean Sea, where Ikaros fell, it was said, from the sky.

146. ὦρορε: ὄρνυμι; transitive.

147. λήιον: 'cornfield'.

148. λάβρος: 'violent'.
ἐπαιγίζων: 'rushing on', specifically of a storm wind.
ἐπί ... ἠμύει: tmesis; 'bends down', 'bends over'; intransitive; the subject is λήιον.

152. ἑλκέμεν: ἕλκειν.
δῖαν: 'bright'.

153. οὐρούς: furrows or channels in the sand, by which the ships were dragged up from, and down to, the sea.

154. ἱεμένων: 'of men eager (for home)'.
ὑπό ... ἤρεον: tmesis; 'took from underneath'.
ἕρματα: 'props'.

155. ὑπέρμορα: A man's fate (μόρος) was established at his birth; Homer sometimes speaks as if it might be theoretically possible to frustrate it, but in practice this does not happen – the gods, if necessary, stepping in to prevent such an upsetting of the balance of the world. So here the Greeks might have gone home contrary to what was fated for them and for Troy, had not Hera taken action.

156. πρός ... ἔειπεν: with double accusative.
Hera and Athene are always on the watch to help the Greeks.

157. αἰγιόχοιο: The *aigis* is a supernatural weapon of the gods, carried by Zeus, but used from time to time by Athene and Apollo. It is normally defensive, like a shield (the popular etymology suggested a goat-skin), but can be used offensively, because when shaken in the face of the enemy it strikes terror in their hearts.
Ἀτρυτώνη: an ancient and obscure title of Athene; supposed to mean 'the unwearied one'.

160. κάδ: the preposition κατά, shortened by *apocope* (the cutting-off of the last syllable), and then with the final consonant assimilated to the first sound of the following word. κάδ ... λίποιεν is yet another example of *tmesis*.
εὐχωλήν: 'triumph', 'cause for boasting'.

161. 'Αργείην 'Ελένην: defining further the εὐχωλή
line.

Helen did not come from the town of Argos but
Homer can use 'Argos' for at least the whole Pel
and the title 'Argives' for all the Greeks.

165. ἄλαδε = εἰς ἅλα (l. 152).

ἀμφιελίσσας: 'curved at both ends'.

166. γλαυκῶπις to Homer doubtless meant 'brigh
eyed'; but this is not inconsistent with the possibi
originally meant 'owl-faced', Athene having at or
shipped in the form of an owl; cp. βοῶπις πότνι
often).

169. Odysseus is the obvious person for the task A
and indeed is the special favourite of the goddess
shows here – coolness of mind, and speed of thou
μῆτιν: accusative of respect; 'like Zeus in inventi

170. ἑσταότα: perfect participle of ἵστημι.

171. μιν ... κραδίην καὶ θυμόν: double object
the part'.

176–81 = 160–5 (with small changes in 176, 179
on the earlier lines.

179. ἐρώει: 'be slow', 'give up'.

180. There may seem to us a slight oddity in At
Odysseus her own instructions from Hera, even
plimentary reference to her powers of persuasion
of oral poetry.

182. ξυνέηκε: συνίημι.

183. βῆ δὲ θέειν: 'started to run'.

κόμισσε: 'picked up'.

185. 'Ατρείδεω: from 'Ατρείδαο (l. 9), by Ionic
(see Introduction, p. xiii).

186. οἱ: 'from him'.

188. ὅν τινα ... κιχείη: indefinite clause in hi
construction as in Attic.

μέν: answered by the δέ in l. 198.

κιχείη: subjunctive, as if from a verb in
provides tenses serving as the aorist system of κι

(διάγω). ἀργειφόντης was traditionally supposed to mean 'the slayer of Argos' (the giant set to watch over the bovine Io), and it may have meant this to Homer. Its true origin, however, is probably not now recoverable.

105. αὖτε: 'in his turn'.

106. Thyestes, Atreus' brother, apparently held the kingship after Atreus, and then left it at his death to his nephew Agamemnon; Homer shows no knowledge of the violent hatred between Atreus and Thyestes which we find in tragedy.

107. Θυέστα = Θυέστης; cp. ἱππότα (nom.), l. 336.
   φορῆναι: Aeolic infinitive, = φορεῖν.

108. Agamemnon's kingdom – 'many islands and all Argos' (i.e. the whole Peloponnese? or all Greece?). This is not consistent with the very restricted kingdom ascribed to Agamemnon in ll. 569–80: Jachmann (*Die homerische Schiffskatalog und die Ilias*, pp. 92 ff.) argues that the general overlordship of Agamemnon is a poetic exaggeration, brought out especially in statements such as this.

109. ἐρεισάμενος: 'leaning on'; a staff, therefore, rather than what we think of as a sceptre.

110–41. Agamemnon's speech is a mixture of arguments for and against departure.

111. μέγα: adverb.
   ἄτη: The Homeric concept of ἄτη is of an infatuation which temporarily destroys a person's judgement, so that he behaves as he would not normally behave; trans. 'recklessness', 'folly'.

112. πρὶν μέν is answered by l. 114, νῦν δέ.

113. ἐκπέρσαντα: accusative, in spite of μοι, became the prime syntactical relationship of the participle is as subject of ἀπονέεσθαι.
   ἀπονέεσθαι: present infinitive, with future meaning.

115. δυσκλέα: for δυσκλεέα (δυσκλεῆ).

116. μέλλει: 'it seems probable that'.

117. πολίων κάρηνα: lit. 'heads of cities', i.e. the crown of towers and walls of the citadel on the acropolis.

119. τόδε: explained by the accusative and infinitive construction in ll. 120 f.
   πυθέσθαι: explanatory infinitive; 'even for future generations to hear of'.

122. πέφανται: φαίνω.

123. εἴ περ γάρ, etc.: a long hypothetical condition, the protasis going on till l. 127. The only difference from later Attic practice here is the κε (= ἄν) in the protasis as well as the apodosis.

124. The throats of the sacrificial victims (ὅρκια) were *cut* at the making of a truce. Trans. 'having made a solemn truce'.

ἀριθμηθήμεναι: infinitive; = ἀριθμηθῆναι.

125. ἐφέστιοι: i.e. οἳ ναίουσι κατὰ πτόλιν (l. 130).

ἔασιν: εἰσίν (also l. 131).

127. ἔκαστοι: i.e. each group of ten Greeks.

128. δενοίατο: δενοῖντο, δέοιντο; 'would lack'.

Agamemnon has chosen a graphic way of showing the great difference of numbers between the Trojans (minus their allies) and the Greeks.

129. τόσσον: adverbial accusative of extent, 'so much more numerous' (πλέας).

πλέας: πλέονας.

131. πολλέων: feminine genitive plural, = πολλάων, by Ionic metathesis of vowels (see Introduction, p. xiii).

132. πλάζουσι: 'distract', 'prevent'.

εἰῶσι: ἐῶσι.

134. βεβάασι: βαίνω.

135. 'The ships planks are rotten and the rigging decayed.' Neuter plural subjects may evidently take either a singular or a plural verb.

137. ἤαται: ἧνται (ἧμαι).

ποτιδέγμεναι: προσδεχόμεναι; ποτί = πρός; δέγμενος is thought to be present participle of *δέγμαι, an alternative form of δέχομαι; cp. δέκτο (l. 420).

ἄμμι: ἡμῖν.

138. αὔτως: strengthens ἀκράαντον, 'simply uncompleted'.

ἱκόμεσθα: a metrically useful variant of ἱκόμεθα (ἱκνέομαι).

139. ἄγετε: cp. l. 72 n.

140. Agamemnon makes his dangerous suggestion of flight.

143. μετά: 'among'; normally with the dative in this meaning, not the accusative.

144. φή = ὡς; a very ancient word, found only twice in the *Iliad*.

145. πόντου Ἰκαρίοιο: defining θαλάσσης; Ikaria was an island near Samos, by the eastern shore of the Aegean Sea, where Ikaros fell, it was said, from the sky.

146. ὦρορε: ὄρνυμι; transitive.

147. λήιον: 'cornfield'.

148. λάβρος: 'violent'.
    ἐπαιγίζων: 'rushing on', specifically of a storm wind.
    ἐπί ... ἠμύει: *tmesis*; 'bends down', 'bends over'; intransitive; the subject is λήιον.

152. ἑλκέμεν: ἕλκειν.
    δῖαν: 'bright'.

153. οὐρούς: furrows or channels in the sand, by which the ships were dragged up from, and down to, the sea.

154. ἱεμένων: 'of men eager (for home)'.
    ὑπό ... ἤρεον: *tmesis*; 'took from underneath'.
    ἕρματα: 'props'.

155. ὑπέρμορα: A man's fate (μόρος) was established at his birth; Homer sometimes speaks as if it might be theoretically possible to frustrate it, but in practice this does not happen – the gods, if necessary, stepping in to prevent such an upsetting of the balance of the world. So here the Greeks might have gone home contrary to what was fated for them and for Troy, had not Hera taken action.

156. πρός ... ἔειπεν: with double accusative.
    Hera and Athene are always on the watch to help the Greeks.

157. αἰγιόχοιο: The *aigis* is a supernatural weapon of the gods, carried by Zeus, but used from time to time by Athene and Apollo. It is normally defensive, like a shield (the popular etymology suggested a goat-skin), but can be used offensively, because when shaken in the face of the enemy it strikes terror in their hearts.
    Ἀτρυτώνη: an ancient and obscure title of Athene; supposed to mean 'the unwearied one'.

160. κάδ: the preposition κατά, shortened by *apocope* (the cutting-off of the last syllable), and then with the final consonant assimilated to the first sound of the following word. κάδ ... λίποιεν is yet another example of *tmesis*.
    εὐχωλήν: 'triumph', 'cause for boasting'.

161. Ἀργείην Ἑλένην: defining further the εὐχωλήν of the previous line.

Helen did not come from the town of Argos but from Sparta. But Homer can use 'Argos' for at least the whole Peloponnese (l. 108), and the title 'Argives' for all the Greeks.

165. ἄλαδε = εἰς ἅλα (l. 152).

ἀμφιελίσσας: 'curved at both ends'.

166. γλαυκῶπις to Homer doubtless meant 'bright-eyed' or 'grey-eyed'; but this is not inconsistent with the possibility that the word originally meant 'owl-faced', Athene having at one time been worshipped in the form of an owl; cp. βοῶπις πότνια Ἥρη (1 551 and often).

169. Odysseus is the obvious person for the task Athene has in mind, and indeed is the special favourite of the goddess for the qualities he shows here – coolness of mind, and speed of thought and action.

μῆτιν: accusative of respect; 'like Zeus *in invention*'.

170. ἑσταότα: perfect participle of ἵστημι.

171. μιν ... κραδίην καὶ θυμόν: double object – of 'the whole and the part'.

176–81 = 160–5 (with small changes in 176, 179 and 180). See notes on the earlier lines.

179. ἐρώει: 'be slow', 'give up'.

180. There may seem to us a slight oddity in Athene passing on to Odysseus her own instructions from Hera, even including the complimentary reference to her powers of persuasion. But this is typical of oral poetry.

182. ξυνέηκε: συνίημι.

183. βῆ δὲ θέειν: 'started to run'.

κόμισσε: 'picked up'.

185. Ἀτρεΐδεω: from Ἀτρεΐδαο (l. 9), by Ionic metathesis of vowels (see Introduction, p. xiii).

186. οἱ: 'from him'.

188. ὅν τινα ... κιχείη: indefinite clause in historic sequence, the construction as in Attic.

μέν: answered by the δέ in l. 198.

κιχείη: subjunctive, as if from a verb in -μι (*κίχημι), which provides tenses serving as the aorist system of κιχάνω, 'find'.

189. δέ: the so-called *apodotic* δέ, introducing the main sentence after a subordinate clause.

ἐρητύσασκε: Tenses in -σκον, formed from either the present or aorist of the verb, are very common in Homer, as *frequentatives*; 'he would restrain him'. Cp. l. 199, ἐλάσασκε, ὁμοκλήσασκε; l. 221, νεικείεσκε.

190. δαιμόνιε: 'This word, always found in the vocative, seems to mean properly one who is under the influence of a δαίμων or unfavourable divine intelligence; that is, one whose actions are either unaccountable or ill-omened' (Leaf). It is used by a person remonstrating with another; trans. 'my friend'.

κακὸν ὥς: 'like a coward'.

δειδίσσεσθαι: At first sight one would expect this to mean 'to be afraid'; but in fact the verb δειδίσσομαι is always transitive in Homer elsewhere, and the meaning of the line is 'it is not right that I should try to *frighten* you as if you were a coward'. This interpretation is supported by xv 196, χερσὶ δὲ μή τί με πάγχυ κακὸν ὣς δειδισσέσθω (where Poseidon is refusing to be bullied by Zeus).

191. κάθησο: imperative of κάθημαι.

192. Ἀτρείωνος: 'son of Atreus' (cp. Κρονίωνι, l. 102).

193. ἴψεται: 'he will chastise, punish'.

195. μή τι, etc.: a warning; 'I am afraid he may, etc.'

ῥέξῃ: ῥέζω; here taking two accusatives – τι κακόν and υἷας Ἀχαιῶν.

197. ἑ: 'him', the singular taken out of διοτρεφέων βασιλήων.

μητίετα: nominative; cp. Θυέστα (l. 107).

198. ὃν δέ: cp. l. 188.

199. Odysseus makes practical use of the ancestral, indestructible, sceptre of Agamemnon.

201–2. The social situation is a simple one. The leaders are, by virtue of their birth, best at both fighting and counsel; the lower orders are less good at either.

204. A much quoted proverb. ἀγαθόν (neuter) = 'is not a good thing'.

205. ἀγκυλομήτεω: genitive, cp. l. 185. It is not known how Kronos, the father of Zeus, earned the epithet 'crooked-thinking', unless it was on account of his practice of swallowing his children.

206. This verse is almost certainly an interpolation; it is missing in the

best manuscripts, and may have been added here in order to give
δῶκε (l. 205) an object. Moreover, the manuscripts which have it end
it with the unmetrical word βασιλεύῃ. βουλεύῃσι has been brought
here from IX 99, which runs σκῆπτρόν τ' ἠδὲ θέμιστας, ἵνα σφίσι
βουλεύῃσθα.

σφίσι: 'them'; this makes no sense in Odysseus' speech here; it is
at home in IX 99.

βουλεύῃσι: The epic dialect possessed, for the three singular persons
of the subjunctive, alternative endings in -ωμι, -ῃσθα, -ῃσι.

210. τε: cp. l. 90 n.

211. ἐρήτυθεν: cp. l. 99 n.

We now meet the only common man who takes any distinctive part
in the *Iliad*, and the only man who is described as ugly. All the other
figures are kings and leaders. Even the minor characters who are
named in order to die in the fighting seem of aristocratic class. Thersites, although later sources give him an aristocratic pedigree, repre-
sents here the ordinary people. Homer's attitude to him, and the
attitude of Homer's audience, is shown by the tendentious description
of him given here. There may be an echo of new political strivings in
Homer's own day – the old aristocracy having become suspect to the
people (cp. Hesiod's βασιλῆες δωρόφαγοι, *Op.* 263), and civil dis-
content breaking out.

212. ἀμετροεπής: 'of immoderate speech'.

213. ᾗσιν: 'his', from the pronominal adjective ὅς.

214. οὐ κατὰ κόσμον: ἄκοσμα (l. 213).

ἐριζέμεναι: explanatory infinitive.

215. A verb of speaking must be understood from the previous lines.
'(He said) what seemed to him to be likely to raise a laugh among the
Argives.'

εἴσαιτο: from εἴδομαι; 'seemed'.

216. αἴσχιστος: 'most ugly'. In the heroic world, good birth =
military prowess = physical beauty.

217 ff. φολκός, φοξός and ψεδνός are found only here in Homer, and
φολκός never recurs in Greek. 'Bandy-legged he was, and lame in one
foot; his shoulders were hunched, brought in upon his chest; above,
his head was pointed; and thin, woolly hair sprouted from it.'

217. τώ . . . ὤμω: dual.

218. συνοχωκότε: perfect participle from συνέχω; intransitive.

219. ἐπενήνοθε: perhaps from ἐπανθέω, 'flower upon'.

220. Followers of Homer took up the suggestion here, and devised a later history for Thersites, in which he eventually met his death at Achilleus' hands (Proclus' summary of the cyclic *Aithiopis*; Quintus Smyrnaeus, 1 722 ff.).

222. κεκλήγων: Aeolic form of κεκληγώς, perfect participle of κλάζω; in fact the manuscripts here read κεκληγώς, but the Oxford editor has altered it on the grounds that the only other case of the participle found in the *Iliad* is the nominative plural, and this (four times) is κεκλήγοντες, not κεκληγότες.

τῷ: Thersites. The Achaians did not approve of the behaviour of their self-chosen champion.

223. νεμέσσηθεν: νέμεσις in Homer is not divine retribution, as later in Attic tragedy; it is the feeling of disapproval aroused in the on-looker by an improper action.

225. τέο: for τοῦ (τίνος), interrogative; 'what are you finding fault with?' Compare the similar uncontracted forms ἕο (οὗ), l. 239; σέο (σοῦ), l. 248.

ἐπιμέμφεαι: second-person singular, Attic -ῃ or -ει; cp. ἐπιδεύεαι (l. 229).

227. ἐνὶ κλισίῃς: ἐν κλισίαις.

τοι: σοι.

228. δίδομεν, ἔλωμεν. Thersites puts himself forward as spokesman of the Greeks. In fact he speaks rather like a parody of Achilleus in the quarrel in book 1; cp. ὅν κεν ἐγὼ δήσας ἀγάγω (l. 231).

229. κε ... οἴσει: κε (ἄν) with the future indicative is not uncommon in Homer.

230. υἱος: genitive.

The practice of taking prisoners with the intention of allowing their relatives to ransom them is mentioned here and there in the *Iliad*. The Greeks were out to enrich themselves, as well as to take vengeance for Helen.

232. γυναῖκα: accusative, because the original construction with ἐπιδεύεαι (l. 229) has now been forgotten, and the objects of Aga-memnon's supposed desires have been accusative for some time (ὅν, l. 229; ὅν, l. 231).

μίσγεαι, 233. κατίσχεαι: These must be subjunctives, although the normal ending would be -ηαι (Attic -η).

233. κατίσχεαι: subjunctive, with the effect of a future.

μέν: μήν.

234. ἐπιβασκέμεν: transitive, with κακῶν, 'make them embark on evil', 'bring them into trouble'.

235. πέπονες: 'soft', 'weaklings'.

236. περ: This enclitic particle puts a slight stress on the preceding word.

237. πεσσέμεν: 'digest', 'enjoy at leisure'.

ἴδηται: 'he may see'; the middle is used in the same sense as the active.

238. ἤ . . . ἦε: indirect question.

χἠμεῖς: καὶ ἡμεῖς, 'we also'.

239. ἔο: cp. l. 225 n.

240. ἀπούρας: aorist participle, an interesting form in which the original digamma (ἀπο-Fρας) as been vocalised as a υ.

242. ἦ γὰρ ἄν, etc.: 'for otherwise . . .'; Achilleus had said this in his quarrel with Agamemnon (I 232).

245. ὑπόδρα ἰδών: 'frowning'.

ἠνίπαπε: ἐνίπτω.

246. λιγύς: 'clear-voiced', a complimentary term for an orator.

περ: cp. l. 236 n. Here, as often, περ has a concessive effect like the later καίπερ.

247. ἴσχεο: middle imperative; 'restrain yourself'.

248. χερειότερον: This looks like a comparative of a comparative (χερείων), just as l. 228 above had πρωτίστῳ, a superlative of a superlative (πρῶτος).

249. Ἀτρείδης: dative plural, referring to both Agamemnon and Menelaos, the two sons of Atreus.

250. τῷ: 'therefore'.

οὐκ ἄν + optative: 'you had better not'.

252. ἴδμεν: ἴσμεν (οἶδα).

253. ἤ . . . ἦε: indirect question (cp. l. 238).

257. 'But I will tell you outright, and it will be fulfilled.'

258. κιχήσομαι: probably aorist subjunctive, not future indicative; cp. l. 72 n.

νυ: the same as the enclitic νυν.

258-64. A long sentence, in which, after the protasis of the condition, the apodosis consists of a wish, with a second condition dependent on it. 'If I find you again . . . may I no longer . . ., if I don't . . .'

260. Τηλεμάχοιο πατήρ: Odysseus is the only person in the *Iliad* who describes himself (here and IV 354) in this way, in relation to his loved ones at home. Strong family attachment is one of the facets of this many-sided character, as may be seen in the *Odyssey*.

261. ἀπό . . . δύσω: probably subjunctive; but ἀφήσω (l. 263) must be future.

φίλα εἵματα: '*your* clothes'; φίλος with parts of the body, possessions, or close relatives is approximately the same as the personal pronoun.

262. τά τ' αἰδῶ ἀμφικαλύπτει: Probably τά τε is simply the relative (τε having the slight generalising sense mentioned in l. 90 n.), referring to the χλαῖνα and the χιτών. The alternative, followed by many commentators, is that these words refer to a *third* article of clothing (τε meaning 'and'), a loin-cloth (ζῶμα). In either case Odysseus is choosing his words to frighten and humiliate Thersites.

264. πεπλήγων: cp. l. 222 n.

266. θαλερόν: 'large'.

268. χρυσέου: The sceptre was not made of gold, but it had golden studs or nails for ornament (I 246).

269. ἀχρεῖον ἰδών: 'with a helpless look'.

270. ἀχνύμενοί περ: They were upset because morale was low, because of the plague and the quarrel between their leaders, perhaps because they were not being allowed to depart for home; they were not at all upset at the treatment of Thersites.

272. ἔοργε: ἔρδω.

275. ἐπέσβολον: 'wild-speaking'.

τόν is the demonstrative, not the article (cp. l. 3), and the words λωβητῆρα ἐπέσβολον are in apposition to τόν. This word-order would be impossible in later Greek, when τόν would be the article and the descriptive epithet (ἐπέσβολον) could not stand outside the article—

noun complex. Cp. 1 340; τοῦ βασιλῆος ἀπηνέος, 'of him, the ruthless king'.

ἔσχ' ἀγοράων: 'put a stop to his public speaking'.

278. φάσαν: plural verb, with a collective noun.

πτολίπορθος: It is not clear what cities Odysseus sacked, apart from Troy, which he has not sacked yet.

279. παρά: adverb, 'by his side'.

The poet says that Odysseus stood up to speak, and by his side stood *Athene* in the guise of a herald, calling for silence from the crowd.

It is difficult for our rational minds to accept the actions of the gods in the way primitive people saw them. When a leading figure rose to speak in the assembly, a herald stood beside him, giving him the sceptre which was the outward sign that he had authority to speak. When Odysseus rose, there was a general and profound silence; the audience, after the tumult of the rush for the ships, and the disturbance caused by Thersites' insubordination, was hushed and expectant. The silence seemed almost uncanny. And therefore, according to the poet, it was no ordinary herald, but Athene in the guise of a herald, who stood by Odysseus' side. Compare the very similar situation explained in the note on l. 791.

284 ff. A fine oration by Odysseus. He begins by addressing Agamemnon, both as a matter of propriety and to bolster his authority as king; but later (l. 299) he turns directly to the army, encouraging them to persevere with the war and reminding them of the prophecy at Aulis nine years before, according to which the war should now be in its last stages.

285. ἐλέγχιστον: 'most dishonoured'.

μερόπεσσι: an epithet whose meaning was almost certainly lost even for Homer; it is used only in formulas with ἄνθρωποι, apart from the example here with βροτοί. A man called Merops appears in l. 831.

286. ἐκτελέουσιν: future.

ὑπέσταν: ὑπέστησαν.

288. ἐκπέρσαντα: understand σε; cp. l. 113.

289. ἤ ... τε: If the former word is correct (many editors follow Bekker in reading the intensive particle ἦ in place of ἤ), there is a strange confusion here of ἤ ... ἤ ('either ... or') and τε ... τε ('and').

290. νέεσθαι: a sort of object of ὀδύρονται; 'they moan to each other to return home'.

291. A difficult line. On the authority of Aristarchus, the Alexandrian scholar, we may take it as if there was a ὥστε before ἀνιηθέντα; 'indeed, there *is* trouble enough to make a man return home in despair'. Alternatively, and perhaps more simply, we could translate 'but surely to return home in despair is also troublesome' (cp. ll. 297–8).

295. περιτροπέων: 'revolving'.

296. μιμνόντεσσι: μίμνουσι.

νεμεσίζομαι: cp. l. 223 n.

298. αἰσχρόν: understand ἐστί, 'it is a shameful thing'.

299. ἐπὶ χρόνον: 'for a time'.

δαῶμεν: from ἐδάην, aorist; 'learn'.

300. ἐτεόν: an internal accusative, 'truly'.

302. κῆρες θανάτοιο: κήρ is the special form of death which comes for each person. Here and at XVIII 535, the κῆρες seem to be like demons of the underworld, physically dragging their victims away.

303. χθιζά τε καὶ πρωιζά: 'yesterday or the day before', i.e. 'very recently'. The temporal adverbs are the antecedent of ὅτε, and have the same effect as the English expression 'it seems just like yesterday'. The main sentence comes with ἔνθ' ἐφάνη in l. 308.

ἐς Αὐλίδα: Aulis, the small town and port in Boiotia, where the Greek fleet was said to have assembled before setting out for Troy.

305. ἀμφὶ περί: a duplication, in which ἀμφί is an adverb, περί a preposition; trans. 'round and about'.

306. ἔρδομεν: ἔρδω (ἔρδω), the same as ῥέζω, is the proper word for 'making' sacrifices.

τελήεσσας: stock epithet of sacrifices – 'perfect', and so promising success.

ἑκατόμβας: supposedly of a 'hundred' animal victims, but used of any large sacrifice.

308. δαφοινός: 'blood-red'.

310. ὑπαίξας: 'darting out from underneath'.

311 ff. The use of human terms (μήτηρ, νήπια τέκνα, etc.) has a pathetic effect; cp. Virgil's frequent treatment of small creatures as having human feelings and aspirations.

312. ὑποπεπτηῶτες: ὑποπτήσσω.

314. ἐλεεινά: to be taken with τετριγῶτας.
τετριγῶτας: τρίζω; 'squeak'.

316. ἐλελιξάμενος: 'having coiled himself up'.
πτέρυγος: normal genitive with verbs of touching and holding.
ἀμφιαχυῖαν: a perfect participle without reduplication, from
ἀμφι-ιάχω.

318. τὸν μέν: the snake.
ἀρίζηλον: 'conspicuous'; ἀρι- (strengthening prefix) + δῆλος.

318–19. It is probable that an ancient corruption has reversed the
original meaning here. The word ἀρίζηλον may hide a word meaning
'unseen' (ἀίζηλον or even ἀειδέλιον). Once l. 318 appeared to state
that the snake became a notable monument (instead of disappearing),
l. 319 was added to show how this happened.

320. ἐτύχθη: τεύχω.

320–1. It would be more consonant with Homeric style to put a
comma at the end of l. 320, and a full stop at the end of l. 321. In this
way l. 321 is an expansion of οἷον ἐτύχθη in l. 320, and Κάλχας δέ in
l. 322 answers ἡμεῖς δέ in l. 320. If the sentence is punctuated in this
way, ὡς οὖν in l. 321 is an example of a particular Homeric use of οὖν,
in a subordinate clause with ἐπεί or ὡς, stressing the completion of an
action (cp. l. 661).

As printed in the Oxford text and by Leaf, there is a full stop at the
end of l. 320. οὖν then becomes an ordinary connecting particle, and
the δέ following Κάλχας in l. 322 is an *apodotic* δέ (cp. l. 189).

321. δεινὰ πέλωρα: 'the frightening monster'.

323. τίπτε: for τί ποτε, 'why'.
ἄνεῳ: more properly ἄνεω, adverb, 'silently'; but here to be translated as an adjective, 'silent'.
κάρη κομόωντες: cp. l. 11.

330. τώς: οὕτως.

331. ἄγε: 'come'. The imperative of ἄγω is used in this way, as an exclamation, here even with a plural verb. We have had ἄγετε twice in
this sense in book II (ll. 72, 83).
ἐυκνήμιδες: greaves were shin-guards, worn particularly as a protection against stones and arrows.

333. ἴαχον: 'shouted'.

Odysseus' speech has been successful in pleasing the crowd and distracting them from taking to the ships. Nestor can now afford to be tougher and more critical.

335. ἐπαινήσαντες: nominative, agreeing with Ἀργεῖοι (l. 333), the intervening clause being treated as a parenthesis.

336. Γερήνιος ἱππότα Νέστωρ: an ancient formula.

Γερήνιος: another word whose origin is quite uncertain. Ancient commentators referred it to a place Gerenia or Gerenon in Messenia, where Nestor was said to have been brought up.

ἱππότα: first-declension nominative masculine (cp. l. 107 n.), 'driver of chariots'; a heroic title, not particularly applicable to Nestor in the *Iliad*.

337. ἀγοράασθε: for ἀγοράεσθε; *diektasis* (cp. l. 11). The first syllable has been lengthened for ease of scansion; cp. the common ᾱθάνατος.

339. βήσεται: i.e. 'what will become of them?'

340. μήδεα: 'plans'.

341. σπονδαὶ ἄκρητοι: 'libations of unmixed wine'; the ancients normally drank their wine diluted with water.

ἐπέπιθμεν: pluperfect (intransitive) of πείθω.

345. ἄρχευε: ἡγεμόνευε.

346. τούσδε δ' ἔα φθινύθειν: 'let these people rot'.

Ἀχαιῶν: with νόσφιν (l. 347).

348. πρίν ... πρίν: adverb ... conjunction (cp. 1 97 n.).

πρὶν Ἄργοσδ' ἰέναι: depends on βουλεύωσι (l. 347).

353. ἐπιδέξια: on the right; i.e. to the east, for the Greeks faced north for augury (XII 239).

ἐναίσιμα σήματα φαίνων: a comment on the first half of the line; the σήματα were the lightning.

354–5. πρίν ... πρίν: as l. 348.

356. 'Avenge the struggles (ὁρμήματα) and lamentations of Helen.' This line, which has caused an unnecessary amount of discussion, recurs at l. 590 of this book, in reference to the intentions of Menelaos. It is true that our general impression of Helen is of one who co-operated willingly in her own abduction; from the Greek point of view, however, and according to what was no doubt a fairly common theme, princesses who are abducted struggle and cry. Helen's

ὁρμήματα and στοναχαί find a close parallel in Hektor's words to his wife in VI 464–5:

ἀλλά με τεθνηῶτα χυτὴ κατὰ γαῖα καλύπτοι
πρίν γέ τι σῆς τε βοῆς σοῦ θ' ἑλκηθμοῖο πυθέσθαι.

'May the piled earth cover my ashes, before I hear you crying and being dragged away.'

357. Now Nestor threatens that anyone who tries to leave will be lynched; this was not quite what he said in l. 346, which was more a curse than a threat.

358. For the genitive, cp. l. 316.

359. πρόσθε: of space, 'in front of'.
     ἐπίσπῃ: ἐφέπειν.

360. μήδεο, πείθεο: present imperative middle, Attic -ου.

362. Nestor ends his speech with advice to Agamemnon about the battle order of the army. This prepares the way for the 'Catalogue of Ships' in the second half of this book.
     κρῖνε: 'separate'.
     φρήτρας: 'clans'.

363. φρήτρηφιν: The suffix -φι seems in the earliest time to have been an instrumental or locative case-ending; but its use had been greatly widened in the epic dialect. Here φρήτρηφιν is obviously the exact grammatical equivalent of the dative φύλοις.

366. ἔῃσι: ἧ; cp. βουλεύῃσι (l. 206).
     κατὰ σφέας γὰρ μαχέονται: 'They will fight in their own sections.' Cp. I 271, where Nestor says that when he went to assist the Lapiths he fought as an independent:

                    καὶ μαχόμην κατ' ἔμ' αὐτὸν ἐγώ.

367. θεσπεσίη: adverbial dative of a noun formed from the feminine of the adjective, 'by the will of the gods'.
     ἀλαπάξεις: future; van Leeuwen well explains the slightly confused thought: 'If you do not take the city, then you will know whether it is through divine will or by the cowardice and inefficiency of your troops.'

368. For ἦ (O.C.T.) read, with most other editors, ἤ ('or').

370. ἦ μάν: Attic, ἦ μήν; a strong asseveration.
     αὖτε: 'once again'.

371. αἰ γάρ: a wish, as in Attic.

373. 'In that case, the city of Priam would soon fall'; for ἠμύω, cp. l. 148.

374. ἁλοῦσα: aorist participle, ἁλίσκομαι.

376. μετά with accusative: 'among'.

377. καὶ γάρ: introduces a particular piece of evidence for a general statement just made; almost equals 'for example'.

εἵνεκα κούρης: with stress at the end of the line, as a trivial reason for two such important men to fall out over.

379. ἐς μίαν: A feminine noun must be understood; perhaps βουλήν (from βουλεύσομεν).

380. οὐδ' ἠβαιόν: 'not even a little'. Cp. also l. 386.

381. Ἄρηα: 'war', as often; cp. l. 385.

382–90. A fine rhetorical passage, with *anaphora* (repetition of the same word at the beginning of successive clauses) both of εὖ in ll. 382–4 and of ἱδρώσει in ll. 388 and 390.

384. ἅρματος ἀμφὶς ἰδών: 'having looked all round (carefully inspected) his chariot'.

πολέμοιο μεδέσθω: 'prepare for war'.

385. κρινώμεθ' Ἄρηι: 'be separated, sorted out, come to a decision, in war'. Cp. διακρινέει (l. 387), 'will separate, part'.

386. μετέσσεται: 'will come among us, intervene'.

388. τευ: του, τινός, 'of somebody' and thus of everybody.

τελαμών: Up to the time of the introduction of the hoplite shield with its arm-band and hand-grip about 700 B.C., shields were supported by a strap over the shoulder.

στήθεσφιν: For the ending, cp. l. 363.

389. ἀμφιβρότης: This epithet clearly originated as a description of the Mycenaean body-shield; but on the three other occasions when it occurs in the *Iliad* it refers to an explicitly stated or implied round shield (XI 32, XII 402, XX 281).

χεῖρα: accusative of respect, of a part of the body, as often.

392. μιμνάζειν: depends on ἐθέλοντα, not on νοήσω.

392–3. 'There will not thereafter be any satisfactory way for him to escape the dogs and birds.'

ἄρκιον: This is an adjective meaning 'sufficient', 'sure'.

ἐσσεῖται: One of four metrically different forms available to the epic poet for the third-person singular of the future of the verb εἰμί (ἔσται, ἔσεται, ἔσσεται, ἐσσεῖται).

κύνας ἠδ' οἰωνούς: i.e. he will be left unburied. The leaving of the body of an enemy for the dogs and birds to eat is constantly referred to in the *Iliad*, mostly as a threat.

394. ὡς ὅτε: understand ἰάχῃ.

396. προβλῆτι σκοπέλῳ: 'a headland jutting out to sea'; in apposition to, and defining more clearly, ἀκτῇ ἐφ' ὑψηλῇ (l. 395), 'against a high cliff'.

397. ἔνθ' ἢ ἔνθα: 'on this side or that'; the subject of γένωνται is κύματα.

398. ἀνστάντες: ἀναστάντες, by apocope (l. 160).

ὀρέοντο: perhaps the imperfect of a verb ὀρέομαι, equivalent to ὄρνυμι.

399. κάπνισσαν: 'they made smoke', and therefore fire.

400. ἔρεζε: cp. l. 306 n.

401. There is a mild zeugma in the use of φυγεῖν; they pray to escape death, and to come safely out of the turmoil of fighting.

405 ff. These then are the chief leaders of the Greeks, Agamemnon's council: Nestor, Idomeneus, Aias son of Telamon, Aias son of Oileus, Diomedes, Odysseus. Achilleus would naturally be added if he were available. Menelaos, as brother of Agamemnon, and mascot as it were of the Greeks (seeing that the war was being fought on his behalf), is present in the council, but does not seem quite to have the standing of the great chiefs.

406. Τύδεος υἱόν: Diomedes, the son of Tydeus.

407. μῆτιν ἀτάλαντον: cp. l. 169.

408. αὐτόματος: 'uninvited'.

βοὴν ἀγαθός: 'good at the war-cry'; βοήν is another example of the Greek accusative of respect (cp. l. 58 n.) – if not a part of the body, it is at least a bodily function.

The heroes shouted in battle, to encourage their own men and frighten the enemy; cp. βοὴ δ' ἄσβεστος ὀρώρει, 'unceasing shouts arose' (XI 500).

409. 'For he knew in his heart how troubled his brother was'; lit. 'his brother, how he was busy', by a common Greek idiom.

410. οὐλοχύτας: Barley grains were sprinkled between the horns of the sacrificial victim.

ἀνέλοντο: 'took up in their hands' from a basket.

412. κύδιστε: superlative formed from the noun κῦδος.

413–14. There are three examples of *tmesis* in these two lines.

μὴ πρὶν ἐπ᾽ ἠέλιον δῦναι: This is Agamemnon's prayer, expressed by μή and the infinitive; we must understand a word meaning 'grant'.

πρίν . . . πρίν: cp. ll. 348, 354.

414. πρηνές: the same as 'prone'; 'flat on the face' (l. 418), 'headlong'. The word is to be taken predicatively with καταβαλέειν.

415. αἰθαλόεν: 'smoke-blackened'; the hall would have a central fire, the smoke from which would get out where it could.

417. χαλκῷ: Although iron was in common use in Homer's own day, the epic tradition is nevertheless very consistent in keeping bronze as the metal for weapons, as it had been in the Mycenaean age; cp. χαλκοχιτώνων (l. 47).

ῥωγαλέον: from ῥήγνυμι; 'broken', 'torn'. The word is to be taken predicatively with δαΐξαι.

418. ὀδὰξ λαζοίατο γαῖαν: as we say, 'bite the dust'.

λαζοίατο: λαμβάνοιεν. Optative for a wish.

420. δέκτο: imperfect; cp. l. 137.

ἱρά: ἱερά.

ὄφελλεν: 'increased'; not to be confused with ὀφέλλω (ὀφείλω), 'owe'.

421–32 = 1 458–69, except that ll. 425 and 426 replace two similar lines in the passage in book 1.

This is a complete description of the procedure at a sacrifice. After a prayer, and the scattering of the grains of barley between the horns of the victim (l. 421), they pulled the head back to expose the neck, cut its throat and skinned it (l. 422); then they cut out the thigh-bones, covered them with a layer of fat above and below, and laid on top of them pieces of flesh from the other parts of the body, to symbolise the offering of the whole animal (ll. 423–4). These pieces were then burnt as an offering to the god; and meanwhile they put the entrails (heart, liver, lungs, kidney, stomach) on spits and started to roast them over the fire (ll. 425–6). These entrails were eaten, or perhaps just ritually tasted, as a first course, and then they cut all the meat up small, pierced in on the spits, and roasted it (ll. 427–9).

422. αὐέρυσαν: from ἀν-Ϝερυσαν, 'they lifted up'.

425. ἀφύλλοισιν: i.e. dead wood.

426. ἀμπείραντες: ἀναπείραντες.

ὑπείρεχον: ὑπερεῖχον; the augment is, as often, dispensed with, and the second syllable is lengthened for the sake of the metre.

Ἡφαίστοιο: 'fire', just as Ἄρης for 'war' (l. 381, etc.).

430. τετύκοντο: reduplicated aorist middle of τεύχω.

431. ἐίσης: 'equally apportioned', the same for all.

432. ἐξ ἔρον ἔντο: 'put away from themselves (ἐξίεμαι) their desire', i.e. had satisfied it. The whole line is a recurring formula meaning 'when the meal was over'.

435. λεγώμεθα: 'speak', 'converse'.

436. ἀμβαλλώμεθα: 'postpone'.

ἐγγυαλίζει: 'puts into our hands'.

437. Ἀχαιῶν: with λαόν.

438. κηρύσσοντες: 'making proclamations'.

ἀγειρόντων: third-person imperative.

439. ἀθρόοι ὧδε: 'together as we are'.

440. ἴομεν, ἐγείρομεν: ἴωμεν, ἐγείρωμεν (cp. l. 72).

θᾶσσον: This, the comparative adverb of ταχύς, is used without any particular comparative sense; 'quickly'.

445. οἱ ἀμφ' Ἀτρείωνα: 'Agamemnon and those with him'.

446. θῦνον: 'hurried about'.

κρίνοντες: 'marshalling the army', as suggested by Nestor in l. 362.

μετά: adverb, 'in their midst'.

447. αἰγίδα: cp. l. 157 n.

448. θύσανοι: 'tassels', round the edge of the aigis.

ἠερέθονται: 'wave in the air'.

449. ἑκατόμβοιος: Each tassel, being wholly of gold (παγχρύσεοι, l. 448), is worth a hundred oxen.

450. παιφάσσουσα: 'rushing in and out'.

451–2. ἑκάστῳ, καρδίη: Both are the indirect object of ἐνῶρσεν, by the construction called that of the 'whole and the part'.

453. 'To them immediately war became more attractive than to return.'

455–83. In his build-up towards the long and detailed list of the Greek contingents (followed by the shorter Trojan list) the poet brings in a succession of no less than five major similes, not to mention other incidental comparisons, in order to describe the Greek army as it gets ready for battle. The similes describe (*a*) the Greek armour as shining like fire; (*b*) the noise as like that of flocks of birds; (*c*) the numbers as like flies; (*d*) the leaders as like goatherds; (*e*) Agamemnon as like a great bull in a herd.

It is noticeable everywhere in the *Iliad* that accumulation or expansion denotes importance. A longer description of the arming of a hero gives that hero more significance than a shorter description. Again, when a hero of the second rank is due to be killed by a major hero, it is normal to give the loser a number of successes first, in order to enhance his status and make him a worthier victim. Similarly here, the five similies strengthen the feeling that something very important is coming – the Catalogue of Ships.

455. ἀίδηλον: from ἀ-ιδηλός (ἰδεῖν) with active meaning, 'making unseen', 'destroying'.

456. οὔρεος: ὄρεος, ὄρους.

458. αἰθέρος: the upper air, above the clouds.

461. Ἀσίῳ: 'Asian'; the word was still limited to a small area of Lydia, on the coast of Asia Minor.

λειμῶνι: flat water-meadows by the outflow of the river to the sea, where great flocks of birds would be seen. The eighteenth-century French editor Villoison, who had visited Asia Minor, reported great numbers of swans in winter on the banks of the Kaystros.

462. ἀγαλλόμενα: agreeing with ἔθνεα; 'delighting in', 'making a fine show with'.

463. προκαθιζόντων: agreeing with ὀρνίθων (l. 459), 'settling'.

σμαραγεῖ: trans. 'is filled with the sound'.

465. Σκαμάνδριον: Skamandros, also called Xanthos, is the main river through the plain of Troy; the other river, Simoeis, flows into it.

ὑπό: This must be an adverb, 'beneath'; it is too far away to be a preposition controlling ποδῶν of the next line.

466. σμερδαλέον: adverbial neuter; 'fearfully'.

ποδῶν αὐτῶν τε καὶ ἵππων: a kind of causal genitive, ποδῶν, on which the other two genitives depend; 'from the feet of them and their horses'.

468. ὥρη: 'the season', i.e. springtime.

469. ἀδινάων: The adjective suggests quick, restless movement, and was used of bees in l. 87. Trans. 'swarming'.

470. 'which fly around in a sheep fold'.

471. γλάγος: 'milk' (γάλα).
δεύει: 'wets', and so 'fills'.

473. μεμαῶτες: 'eager'; a participle from the shorter stem of the perfect μέμονα.

474. πλατέα: We are told that goats grazing spread out more than sheep; 'wide-ranging'.

475. διακρίνωσιν: cp. κρίνοντες (l. 446); 'separate'.
νομῷ: 'pasture'; the accent is different from that of νόμος, 'law'. The dative is locative.
μιγέωσιν: aorist subjunctive passive; 'when the different flocks have become mixed together in the pasture'.

477. μετὰ δέ: cp. l. 446.

478–9. Homer does not often give a physical description of his characters, but compare Priam's view of Agamemnon (III 168–70):

ἤτοι μὲν κεφαλῇ καὶ μείζονες ἄλλοι ἔασι,
καλὸν δ᾽ οὕτω ἐγὼν οὔ πω ἴδον ὀφθαλμοῖσιν,
οὐδ᾽ οὕτω γεραρόν· βασιλῆι γὰρ ἀνδρὶ ἔοικε.

For the method of description, compare Hamlet on his father (III iv 56 ff.):

> Hyperion's curls; the front of Jove himself;
> An eye like Mars, to threaten and command;
> A station like the herald Mercury
> New-lighted on a heaven-kissing hill.

ὄμματα, κεφαλήν, ζώνην, στέρνον: accusatives of respect.

479. Note the *chiasmus*.
ζώνην: generally the middle part of the body; here 'thighs' not 'waist'. The thighs show the strength of the lower part; Odysseus, when stripped for wrestling, impressed the suitors by the size of his thigh muscles (*Od.* XVIII 67 ff.).

480. ἀγέληφι: locative.
μέγα: adverbial, 'far', 'by a long way'.
ἔπλετο: the common *gnomic aorist*, i.e. the aorist found in pro-

verbial or general statements, of things which do happen now and always have happened.

481. ταῦρος: agreeing with βοῦς.

μεταπρέπει: 'is outstanding among'.

ἀγρομένῃσι: participle of the second aorist middle of ἀγείρω, 'assemble', 'come together'.

483. 'outstanding in the crowd, and pre-eminent among the heroes'. It is probably better to take this line so, as two separate halves, than to make πολλοῖσι agree with ἡρώεσσιν; the latter would produce a more complex word-order than is natural in Homer.

484–93. After the similes comes a conventional appeal to the Muses to direct the poet's words. Such an invocation always enhances the importance of what is to follow.

484. ἔσπετε: for ἐν-σπέτε, aorist imperative of ἐνέπω (cp. present imperative ἔννεπε in the invocation of the first line of the *Odyssey* – ἄνδρα μοι ἔννεπε, Μοῦσα); 'tell'.

486. κλέος: 'hearsay'.

οἶον: 'only'.

488. μυθήσομαι could be either future indicative or aorist subjunctive (l. 72). But ὀνομήνω can only be aorist subjunctive, and it is reasonable to take both verbs together. In any case it makes little difference to the sense, as the subjunctive, with or without ἄν, is close to a future in Homeric Greek. 'I cannot', 'will not'.

489. οὐδ' εἰ + optative: The condition is more remote than the main sentence; 'not even if I *had*, etc.'.

491. εἰ μὴ 'Ολυμπιάδες Μοῦσαι, etc.: There is some confusion of thought here. After asking the Muses to tell him the names of the leaders of the Greeks, he says that he could not under any physical circumstances recount the mass of ordinary troops *unless the Muses gave him a list*, but that he will tell the names of the captains, and the numbers of the ships. 491–2 are illogical.

492. μνησαίατο: μνήσαιντο (cp. l. 25); 'recounted', 'told'.

493. ἀρχοὺς νηῶν: From the point of view of the situation in the *Iliad*, where all are on land, there is no particular reason for describing the leaders as ἀρχοὶ νηῶν. Compare what is said about the Catalogue in the next note.

αὖ: i.e. as opposed to the mob (πληθύν, l. 488).

494–759. The rest of book II consists of (1) The Catalogue of Ships (the list of the Greek contingents) (ll. 494–759); (2) some comments thereon (ll. 760–85); (3) a connecting passage to introduce the Trojans (ll. 786–815); (4) the catalogue of the Trojans and their allies (ll. 816–77). Of these, the first and longest (the Catalogue of Ships) is of the greatest importance. Some preliminary comments must be made.

First, this long list (of 29 contingents, 44 leaders, 175 towns or other localities, 1186 ships and, according to a plausible calculation, *c*. 100,000 men) was not created for its present place in the second book of our *Iliad*. The evidence for this is threefold:

(*a*) Contingents that are important here have no particular part to play in the rest of the *Iliad*; in particular, the Boiotians head the list in the catalogue, and are given the largest number of named leaders and towns, but their significance in the later *Iliad* is minimal.

(*b*) The imperfect tenses throughout, and the insistence on the numbers of *ships* (cp. also ἀρχοὺς νηῶν, l. 493) would better suit the beginning of the war, and even the assembly of the whole army at Aulis, than the situation found in the *Iliad*.

(*c*) In three cases the poet seems to have inserted lines to assimilate the Catalogue to the *Iliad* situation; he had to do this because three of the original leaders are not appearing on the field of battle this day, and some explanation seems required. The three are Philoktetes (sick), Protesilaos (dead) and Achilleus (sulking).

These considerations compel the belief that a separately existing catalogue has been inserted into the *Iliad*, with a few modifications which we can see, and perhaps others which we cannot.

If this is so, where did the Catalogue come from? There is evidence associating 'catalogue poetry' with Boiotia. Our Catalogue of Ships begins with the Boiotian contingent, and puts much more emphasis on it than could be justified by the Boiotians' part in the later *Iliad* or in any other version of the Trojan War known to us. An origin connected with the Boiotian school of poetry may therefore be suspected.

Secondly, what about the geographical information in the Catalogue? Is it fact or fiction? All shades of opinion are held, ranging from those who argue that the Catalogue is a poor invention interpolated into the *Iliad* by a late and decadent poet, to those who see in it a miraculously preserved record of the historical army of Agamemnon. While the latter is certainly an overstatement, it is probably

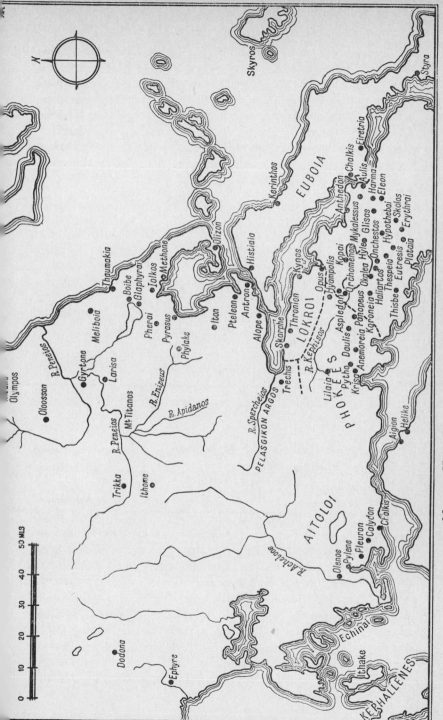

MAP I. Homeric geography: northern and central Greece

the nearer to the truth. Because of the general conformity with our other knowledge of the Mycenaean world (most of which comes from the findings of archaeology), and because of a number of descriptive epithets for towns whose very existence – not to mention importance – had been forgotten in the classical period, we may accept that the Catalogue contains (preserved down the centuries presumably in verse) invaluable evidence about Greece in the late Mycenaean period, before the arrival of the Dorians.

BIBLIOGRAPHY

Allen, T. W., *The Homeric Catalogue of Ships* (Oxford, 1921).

Hope Simpson, R., and Lazenby, J. F., *The Catalogue of the Ships in Homer's Iliad* (Oxford, 1970).

Page, D. L., *History and the Homeric Iliad* (Berkeley, 1959), pp. 118–77.

Thomas, Helen, and Stubbings, F. H., 'Lands and Peoples in Homer', in *A Companion to Homer* (London, 1962), pp. 283–310.

The Catalogue describes the Greek world in five major areas. They are (*a*) Greece north of the Isthmus of Corinth (ll. 494–558); (*b*) the Peloponnese (ll. 559–624); (*c*) the western islands and west Greece (ll. 625–44); (*d*) the south-eastern islands (ll. 645–80); (*e*) north Greece (ll. 681–759).

(*a*) *Greece north of the isthmus: Boiotia, Minyan Orchomenos, Phokis, Lokris, Euboia, Athens, Salamis.*

494–510: Boiotia.

As has been explained in the introduction to the Catalogue, there is no reason inherent in the *Iliad* why the Boiotian contingent should have the honour of being named first, nor why it should have more leaders and come from more named towns than any other contingent. The explanation offered for these facts is that they reflect the patriotism of a Boiotian school of catalogue poetry. Added uncertainty about this entry is caused by Thucydides' statement (1 12.3) that the Boiotians did not move into the land called after them Boiotia until sixty years after the fall of Troy, though still twenty years before the Dorian invasion.

Interesting, however, and producing a strong impression of historical verisimilitude, is the fact that neither Thebes nor Orchomenos finds a place in the list of Boiotian cities. And yet these were the two most important cities in later Boiotia, and had been places of great wealth and significance in the Mycenaean age (ix 381). The reasons for their non-appearance here are that Thebes was in a state of temporary non-existence because of the success of the Epigonoi (see l. 505 and note), while Orchomenos was still independent of Boiotia (ll. 511 ff.)

499. ἀμφί . . . ἐνέμοντο: tmesis; 'lived round'.

505. Ὑποθήβας: i.e. the lower town, around the foot of the acropolis of Thebes; the upper town, called Kadmeia, had (mythologically speaking) been destroyed by the Epigonoi just before the war against Troy (see Introduction, p. xvi).

508. Νῖσαν: Some have thought to see in this Nisa the old name of Megara, which (unless here) does not appear in the Catalogue. Megara, however, does not naturally belong to Boiotia.

510. On two occasions in the Catalogue, of which this is one, Homer mentions the number of men carried by each ship in a contingent; the other number (l. 719) is fifty. Thucydides (1 10.4) suggested that Homer may be giving us the largest and smallest complements; and therefore we might take the mean of these two numbers (85), and multiply it by the number of ships (1186) to find the total strength of the army. The result is a little more than 100,000.

511–16: Minyan Orchomenos.

The Minyans are a shadowy people, whose half-forgotten exploits date from an earlier age. They are associated with seafaring (although Orchomenos was far from the coast, being on the inland lake Kopais), and had connections with Iolkos and the Argonauts' quest for the Golden Fleece, and with Nestor's Pylos (Nilsson, *The Mycenaean Origin of Greek Mythology*, pp. 127–50).

511. ἰδέ: alternative form of ἠδέ, 'and'.

513. δόμῳ ῎Ακτορος ᾿Αζείδαο: 'in the house of (her father) Aktor son of Azeus'.

τέκεν: This verb is used in this sentence in a rather confused way, for the two different moments of conception and birth. In l. 513 the statement is that Astyoche was mother of Askalaphos and Ialmenos; in ll. 514–15, however, the poet is describing the earlier occasion when the girl went up to her bedroom and Ares lay with her secretly there (cp. ll. 820–1).

D

517–26: Phokis.

518. Ἰφίτου: This is one of the words used to show that there was originally a genitive of the -ος declension in -οο, as well as the common forms in -οιο and -ου. The second syllable of Ἴφιτος was short; and there is great likelihood that the line should run υἷες Ἰφίτοο μεγαθύμου Ναυβολίδαο, with the last syllable of Ἰφίτοο lengthened before the μ of μεγαθύμου. Cp. xv 66, Ἰλίου προπάροιθε (i.e. Ἰλίοο).

519. Πυθῶνα: Delphoi.

525–6. These two lines are obviously an addition to the pre-Iliadic catalogue, because they refer to the army on land, not to the ships.

525. οἱ μέν: Schedios and Epistrophos.

ἵστασαν: transitive imperfect of ἵστημι, 'set in order'.

526. ἔμπλην: with Βοιωτῶν, 'next'.

527–35: Lokris.

Here we have the first major hero – Aias the son of Oileus. The Lokrians are described elsewhere in the *Iliad* (XIII 713–18) as light-armed troops, with bows and slings instead of the usual heavy armour; this fits the description of Aias here as λινοθώρηξ (l. 529). A glance at a map of classical Greece will show that the Lokrians at that time occupied two separate areas: west of Delphoi, and on the coast north of Boiotia. The latter area only is involved here.

527. Ὀιλῆος: understand υἱός.

529–30. Three objections are made to these lines, supporting the view of the Alexandrian scholar Aristarchus that they are spurious: (1) The thick linen jerkin instead of the universal metal breastplate differentiates Aias too much from the other leaders. (2) The rest of the *Iliad* does not support the statement here that the lesser Aias was the best spearman of the Greeks (though he was not bad either, being un-usually quick to kill his man (XIV 442, 521)). (3) Πανέλληνας is unique in the *Iliad*; and as Hellas still meant a small area of north Greece (l. 683), the expression 'all the Hellenes' for 'all the Greeks' (if that is what it means) is an anachronism. Παναχαιοί (l. 404) is unexceptionable.

530. ἐκέκαστο: pluperfect from a perfect κέκασμαι, 'excel', 'surpass' (καίνυμαι).

535. πέρην: 'opposite'.

536–45: Euboia.

536. μένεα πνείοντες: 'breathing might'.

540. ὄζος Ἄρηος: 'of the stock of Ares'.

542. ὄπιθεν κομόωντες: i.e. growing the hair at the back of the head only, having shaved the front. Contrast the κάρη κομόωντες Achaians (l. 11, etc) and the ἀκρόκομοι Thrakians (IV 533).

543. μεμαῶτες: cp. l. 473.

ὀρεκτῇσιν: adjective formed from the verb ὀρέγνυμι, 'stretch out'; trans. 'thrusting with their spears'.

544. ῥήξειν: The future infinitive with μεμαῶτες implies 'hope'.

If we treat δηίων as two long syllables by *synizesis*, this line consists of six spondees and no dactyl at all.

546–56: Athens.

We approach the Athenian contingent with interest, because of the importance of later Athens, which was in any case also a significant Mycenaean citadel. Moreover, the *Iliad* was almost certainly edited at Athens in the sixth century, so that one might expect some patriotic enhancement of the city's prestige. In practice, however, the Athenian entry is unimpressive: no other places of Attica are mentioned except Athens itself, and the leader is the obscure Menestheus, not the son or sons of Theseus as in the epic cycle and later Athenian poetry.

547. Ἐρεχθῆος: Erechtheus, mythical king of Athens, was worshipped with Athene on the acropolis. Here he is described as having been spontaneously generated from a ploughed field, in allusion no doubt to the frequent claim of the Athenians to have been the original, *autochthonous*, inhabitants of their land. (Herodotus, VIII 55: Ἐρεχθέος τοῦ γηγενέος λεγομένου εἶναι.)

548. A ὕστερον πρότερον, Ὁμηρικῶς as Cicero puts it; first Erechtheus was born in the field; then Athene looked after him.

549. κάδ (κατά) . . . εἶσεν: *tmesis* (καθίζω).

550. μιν: Erechtheus.

551. περιτελλομένων ἐνιαυτῶν: i.e. annually.

552. Πετεῶο: genitive of Πετεώς.

553 ff. Skill at marshalling the troops is a useful, if rather unheroic, quality (the mention of Nestor helps). In the rest of the *Iliad* Menestheus never in practice shows this skill.

554. ἵππους: i.e. chariots.

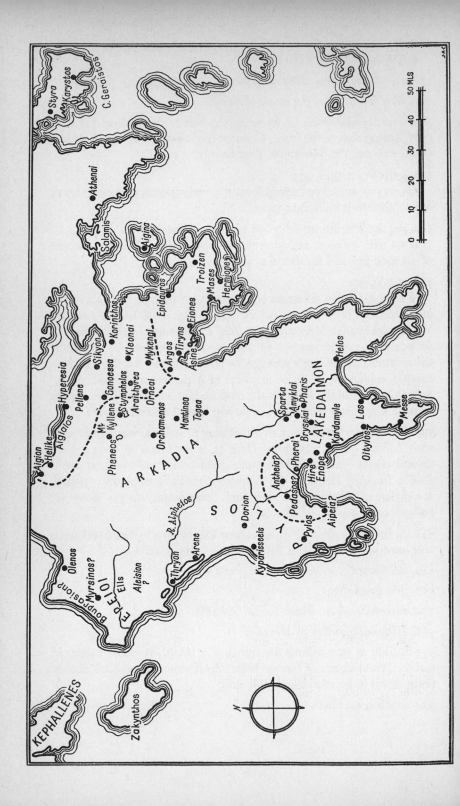

557–8: Salamis.

These two lines raise many doubts. Aias could not of course help coming from the little island of Salamis, and so having a very small number of ships. But two lines are far too meagre for such a great hero; they do not even give him his usual title 'son of Telamon', to distinguish him from the other Aias (l. 527). Moreover, much repeated in the ancient world was the accusation that l. 558 was invented by an Athenian (Solon or Peisistratos) and inserted into the *Iliad* in order to support Athens' claim to the possession of Salamis in opposition to Megara in the sixth century. If this story is true, l. 558 may have displaced a longer description of Aias.

558. The statement that Aias 'drew up his ships next to the Athenians' involves a complete reversal of his status in the *Iliad*. In any case, VIII 224 (=XI 7) describes Aias as holding one of the two positions of honour and danger, the extreme ends of the Greek line of ships. If the Athenians were beside him, they were next to Aias, not he next to them.

(b) The Peloponnese: Argos, Mykenai, Lakedaimon, Pylos, Arkadia, Elis.

559–68: Argos.

A surprising fact about the geographical area described in this section is that it not only cuts the king of Mykenai off from his natural access to the Aegean sea, but also removes from his domain the city and the fortress on the Argive plain (Argos and Tiryns). Agamemnon is left with an apparently much less useful kingdom to the north and west of Mykenai; Diomedes controls the east and south.

559. τειχιόεσσαν: the walls still admired by the visitor to the ruins of Tiryns.

560. κατά . . . ἐχούσας: 'occupying'.

563. βοὴν ἀγαθός: cp. l. 408 n.

564. Kapaneus was one of the Seven against Thebes, as was Tydeus, the father of Diomedes, and Mekisteus, the father of Euryalos.

566. Ταλαιονίδαο: Mekisteus' father was Talaos. The form here is a confusion of two possible patronymics – Ταλαίων and Ταλαΐδης.

569–80: Mykenai.

On the division between Agamemnon's kingdom and Diomedes', see the note on ll. 559–68. Agamemnon is not completely cut off from the Aegean, as he has Corinth, which is on both seas; but his kingdom is strangely limited. It has been suggested with some probability that the Catalogue is here describing the situation at the end of the Mycenaean age, when the king of Mykenai had been shorn of some of his power.

570. ἀφνειόν: a very accurate epithet. Corinth was certainly wealthy in classical times, and in pre-classical (when she was a powerful mercantile city). No doubt her geographical position had always given her this advantage. A wealthy citizen of Corinth appears at XIII 664.

572. Adrastos, the leader of the Seven against Thebes, was king of Sikyon before he became king of Argos.

575. Αἰγιαλὸν πάντα: i.e. all the coastal strip, later called Achaia.

576. τῶν: 'of these people', depending on νηῶν.

577. πολὺ πλεῖστοι καὶ ἄριστοι: In fact the Mykenaians are hardly mentioned in the fighting in the *Iliad*.

578. ἐδύσετο: cp. ἀπεβήσετο (l. 35).

νώροπα: an adjective of unknown derivation, used only to describe bronze armour; trans. 'shining'.

580. ἄριστος: 'most powerful'; cp. l. 82.

581–90: Lakedaimon.

581. κοίλην: 'hollow', i.e. surrounded by hills.

κητώεσσαν: 'with many ravines'. Lakedaimon is the country; Sparta (l. 582) the town.

586. οἷ: 'his' (lit. 'to him'), referring back to Agamemnon.

587. ἀπάτερθε δὲ θωρήσσοντο: i.e. separately from Agamemnon's Mykenaians.

590. See l. 356 n.

591–602: Pylos.

There has been dispute since ancient times about the location of the famous city of Pylos. Three sites have been discussed, all near the west coast of the Peloponnese, one in the north (in Elis), one in the centre (near the river Alpheios) and one in the south. Excavations since 1939 have solved the problem. There is now no doubt that Nestor's palace was a little inland of the southern Pylos (famous in another context in book IV of Thucydides), on the coast of Messenia.

594–600. The story of Thamyris, a singer (i.e. poet) who was rash enough to challenge the Muses to compete with him. This is a common theme: a mortal gets above himself, forgets the limitations of humanity, and tries to equate himself with the gods; the result is always disastrous. Compare Lykourgos in VI 129–41, Bellerophontes in VI 200–2 and Niobe in XXIV 602–9.

595. ἀντόμεναι: 'meeting him'.

596. Oichalia was in Thessaly (l. 730). Eurytos is 'the Oichalian', as king of the town.

597. στεῦτο: 'he undertook', 'promised', 'declared' (στεῦμαι).

599. πηρόν: This word properly means 'crippled', 'disabled', but is traditionally understood to mean specifically 'blind' here. Cp. Milton's reference to his own blindness in *Paradise Lost*, III 33 ff.

> Those other two equal'd with me in Fate
>
> .   .   .   .   .
>
> Blind *Thamyris* and blind *Maeonides*,

referring (in Maeonides) to the ancient story that Homer himself was blind (*Hymn. Apoll.*, 172):

> τυφλὸς ἀνήρ, οἰκεῖ δὲ Χίῳ ἔνι παιπαλοέσσῃ.

600. ἐκλέλαθον: a *reduplicated aorist*, an old tense-formation of which numerous examples are found in Homer; it is transitive in meaning, 'they made him forget'.

601. Γερήνιος ἱππότα Νέστωρ: cp. l. 336 n.

603–14: Arkadia.

604. Αἰπύτιον παρὰ τύμβον: 'by the tomb of Aipytos' (an old hero of Arkadia).

613. περάαν: περᾶν, 'to cross'.

614. μεμήλει: pluperfect of μέλω.

The Arkadians, being an inland people, had no connections with the sea, so Agamemnon provided ships for them.

615–24: Elis.

615. The geographical area is Elis, but the people are Epeians (l. 619).

616. ὅσσον ἔπι: ἐφ' ὅσον, ' so far as'.

621. The Ἀκτορίωνε, sons of Aktor, also called Μολίονε, were Kteatos and Eurytos (who may or may not have been Siamese twins) (XI 709, 750; XXIII 638); here the patronymic is applied to the grandchildren.

(c) The western islands and west Greece: Doulichion and the Echinades, Ithaka and other islands, Aitolia.

625–30: Doulichion and the Echinades.

The Echinades were small islands off the estuary of the river Acheloos by the coast of Akarnania; Doulichion, however, has not been identified. A great difficulty is that Meges has a contingent of forty ships, whereas Odysseus only has twelve; this suggests that Doulichion ought to be somewhere large. Discussion of its where-abouts is connected with the wider argument whether the Homeric Ithaka was the same as classical Ithaka, or is rather to be identified with Leukas. Fortunately all this is of more concern to the *Odyssey* than the *Iliad* (see Stanford, *Homer, Odyssey I–XII*, pp. xxxv–xli). What does seem probable is that the poet of neither epic had a clear idea of the geography of these western islands.

626. 'Across the sea opposite Elis' is a slightly odd description of the Echinades, which are quite a long way north of Elis, and just off the coast of Akarnania.

629. ὅς: traditionally taken to be Phyleus, not Meges.

631–7: Ithaka and other islands.

632. Neritos is the mountain on Ithaka.

635. 'Who held the mainland, and dwelt in the land opposite.' It is uncertain whether this line is saying the same thing twice – i.e. that some of Odysseus' followers came from the mainland opposite Ithaka, namely Akarnania – or whether ἀντιπέραια means opposite to the ἤπειρον, and thus the coast of Elis. The former is more probable.

637. μιλτοπάρῃοι: trans. 'with painted bows'.

638–44: Aitolia.

641–2. The poet feels he should explain why Thoas is leader, and not one of the famous heroic family of Aitolia – Oineus and his sons Tydeus and Meleagros.

643. ἐπί . . . ἐτέταλτο: ἐπιτέλλω.
πάντα is subject of the verb; ἀνασσέμεν explanatory infinitive.

(d) The south-eastern islands: Crete, Rhodes, other islands.

This group of contingents raises an exceptionally interesting question. The Dorian invasion was called by the Greeks 'the Return of the Herakleidai'. In general the archaising of the heroic tradition of poetry was strong enough to prevent any mention of Dorians; but (i) Tlepolemos (l. 653) was a son of Herakles, and Pheidippos and Antiphos (l. 678) grandsons; (ii) there is a reference to a threefold tribal division (a typical Dorian feature) at Rhodes in ll. 655 and 668; (iii) the one actual mention of the Dorians in either of the two epics comes at *Odyssey* XIX 177, in a list of the different peoples found in Crete: Δωριέες τε τριχάικες δῖοί τε Πελασγοί

(τριχάικες is probably another reference to the three Dorian tribes; cp. τρίχα, l. 655).

It is not easy to draw historical conclusions from this evidence (because, of course, the date of the Catalogue's information must remain uncertain), and any theory of Dorians inhabiting the islands before they reached the mainland of Greece is not supported by the findings of archaeology; but we are left with the feeling that here, if anywhere in the *Iliad*, we are in touch with the Dorians.

645-52: Crete.

The history of Crete in the period 1450-1200 is much in dispute at the present time. One difficulty is to bring together the archaeological and the literary evidence. According to orthodox archaeological opinion, Knossos was destroyed about 1400 B.C., and Crete as a whole reduced to insignificance during the whole of the following period. In the *Iliad*, however, and more particularly here in the Catalogue of Ships, Idomeneus is ruler of a powerful kingdom, and brings to Troy eighty ships, a number only exceeded by Mykenai and Pylos. It hardly seems possible to reconcile the two pictures.

The towns named in ll. 646-8 are all from a strip in the centre of the island. Reference to the 'hundred cities of Crete' (l. 649) may well be a reminiscence of earlier days.

647. ἀργινόεντα: 'with chalk cliffs'; cp. also l. 656.

651. Ἐνναλίω ἀνδρειφόντῃ: A violent *synizesis* of ω and α is the only way to make this ancient formula (as it has come down to us) scan; Enyalios is an epithet of Ares.

653-70: Rhodes.

Rhodes was an Achaian colony before it was a Dorian, and the three cities Lindos, Ialysos and Kameiros were already there in Mycenaean times. The small number of ships, however, (nine) suits a very new foundation, as described in the text here. Tlepolemos' story is told in similar terms, but with more detail, by Pindar in the *Seventh Olympian*, 20-34.

653. ἠΰς: This, and ἐΰς (l. 819), are the adjectives corresponding to the adverb εὖ.

654. ἀγερώχων: 'proud'.

655. διὰ τρίχα κοσμηθέντες: i.e. τρίχα διακοσμηθέντες; see the introductory remarks to section (d) above.

656. ἀργινόεντα: cp. l. 647.

658. βίη Ἡρακληείη: 'the might of Herakles', a periphrasis for Ἡρακλῆι; cp. also l. 666.

659. There were several cities called Ephyra, including Corinth. This one was in Thesprotia in north-west Greece.

661. ἐπεὶ οὖν: see the note on ὡς οὖν, ll. 320–1.
   τράφε: intransitive aorist.

662. His father's maternal uncle would be Alkmene's brother.
   Homicide was regularly put forward in mythology as an explanation for tribal movement or colonisation, blood guilt compelling a hero to leave home.

663. ὄζον Ἄρηος: cp. l. 540.

665. οἱ: dative of the pronoun, 'to him'; not the article.

668. τριχθὰ δὲ ᾤκηθεν καταφυλαδόν: cp. l. 655 and the introductory remarks to section (d). καταφυλαδόν certainly refers to tribal division.
   ᾤκηθεν, ἐφίληθεν: -ηθησαν (l. 99).

670. Pindar affects to take the metaphor in κατέχευε here literally, and speaks of a golden cloud raining on the city (*Seventh Olympian*, 34).

671–5. Syme, a small island north of Rhodes.

671–3. Note the threefold repetition of Νιρεύς at the beginning of the lines. Nireus was κάλλιστος, just as Aias was the best fighter (l. 768) and Eumelos had the finest horses (l. 763) – *always excepting the son of Peleus*. Achilleus was pre-eminent in all respects.

676–80: Other islands.

677. Εὐρυπύλοιο: Eurypylos was the king of Kos whose daughter Chalkiope was mother of Thessalos (l. 679) by Herakles. This Eurypylos is not to be confused with two others of the same name – Eurypylos son of Euaimon, leader of the contingent described in ll. 734–7, and Eurypylos son of Telephos who came to defend Troy after the end of the *Iliad*, and was killed by Neoptolemos (*Od.* XI 520).

(e) North Greece.

Nine principalities, the geographical limits of which are not clear, take the place of what in post-Homeric and classical times was Dorian Thessaly. The uncertain state of affairs in this area seems to suit the situation as it must have been towards the end of the Mycenaean age, with peoples on the move and pressure from the north.

681–94: Pelasgian Argos.

This northern area was, as it were, the matrix of Greece, for the tribes paused in Thessaly on their way south, and we find here names with limited connotation which were later to have much wider meaning. So Argos, Achaia and (pre-eminent in the end) Hellas.

681. νῦν αὖ τούς: He begins the new section as if he will use a verb such as ἐρέω (l. 493); but the verb does not come, and τούς is picked up by τῶν (l. 685).

684. Myrmidons and Hellenes and Achaians were still obviously limited tribal names when this line was first applied to the people of Achilleus. Hellenes are not mentioned again in the *Iliad*; for the more striking Panhellenes, see ll. 529–30 n.

686–94. These lines are an obvious addition, made to fit the catalogue to its present place in the *Iliad*; cp. ll. 699–709, 721–8.

687. ἐπὶ στίχας: 'to the battle line' (cp. III 113).

ἡγήσαιτο: potential optative, but without the particle ἄν or κεν.

689. κούρης: genitive of cause.

690–3. For Achilleus' expedition, on which he took the two towns of Lyrnessos and Thebe, see I 184 n.

692. Mynes was king of Lyrnessos (XIX 296).

695–710: Phylake and other places.

696. τέμενος: 'sanctuary', 'precinct'.

699–709. Another addition to make the information of the Catalogue suit the situation of the *Iliad*; cp. ll. 686–94, 721–8.

699. ἔχεν κάτα: κατεῖχεν.

700. ἀμφιδρυφής: The adjective really applies to the cheeks of the mourning wife, which are 'torn on both sides', as in XI 393, τοῦ δὲ γυναικὸς μέν τ' ἀμφίδρυφοί εἰσι παρειαί. Here it is transferred to the wife herself.

701. Δάρδανος ἀνήρ: in later versions it was Hektor who killed Protesilaos as he leapt ashore first of the Greeks; here the killer is anonymous.

703. οἴ: 'they'.

μέν: μήν; also l. 709.

711–15: Pherai and other places (including Iolkos).

711. παραί: παρά.

712. Iolkos was a famous city in the legends of the Aiolians. Pelias was king there, and Iason assembled his company of Argonauts there. It is strange that this important area should contribute only eleven ships.

716–28: Methone and other places.

719. πεντήκοντα: For a calculation based in part on this figure, see l. 510 n.

720. ἶφι: instrumental case, formed by adding the suffix -φι to the dative of the noun (F)ἴς (Latin *vis*).

721–8. The third major addition to make the information of the Catalogue suit the situation of the *Iliad*; cp. ll. 686–94, 699–709.

724. Philoktetes came to Troy soon after the end of the *Iliad* story, brought by the Greeks from Lemnos because of a prophecy that Troy could not be taken without the bow and arrows of Herakles, which were in his possession. He killed Paris.

726 = 703.

729–33: Trikka and other places.

729. κλωμακόεσσαν: 'rocky'.

730. cp. l. 596 n.

731. Ἀσκληπίου: the great healer, son of Apollo; the oldest sanctuary of Asklepios was at Trikka (l. 729). (This should be Ἀσκληπίοο; cp. l. 518 n.)

734–7: Ormenion and other places.

735. λευκά: 'white', because these are chalk hills; cp. also l. 739.

κάρηνα: 'hill tops'.

738–47: Argissa and other places

741. Πειριθόοιο: king of the Lapiths; cp. 1 262–73.

742. τέκετο: 'bore'. There is some uncertainty about this, because

the later tradition makes the fight between the Lapiths and the Centaurs break out at the marriage feast of Peirithoos and Hippodameia; if Homer agrees with that version, then τέκετο must mean 'conceived' (cp. l. 513 n.). On the other hand Homer does not say anything about the marriage feast; ἐτείσατο (l. 743), 'punished', suggests a planned campaign, as does the driving of the Centaurs from Pelion right across Thessaly (l. 744), and Nestor's claim to have been invited to participate in the war (I 270). We may therefore give τέκετο its natural meaning 'bore'.

743. φῆρας: 'Centaurs'. φήρ was the Aeolic form of θήρ, 'wild beast', and is used by Homer specifically for these Aiolian wild creatures; cp. I 268.

744. The Centaurs lived on Mount Pelion; they were driven by Peirithoos to the land of the Aithikes, Mount Pindos west of Thessaly.

745. οὐκ οἶος: picks up ἡγεμόνευε of l. 740.

746. Kaineus was among those named by Nestor (I 264).

748–55: Kyphos and other places (including Dodona).

750. περὶ Δωδώνην: Dodona is far to the west, in Epiros, near the Thesprotians; it was famous for its ancient oracle of Zeus. Achilleus prays to Zeus of Dodona in XVI 233 ff.

751. ἔργα: cultivated fields.

752–4. The waters of the tributary Titaressos (MSS Titaresios) flow pure and clear into the muddy stream of Peneios.

755. ὅρκου δεινοῦ: These words are in apposition to Στυγός, which was the 'dread oath' of the gods (XV 37).

756–9: Magnesia.

757. The river Peneios, whose upper waters are referred to in ll. 753 ff., flows to the sea through the valley of Tempe; Mount Pelion is to the south. Perhaps these two names are given as the limits of Prothoos' kingdom.

758. Πρόθοος θόος: a play on words.

The Catalogue names forty-four Achaian leaders, of whom ten are killed in the course of the *Iliad*, three by Hektor.

760–85: a pendant to the Catalogue of the Achaians.

761. ὄχα: 'by far'; the word only occurs in the phrase ὄχ' ἄριστος.
    ἔννεπε: see l. 484 n.

763. Φηρητιάδαο: for Φερητιάδαο, the first syllable lengthened for metrical reasons; the son of Pheres was Admetos, whose son Eumelos (l. 714) now drove the horses, and indeed competed with them in the chariot race of XXIII 262 ff.

765. Equal in colour, age and size.

ὄτριχας οἰέτεας: The o- prefix has the force of 'the same'; cp. XI 257, ὄπατρον, 'having the same father'.

σταφύλῃ, etc.: lit. 'equal on their backs by a builder's level'.

766. Apollo served Admetos as a herdsman.

Πηρείη is either a variant spelling of Φεράι, the home of Admetos (l. 711), in which case there has been a similar uncertainty about the length of the first vowel as in Φηρητιάδαο in l. 763; or else it is a small village whose existence is attested in *I.G.*, IX 2.205, near Melitaia in Achaia Phthiotis, a long way to the south-west of Pherai.

769. ὄφρα: 'so long as'.

770. ἵπποι τε: understand 'were far the best' from the previous line.

774. ἱέντες: with all three nouns δίσκοισιν, αἰγανέῃσιν, and τόξοισιν. No single verb will do in English.

777. πεπυκασμένα: 'covered', i.e. with cloths to protect them from the dust; cp. V 193–5:

ἀλλά που ἐν μεγάροισι Λυκάονος ἔνδεκα δίφροι
καλοὶ πρωτοπαγεῖς νεοτευχέες· ἀμφὶ δὲ πέπλοι
πέπτανται.

778. οἱ δέ: the Myrmidons.

780. οἱ δ' ἄρ' ἴσαν: The poet now returns to the advance of the Greeks, taking up again the situation of the five similes of ll. 455–83. In particular, he repeats the first simile (of fire, l. 455), and stresses again the noise (cp. l. 465).

νέμοιτο: passive, 'were consumed'.

The comparison with fire is of the shine of the weapons of the Greek army.

781. Διὶ ὣς τερπικεραύνῳ: dative dependent on ὑποστεναχίζει understood in the ὣς clause.

782. Τυφωέι: Typhoeus was the last of the opponents of Zeus, a monstrous creature, not human in shape as the giants and titans were. He was cast down beneath the surface of the earth by the thunderbolts of Zeus, and trapped on a hard bed of stone, his stirring on which was an explanation for local earth tremors and volcanic activity.

γαῖαν ἱμάσσῃ: When there was a thunderstorm in the mountains with lightning flashing down, the people would say that Zeus was 'lashing the earth' with his thunderbolts, in anger against Typhoeus.

783. εἰν 'Αρίμοις: whether this is Arima (a place), Arimoi (mountains) or Arimoi (a people) was uncertain even in ancient times; the location was thought to be Kilikia, on the south-east coast of Asia Minor. Pindar, in his *First Pythian*, has Typhoeus born in Kilikia, but suppressed by Zeus under the volcanic Mount Etna in Sicily, where (l. 28) στρωμνὰ χαράσσοισ' ἄπαν νῶτον ποτικεκλιμένον κεντεῖ ('his bed scratches and pricks his whole back as he lies there').

785. διέπρησσον: Attic διέπραττον; 'traversed', 'crossed', with genitive of the ground covered.

786. Τρωσὶν δέ, etc.: a sudden switch, preparing the way for the Trojan catalogue.

788. ἀγορὰς ἀγόρευον: 'were holding an assembly'.

789. ἠμέν: 'both', corresponding to ἠδέ.

791. εἴσατο: εἴδομαι.

φθογγήν: accusative of respect. In fact it is clear from the situation (and from l. 795) that Iris is in the physical shape of Polites, not only speaking with his voice.

It is a little difficult for our more rational minds to see what exactly is meant by the statement that Iris came in the shape of Polites, who had been watching for the Greek advance. We, and for that matter the Alexandrian scholars, assume instinctively that the person who came must have been *either* Iris *or* Polites. If the former, then what was Polites doing while Iris was addressing the Trojans? Still sitting on the tomb of Aisyetes (l. 793)? If, on the other hand, it was really Polites who came, and Homer is using the concept of Iris merely as a manner of speaking, then we are surprised by Polites' language to his father in l. 796 and to his brother in l. 802.

The answer is that Polites indeed came running from his look-out post on Aisyetes' tomb; his message was of urgent importance, and suddenly there was new fire and life in the Trojan assembly. In this enhanced vividness, the Greeks saw the presence of a god; and what god but Iris, the divine messenger? So Iris was there in the shape of Polites, and (as Homer tells us) it was Iris that spoke to Priam and Hektor. Cp. l. 279 n.

793. The tomb of ancient Aisyetes (mentioned only here) was clearly

a landmark on the plain; cp. the tomb of Aipytos in Arkadia (l. 604) and Myrine's mound (l. 814).

794. δέγμενος: present participle of *δέγμαι (δέχομαι); cp. l. 137 n.
    ναῦφιν: for genitive plural of ναῦς.

795. Take τῷ with ἐεισαμένη, μιν with προσέφη; cp. l. 22.

796. ἄκριτοι μῦθοι ἀεί σοι φίλοι εἰσίν.

798. πολλά: adverbial, 'often'.

This line is more suitable to the *persona* of Polites than to Iris; ll. 796 and 802, however, come more easily from the goddess; cp. l. 791 n.

801. πεδίοιο: for the genitive of ground covered; cp. l. 785 n.
    προτί: πρός.
    προτὶ ἄστυ: to be taken with ἔρχονται.

802. ῥέξαι: infinitive for imperative.

803. γάρ: This introduces the reason for the following instruction; trans. 'in that', 'because'.
    Iris–Polites proposes a similar review to that suggested by Nestor in ll. 362–8, and thus prepares the way for the Trojan Catalogue.

806. τῶν: genitive depending on ἐξηγείσθω; 'let him lead them out'.

807. οὐκ ἠγνοίησεν: 'recognised'.

809. πᾶσαι πύλαι: 'the whole gate'; πύλαι is not found in the singular in Homer.

810. ὀρώρει: pluperfect.

811. πόλιος: dissyllabic by *syni̯zesis*.

812. i.e. it was an isolated mound, standing on its own (ἀπάνευθε) on the plain.

813–14. On four occasions in the *Iliad* different names are quoted from the languages of gods and of men. They are

I 403 (a giant)	Βριαρέως/Αἰγαίων
II 813 (a hill)	σῆμα Μυρίνης/Βατίεια
XIV 291 (a bird)	χαλκίς/κύμινδις
XX 74 (the river)	Ξάνθος/Σκάμανδρος

(gods' names first). The accepted explanation is that the gods' language is the transmitted poetical language from the past, while the language of men is the common and everyday terminology known to the poet.

814. πολυσκάρθμοιο: 'much-leaping', i.e. 'nimble', 'agile'.

Μυρίνης: supposedly one of the Amazons who had fought against the Phrygians (III 189).

816–77. The Trojan Catalogue.

This is far shorter than the Greek Catalogue of Ships, and the geographical and other information contained in it is briefer and more factual. Some of the names and tribes are outlandish enough. The method of presentation is geographical also, but on a different scheme from that of the longer Catalogue of Ships. Here, after (*a*) a list of the contingents from Troy itself and the surrounding country (ll. 816–43), the remaining peoples are listed as if on four lines radiating outwards from Troy. These are (*b*) the European allies (ll. 844–50); (*c*) those to the east, along the south shore of the Black Sea (ll. 851–7); (*d*) those to the east again, along a slightly different line (ll. 858–63); (*e*) those to the south, along the coast of Asia Minor (ll. 864–77). By an unexpected convention, the poet tells us when we have reached the limit of one particular directional line from Troy by using the adverbs τηλόθεν (ll. 849, 857, 877) and τῆλε (l. 863) in connection with the most remote locality in each direction.

The Trojan Catalogue has less claim to a pre-Iliadic existence than the Achaian (see the note to l. 877). This, however, does not invalidate the fact that it contains valuable information about the demography of Asia Minor and Thrace at an early time, before the Ionian migration. It is striking that important later Greek cities like Smyrna and Ephesos are not mentioned at all, Miletos is named as the home of barbarous-speaking Kares, and the islands of the Aegean, such as Chios and Samos, are disregarded.

(*a*) *Troy and the Troad.*

816–18: The city of Troy itself.

818. μεμαότες = μεμαῶτες (l. 473).

819–23: Dardanians.

821. Ἴδης ἐν κνημοῖσι: where Anchises was herding cattle (cp. l. 513 n.). Here again the poet is referring simultaneously to the birth of the child and the circumstances of its conception.

824–7: 'Troes' living under Mount Ida.

There is a complication here, in that Pandaros is elsewhere called Lykian (v 105, 173), while the true Lykians lived far away, at the

MAP 2   Homeric geography: Asia Minor, etc.

south-west corner of Asia Minor (l. 876). Aristarchus' solution is a 'Trojan Lykia' beneath Mount Ida.

824. ὑπαί: ὑπό, cp. παραί (l. 711).

827. The statement that Apollo had given Pandaros his bow has been held to be inconsistent with the detailed description in iv 106–11 of how Pandaros got the bow for himself. Homer has made the gods so human that we are tricked into treating them as if they acted on the same plane as human beings (cp. l. 791 n.). In fact particular skill with the bow would make that bow the gift of the god of archery. In an exactly similar way, Aias speaks to Teukros in xv 440, 'Where are your arrows and bow, which Phoibos Apollo gave you?'

828–34: Adrasteia and other towns.

828. Ἀδρήστειαν: The town seems to take its name from its king, Adrastos (l. 830).

830. λινοθώρηξ: cp. l. 529.

831. Μέροπος: Apart from its use here as a proper name, the word is always an epithet for mankind – its significance quite lost to us; cp. l. 285.

Περκωσίου: Presumably he had come from Perkote (l. 835).

περὶ πάντων: 'beyond all men'.

832. οὖς: 'his'.

οὐδὲ . . . ἔασκε: 'he tried to dissuade them'.

834. The death of these two sons of Merops is described in xi 329 ff.

835–9: Cities on the shore of the Hellespont.

836. Σηστόν: This city alone is on the other side, the north side, of the Hellespont.

840–3: 'Pelasgians' from Larisa.

These must be a branch of this ancient tribe, which gave its name also to Pelasgian Argos (l. 681).

(b) *The European allies – Thrake and the country towards Makedonia.*

844–5: Thrakes.

845. ἐντὸς ἐέργει: 'is the boundary'.

846–7: Kikones.

This tribe is famous as the victims of Odysseus' first adventure, *Od.* ix 39 ff.

848–50: Paiones.

849. τηλόθεν: see ll. 816–77 n.

850. ἐπικίδναται: ἐπισκεδάννυται.

(c) *Allies along the south shore of the Black Sea.*

851–5: Paphlagones.

851. Πυλαιμένεος λάσιον κῆρ: cp. βίη Ἡρακληείη (l. 658) and the
Odyssean ἱερὴ ἷς Τηλεμάχοιο for Τηλέμαχος.

λάσιον: 'shaggy', 'hairy', and so 'tough'; used more properly of
the chest (1 189, στήθεσσιν λασίοισι).

852. Ἐνετῶν: These may well be remote ancestors of the Venetians
(Livy 1 1).

856–7: Halizones.

857. τηλόθεν: see ll. 816–77 n.

ἐξ Ἀλύβης: The Halizones from Alybe cannot be firmly identified;
but the names are reminiscent of the river Halys and the Chalybes,
famous metal-workers.

(d) *Allies from north-central Asia Minor.*

858–61: Mysoi.

858. οἰωνιστής: an *augur*, who prophesied by the flight of birds.

859. ἐρύσατο: 'kept off' (ἐρύω).

860. Ennomos' death in the river at the hands of Achilleus is not in
fact mentioned when the river battle takes place in book XXI; this is
not of great significance; cp. l. 874.

Αἰακίδαο: Achilleus was *grandson* of Aiakos.

862–3: Phryges.

863. τῆλε: see ll. 816–77 n.

μέμασαν: pluperfect.

(e) *Allies from the west coast of Asia Minor.*

864–6: Meiones.

865. Γυγαίη τέκε λίμνη: i.e. the nymph of the lake.

866. ὑπὸ Τμώλῳ γεγαῶτας: 'born beneath Mount Tmolos'.

γεγαῶτας: participle of the active-form perfect γέγαα (alternative to
γέγονα) from γίγνομαι.

867–75: Kares.

867. βαρβαροφώνων: Sometimes Homer admits that the Trojan allies spoke non-Greek languages; cp. l. 804, ἄλλη δ' ἄλλων γλῶσσα πολυσπερέων ἀνθρώπων.

868. Μίλητον: not yet a Greek city.

ἀκριτόφυλλον: of a mountain thickly wooded, so that individual trees cannot be distinguished.

872. ὅς: ambiguous; perhaps it is best (following Cauer) to treat l. 871 as purely parenthetical, and refer ὅς back to Nastes in l. 870.

χρυσόν: ornaments of gold.

873. νήπιος: cp. l. 38.

ἐπήρκεσε: 'kept off'.

874–5. Nastes' (or Amphimachos') death is not mentioned in the river battle of book XXI; cp. l. 860.

875. ἐκόμισσε: 'took possession of'.

876–7: Lykioi.

876. Sarpedon and Glaukos are the most important and most sympathetically treated of the Trojan allies.

877. τηλόθεν: see ll. 816–77 n.

The Trojan Catalogue names twenty-seven leaders, of whom seventeen are killed in the course of the *Iliad*, four falling to Aias and three each to Achilleus and Diomedes. This heavy casualty rate suggests that the Trojan Catalogue was composed for the *Iliad*; the geographical information, however, seems much older (see ll. 816–77 n.).

BOOK III

*Preparations for the Single
Combat between Paris and
Menelaos; the View from the Wall;
the Single Combat; Paris and Helen*

1. κόσμηθεν: ἐκοσμήθησαν: The omission of the augment is very frequent in Homer; cp. φύγον (l. 4). The ending is an alternative shorter form; cp. ἔβαν (l. 113) for ἔβησαν.

ἡγεμόνεσσιν: Aeolic dative ending (Attic ἡγέμοσιν).

ἕκαστοι: 'each set of men', 'each contingent'. This refers to the Catalogues of Greeks and Trojans in book II (second half).

2. Τρῶες μέν: answered by οἱ δέ ... Ἀχαιοί (l. 8).

ἴσαν: imperfect of εἶμι, 'go'.

ὥς: 'like'; here following its word, and for that reason accented.

3–7. The expression ὄρνιθες ὥς is expanded into a simile describing the flight of cranes to the south in autumn.

3. ἠύτε περ: 'just as'. The enclitic particle περ has a slight intensive effect.

οὐρανόθι πρό: i.e. πρὸ οὐρανοῦ, 'in front of', and so 'beneath the sky'. The suffix -θι is really locative, but is used here for the genitive. Cp. Ἰλιόθι πρό, 'before Ilium' (VIII 561).

4. αἵ τε: The enclitic particle τε often accompanies a proverbial or general statement in Homer; it occurs three times in the gnomic ll. 11 and 12 below. It is not to be translated.

ἐπεὶ οὖν: This is a particular Homeric use of οὖν, in a subordinate clause with ἐπεί or ὥς, stressing the completion of an action; cp. ll. 21, 30.

φύγον: For the lack of augment, cp. l. 1 n. The tense is the gnomic aorist, i.e. the aorist found in proverbial or general statements, of things which do happen now and always have happened.

5. ταί: an alternative form of αἱ, the nominative feminine plural of what later Greek knew as the article; in Homer it is still primarily a demonstrative pronoun. Here ταί means 'they', and picks up the relative αἵ of the previous line.

ἐπί + genitive: 'towards'.

'Ωκεανοῖο: The genitive singular of -ος declension nouns may be in -οιο in Homer as well as -ου. The river Okeanos was thought of as flowing round the flat, disk-shaped earth.

ῥοάων: Notice the normal genitive plural of the -α declension in Homer, in -αων (Latin -*arum*).

6. The war between the cranes and the pygmies is a folk story reflecting some knowledge of a diminutive African people. It probably arose from the sight of cranes flying south in formation, uttering cries.

7. ἠέριαι: 'in early morning'; an adjective used predicatively.

ταί: cp. l. 5.

προφέρονται: middle; lit. 'carry forward for themselves', and so 'offer' battle.

8. μένεα πνείοντες: 'breathing might'.

'Αχαιοί: Notice that there are three names used by the poet indistinguishably for the Greeks – Achaians ('Αχαιοί), Argives ('Αργεῖοι) and Danaans (Δαναοί).

The Greeks advance silently, with better discipline than their opponents.

9. μεμαῶτες: 'eager', a participle from the shorter stem of the perfect μέμονα.

ἀλεξέμεν: an alternative form for the infinitive ἀλέξειν.

10. εὖτε: here = ἠύτε (l. 3). Usually εὖτε is a conjunction meaning 'when'.

ὄρεος: genitive; Attic ὄρους.

κορυφῇσι = κορυφαῖς.

κατέχευεν: gnomic aorist; cp. l. 4 n.

11. κλέπτῃ: 'to a thief'.

τε: proverbial; cp. l. 4 n. So also twice in l. 12.

12. 'A man can see only as far as he can throw a stone.'

ἐπί . . . ἵησιν: ἐφίησιν; the elements which later constituted a compound verb are still separable in Homer, with the preposition able to stand by itself as an adverb. The phenomenon is called *tmesis* (from τέμνω, 'cut'). In practice one may treat this as if a verb has been divided into its two parts, although the true situation is that the two parts have not yet coalesced.

13. ὥς: Accented in this way, or with the circumflex ὦς, this word is an adverb = οὕτως, 'so'; the conjunction is not accented, except when it follows its noun in a simile, as in l. 2 above.

τῶν: demonstrative, 'of them'; cp. ταί (l. 5).

ὄρνυτ᾽: i.e. ὤρνυτο.

ἀελλής: adjective; 'swirling', 'eddying', agreeing with κονίσαλος. The noun ἄελλα means 'a storm'.

14. ὦκα: adverb, 'quickly'.

διέπρησσον: Attic διέπραττον; 'traversed', 'crossed'; with genitive of the ground covered, a sort of partitive genitive. The η for α even after ε, ι, ρ is the most obvious Ionic feature of the Homeric dialect.

πεδίοιο: genitive; cp. Ὠκεανοῖο (l. 5).

15 ff. As the two armies come together, we expect a general engagement, but in practice Paris steps forward from the Trojan ranks, and Menelaos immediately comes to meet him from the Greek. This is typical of Homeric fighting; the massed armies are present, but they are often disregarded. The fighting as described consists mostly of clashes between individual leaders, who step out of the ranks as πρόμαχοι.

16. Ἀλέξανδρος: the Trojan prince, also called Paris, who caused the war by carrying off Helen, wife of Menelaos, from Sparta.

17–18. Paris' equipment is abnormal – a leopard-skin over his shoulders, bow and arrows, sword and two throwing spears. Later in the book (ll. 330–8) he puts on the full armour of the Homeric hero.

18. δοῦρε: dual, but the participle that agrees with it is plural.

κεκορυθμένα χαλκῷ: 'tipped with bronze'. Although iron was in common use in Homer's own day, the epic tradition is nevertheless very consistent in keeping bronze as the metal for weapons, as it had been in the Mycenaean age.

19. προκαλίζετο: 'challenged'.

20. ἀντίβιον: adverb.

21. ὡς οὖν: cp. l. 4 n.

22. μακρὰ βιβάντα: 'with long strides'. βιβάς is a reduplicated present of βάς, as from *βίβημι, for βαίνω.

23. ἐχάρη: gnomic aorist.

ἐπί . . . κύρσας: tmesis (l. 12).

σώματι: an animal already killed by the hunters (αἰζηοί, l. 26).

25. πεινάων: Uncontracted forms are normal in Homer.

μάλα γάρ τε, etc.: 'He eats it eagerly (μάλα), even though the dogs and men run at him.'

27. ὧς: cp. l. 13 n.

θεοειδέα: an uncontracted form; but the two final vowels must be treated from the point of view of scansion as a single long syllable; this is called *synizesis* (see Introduction, p. xxv).

28. φάτο: third-person singular, imperfect middle of φημί; here meaning 'he thought'.

τείσεσθαι: from τίνω.

ἀλείτην: 'the wrongdoer', 'transgressor' (ἀλιταίνω).

29. ὀχέων: genitive of the plural neuter ὄχεα, 'chariot'.

ἆλτο: aorist of ἅλλομαι.

χαμᾶζε: 'to the ground'.

31. φίλον ἦτορ: 'in *his* heart'; accusative of respect, a common Greek accusative, most regularly used with reference to parts of the body; cp. εἶδος ἄριστε (l. 39). φίλος with parts of the body, possessions or close relatives is approximately the same as the personal pronoun.

32. ἄψ: adverb, 'back'; also l. 35.

ἑτάρων = ἑταίρων.

ἔθνος: 'throng', 'crowd'.

κῆρα: from κήρ, 'fate', 'death'; as in l. 6.

33. ὡς δ' ὅτε, etc.: This is the fourth simile taken from nature in less than forty lines.

ἀπέστη: gnomic aorist again: also ἀνεχώρησεν (l. 35).

34. οὔρεος = ὄρεος, ὄρους.

βήσσῃς = βήσσαις; cp. κορυφῇσι (l. 10).

ὑπό . . . ἔλλαβε: *tmesis*; ἔλλαβε for ἔλαβε.

35. ὦχρος: noun, 'paleness'.

μιν: the epic form of νιν, accusative third-person pronoun, 'him'.

παρειάς: a second accusative with εἷλε.

36. κατά . . . ἔδυ: *tmesis*; 'he went back into'.

37. δείσας: δείδω.

Ἀλέξανδρος θεοειδής: This is a good example of the Homeric *stock epithet*, for it is the fourth time in twenty-two lines that Alexandros has been unnecessarily described as 'godlike'. Such epithets have a metrical rather than a semantic purpose. They do indeed describe a general characteristic of a person; but, more important, together with his name, they fill a clearly defined part of the hexameter verse (here, from the weak caesura to the end of the line). See Introduction p. xviii.

38. αἰσχροῖς: 'shaming'.

39. This line is a regular, and obviously traditional, way of addressing Paris, especially for his stronger brother Hektor (XIII 769; cp. XI 385); his name has even been fitted into a term of abuse – Δύσπαρι. Parallels to this compound created from a proper name are found in the *Odyssey*, e.g. XXIII 97, μῆτερ ἐμή, δύσμητερ, and XIX 260, Κακοίλιον οὐκ ὀνομαστήν.

εἶδος ἄριστε: 'best in physical appearance'; cp. l. 31 n.

ἠπεροπευτά: vocative of ἠπεροπευτής, 'deceiver'.

40. ἄγονος: 'unborn'. The line means 'You should never have been born; if born, you should have died unmarried.'

ἔμεναι = εἶναι. So also l. 42, and ἔμμεναι (l. 44).

41. κε: κε (κεν) is the alternative form of the *modal* particle ἄν, and is used in the same way.

ἦεν = ἦν. 'I would prefer this, and it would have been far better.'

42. ὑπόψιον ἄλλων: 'viewed with hostility by all others'; ἄλλων is a subjective genitive.

43. καγχαλόωσι: This, from the verb καγχαλάω, would be καγχαλάουσι uncontracted, καγχαλῶσι contracted. By a peculiarity of Homeric Greek (caused no doubt by the opposed pressures of contraction of vowels and the requirements of the metre), the contracted form has suffered a sort of expansion or distension. This, technically called *diektasis*, is found particularly with verbs in -αω. So also κομόωντες (from κομάω) in this same line.

κάρη κομόωντες: κάρη is a neuter noun, here accusative of respect with κομόωντες. The phrase is taken to mean 'with hair growing over the whole head', as opposed to tribes such as the Thrakes, who are described (IV 533) as ἀκρόκομοι (i.e. 'with topknots'). Trans. 'long-haired'.

Hektor's point is that the Greeks are laughing because they *thought* (φάντες) Paris was a leading champion of the Trojans, because of his appearance, but they can now see his lack of courage.

45. ἔπι = ἔπεστι (understand σοι).

46. ἦ: introduces the question.

ἐών = ὤν.

νέεσσι = ναυσί.

47. ἐπιπλώσας: from ἐπιπλώω (=ἐπιπλέω).

ἐρίηρας: accusative masculine plural.

49. ἀπίης: 'distant', adjective from ἀπό, as ἀντίος from ἀντί.

νυόν: lit. 'daughter-in-law'. The wife married into the family and race of her husband, and the Achaian princes were therefore committed to defend and avenge Menelaos' wife; trans. 'related by marriage to'.

50. πῆμα: accusative in apposition to the sentence. Helen herself was not a disaster to Priam, Troy and the Trojans, but the bringing her back was. So also χάρμα and κατηφείην in the next line.

52. οὐκ ἂν δή: 'could you not'.

53. χ': κε (l. 41).

θαλερήν: from θάλλω, 'grow', 'bloom'; so 'full of life', 'strong', 'warm', 'loving'.

54. οὐκ ἄν τοι χραίσμῃ: 'would be of no help to you'; the subjunctive is more vivid, and closer to a future, than the optative, which would be obligatory with ἄν here in later Greek.

τοι: equals the enclitic σοι, the unstressed dative of σύ.

55. μιγείης: optative because this is all within the hypothesis of his defeat at Menelaos' hands if he dared to meet him.

56–7. ἦ τέ κεν ἤδη λάινον ἔσσο χιτῶνα: 'otherwise you would already have been made to wear a *shirt of stones*', i.e. you would have been stoned to death.

ἔσσο: pluperfect passive of ἔννυμι.

57. ὅσσα = ὅσα.

ἔοργας: perfect of ἔρδω.

59. 'Since you criticised me deservedly, and not unfairly.'

αἶσα is a very ancient word, proved in fact to have been part of the 'Achaean' (see Introduction, p. xiii) dialect, meaning 'a part' or 'a portion'. The αἶσα of a man was what had been allotted to him by destiny, i.e. his fate. κατ' αἶσαν would therefore mean 'in accordance with what I am', ὑπὲρ αἶσαν 'beyond my deserts'.

It is part of the character of Paris that he shows an acceptance of his own faults which disarms criticism.

60. κραδίη: καρδία.

πέλεκυς ὥς: 'like an axe'; cp. ὄρνιθες ὥς (l. 2).

61-2. 'which goes through wood wielded by a man who cuts out ship's timber by his skill, and the axe adds effect to the man's effort'.

δουρός: genitive of δόρυ.

ἀνέρος: ἀνδρός.

ἐκτάμνῃσιν: The epic dialect possessed, for the three singular persons of the subjunctive, alternative endings in -ωμι, -ῃσθα, -ῃσι. These forms are regularly used to produce a weak third-foot caesura, as here.

64. μὴ πρόφερε: 'do not bring up against me'.

66. ὅσσα: referring to δῶρα (l. 65); 'the gifts that they (the gods) give, but no one could get for himself'.

67. ἠδέ: an alternative word for 'and'.

70. κτήμασι: the property that Paris carried off with Helen.

73. οἱ δ' ἄλλοι: 'the rest of you'. divided in the following line into <ὑμεῖς μὲν> ναίοιτε, τοὶ δὲ νεέσθων.

ταμόντες: The throats of the sacrificial victims were cut at the making of a truce; so ὅρκια ταμόντες would mean having made a solemn truce'. φιλότητα is also made an object of ταμόντες by an extension of the metaphor.

74. ναίοιτε: a wish; parallel to the imperatives.

75. Ἄργος: The place-name Argos is used indiscriminately in Homer to mean the town (Argos), the surrounding country (Argolid), the the Peloponnese and the whole of Greece, not to speak of Pelasgian Argos in Thessaly (II 681), which is the most probable original reference of the adjective ἱππόβοτον. Here Argos should be taken as the Peloponnese, and Achaiis as north Greece.

76. ἔφατο the imperfect middle of φημί; there is no distinction of meaning from the active.

μέγα: adverbial, with χάρη.

77. ῥα: Homeric verse uses all three forms ἄρα, ἄρ and the enclitic ῥα, merely as required by the metre. The particle has a mild inferential force.

78. μέσσου δουρὸς ἑλών: taking hold of his spear in the middle with both hands, to push back the soldiers.

79. κάρη κομόωντες: cp. l. 43.

80. Take both ἰοῖσιν and λάεσσι with ἔβαλλον: 'and they were aiming at him and trying to hit him with arrows and stones'.

81. ὁ . . . Ἀγαμέμνων: 'he, namely Agamemnon' (cp. l. 5 n.).

83. στεῦται: 'he looks as if he is going to'.

84. ἄνεῳ: more properly ἄνεω, adverb, 'silently'; trans. as an adjective.

86. κέκλυτε: imperative of a *reduplicated aorist*, an old tense-formation of which numerous examples are found in Homer.

μευ: μου.

87. ὄρωρεν: ὄρνυμι.

88–94. Hektor repeats more or less exactly what Paris had suggested in ll. 68 ff. Such repetition is a natural feature of oral poetry.

95. ἀκὴν ἐγένοντο σιωπῇ: a common formulaic phrase. ἀκήν is an accusative used adverbially, 'silently'; σιωπῇ reinforces it.

96. βοὴν ἀγαθός: The heroes shouted in battle to encourage their own men and frighten the enemy; cp. βοὴ δ' ἄσβεστος ὀρώρει, 'unceasing shouts arose' (XI 500). To be 'good at the war-cry' (βοήν is another example of a Greek accusative of respect; though not a part of the body, it is at least a bodily function) was therefore a heroic quality.

97. ἐμεῖο: ἐμοῦ.

98. φρονέω διακρινθήμεναι: ˙φρονέω means 'I intend', and therefore can take an aorist infinitive, not (as we would expect) a future. 'I intend the Greeks and the Trojans to be parted this day.'

διακρινθήμεναι: διακριθῆναι.

99. πέπασθε: second-person plural of an alternative form of the perfect of πάσχω; = πεπόνθατε.

100. 'Because of my quarrel and Alexandros who began it.' (But it may be better, with Zenodotos, to read ἄτης for ἀρχῆς; cp. VI 356.)

101. τέτυκται: τεύχω.

102. τεθναίη: perfect optative; a wish; cp. ναίοιτε (l. 74). Also διακρινθεῖτε.

103. οἴσετε: an imperative, apparently aorist, but created from the future stem. So also ἄξετε (l. 105). οἴσομεν in l. 104 is of course future.

ἄρν': ἄρνε, dual.

Male animals were sacrificed to gods, female to goddesses; white to the Olympians, black to the gods of the underworld.

105. ἄξετε; cp. l. 103 n.

Πριάμοιο βίην: lit. 'the might of Priam', a periphrasis for Πρίαμον;

cp. βίη Ἡρακληείῃ: 11 658.
ὅρκια τάμνῃ: cp. l. 73.

106. οἱ: dative of the third-person pronoun, 'to him', 'his'. Not the article.

108. ἠερέθονται: 'are flighty', 'unstable', 'up in the air'.

109. μετέῃσιν: μετῇ (μέτειμι,; cp. ἐκτάμνῃσιν (l. 62).

ἅμα πρόσσω καὶ ὀπίσσω: 'the immediate future and the more distant future'. The A scholia (scholia are marginal and other notes derived from ancient commentaries on Homer and preserved alongside the text in some of our manuscripts; the A scholia are those in the important manuscript Venetus A) say τά τε παρόντα καὶ τὰ ὕστερον.

110. ὄχα; 'by far'; the word only occurs in the phrase ὄχ' ἄριστος.

112. ἔλπομαι, 'hope' or 'expect', can take an aorist infinitive.

113. ἐπὶ στίχας: 'in their ranks'.
ἐκ δ' ἔβαν: ἐξέβησαν δέ. For the ending, cp. l. 1 n.

115. ὀλίγη δ' ἦν ἀμφὶς ἄρουρα: 'there was little open space around', an indication of the large numbers in the armies.

116. προτί: πρός.

κήρυκας: 'heralds', whose functions included the arrangements for sacrifices, as well as the taking of messages, and general assistance to the kings.

119. The Oxford text reads ἄρνε κέλευεν, which must be a mistake, as the Greeks are providing only one lamb (l. 104). Other editions have ἄρν' ἐκέλευεν or ἄρνα κέλευεν.

120. οἰσέμεναι: aorist infinitive; cp. aorist imperative οἴσετε (l. 103).

121–244. The Teichoskopia, or View from the Wall, a wonderful scene in which we discover more about the personalities and even appearance of the Greek leaders, and meet for the first time Helen, the cause of the war, fills the time between the heralds' departure for Troy (l. 116) and their appearance to summon Priam (l. 245).

121. Iris, the messenger of the gods; compare 11 786 ff., where she addresses the Trojan assembly disguised as Polites.

122. γαλόῳ: 'sister-in-law', husband's sister; the Greeks were well supplied with different names for the different relationships by marriage, and had another word for the sister-in-law who was a brother's wife; cp. VI 378.

E

'Αντηνορίδαο: 'of the son of Antenor'; the old form of the genitive of -α declension masculine nouns was in -αο. For Antenor see l. 148.

124. εἶδος: accusative of respect; cp. l. 39.

126. δίπλακα πορφυρέην is in apposition to ἱστόν, because this is what she was in fact weaving, a large red piece of cloth, which when folded was of the ordinary dimensions of a cloak.

ἐνέπασσεν: lit. 'sprinkled on it'; the word describes the weaving of the designs into the fabric.

127. χαλκοχιτώνων: This is a common formulaic epithet of the Achaians, and must refer to defensive armour worn in the Mycenaean age. Miss Lorimer (*Homer and the Monuments*, pp. 201, 209) refers to figures on the Warrior Vase from Mykenai, who seem to be wearing both *chitons* and jerkins strengthened by metal disks. Trans. 'bronze-clad'.

128. ἔθεν: οὗ, genitive of the third-person pronoun, 'of her'.

ὑπ' Ἄρηος παλαμάων: 'at the hands of Ares'.

There is something very convincing in the picture of the beautiful Helen placidly composing pictorial representations of the battles being fought on her behalf.

129. πόδας ὠκέα: 'swift-footed', another accusative of respect.

130. νύμφα: vocative of νύμφη; the word is often used of a young married woman. Trans. 'my dear'.

ἴδηαι: ἴδῃ, middle subjunctive with active meaning.

132. Ἄρηα: the name of the god of war, used simply for 'war'.

134. ἕαται: for ἧνται; the ν is vocalised as α, because the Greeks found the particular combination of consonants -ντ- uncomfortable, and in certain positions impossible (II 25). From the resulting ἥαται (cp. ἥατο for ἧντο, l. 149) the first vowel has been shortened.

135. 'Leaning on their shields, and with their long spears fixed in the ground beside them.'

παρά . . . πέπηγεν: intransitive perfect (παραπήγνυμι).

138. κε: with the future κεκλήσῃ; ἄν with the future is found occasionally even in Attic prose.

κεκλήσ': future perfect passive.

141. ὀθόνῃσιν: 'veil'.

142. τέρεν: 'round', 'large'.

κατά . . . χέουσα: tmesis.

144. This line presents an ancient problem. Aithra, the daughter of Pittheus, was a figure of Athenian mythological history, being the wife of their king Aigeus and mother of the famous Theseus. The appearance of this aged queen as the handmaid of Helen in Troy seems to call for explanation. This was forthcoming in the story, known as early as the post-Homeric epic cycle, that when Helen was carried off by Theseus and Peirithoos, some time before she married Menelaos, her brothers Kastor and Polydeukes rescued her, and in doing so carried off in revenge Theseus' mother Aithra, who thus became the slave of Helen. The rescue of Aithra by her grandsons was a well-known incident in descriptions of the fall of Troy.

What seems most likely is that Homer *or a predecessor* chose at random from the epic stock a name for the handmaid of Helen, and happened to hit on Aithra daughter of Pittheus; the explanatory legend then arose through the attempts of mythologists and poets to integrate this awkward detail into the total picture.

Κλυμένη τε βοῶπις: There was speculation from the earliest times that Klymene was a relative of Peirithoos, as Aithra of Theseus. βοῶπις is the stock epithet of Hera, but is occasionally used of other women. For its probable origin, see IV 50 n.

145. Σκαιαὶ πύλαι: the only named gates of Troy, facing the plain.

146–8. οἱ δ' ἀμφὶ Πρίαμον, etc.: By a slight illogicality, five of the seven councillors who were with Priam are attracted into the accusative with him after ἀμφί, instead of the nominative as subjects of the sentence.

147. ὄζον Ἄρηος: 'of the stock of Ares'.
These three councillors were Priam's brothers, according to xx 238.

148. Οὐκαλέγων: 'not caring', a very strange name which caught the fancy of Virgil (*proximus ardet Ucalegon*, 'Ucalegon's house next door was on fire', *Aeneid* II 311–12).
Ἀντήνωρ: the most important Trojan outside the royal family.
πεπνυμένω: dual.

149. ἥατο = ἧντο (l. 153); cp. l. 134 n.
ἐπί: 'on', i.e. 'above'.

151. τεττίγεσσιν ἐοικότες: 'like grasshoppers', i.e. chattering away in soft dry voices – a wonderfully imaginative description of the old men. The Greeks thought highly of the sound of grasshoppers.

152. δενδρέῳ ἐφεζόμενοι: *synizesis* and *correption* (see Introduction,

p. xxv) make δενδρέῳ scan as a trochee; cp. χρυσέῳ ἀνὰ σκήπτρῳ (1 15).

λειριόεσσαν: 'lily-like', i.e. 'soft'.

ἱεῖσι: ἵημι, 'emit'.

154 ff. The poet has often been praised for this passage, in that, instead of attempting to describe Helen's beauty, he shows its effect by the reactions of the old councillors of Troy.

155. ἧκα: 'softly'.

ἔπεα πτερόεντα: 'winged words', in that they fly from mouth to ear; an ancient poetic phrase.

156. νέμεσις: Nemesis in Homer is not divine retribution, as later in Attic tragedy; it is the feeling of disapproval aroused in the onlooker by an improper action. Trans. (understanding ἐστί with νέμεσις) 'The Trojans and well-greaved Achaians are not to be blamed for etc.'

ἐυκνήμιδας: Greaves were shin-guards, worn particularly as a protection against stones and arrows.

158. εἰς ὦπα: 'in appearance', 'to look at'.

159. ὥς: cf. l. 13 n.

160. ὀπίσσω: 'for the future'.

λίποιτο: with passive meaning.

162. πάροιθε ... ἐμεῖο: 'in front of me'.

ἵζευ: ἵζου, present imperative middle.

163. πηούς: male relatives by marriage.

164. ἐσσί: εἶ.

166. ὥς: 'so that', introducing another purpose clause, parallel to l. 163.

The true Teichoskopia now begins, with Priam asking Helen to identify particular Greek leaders down below on the plain.

167. ἠΰς: This, and ἐΰς, are the adjectives corresponding to the adverb εὖ.

168. κεφαλῇ: not 'by a head', but 'in height', cp. l. 193.

ἔασι: εἰσί.

172. φίλε ἑκυρέ: Both final syllables are lengthened – ἑκυρέ before an original δϜεινός, φίλε before an original (σϜ)εκυρέ (cp. Latin socer, German Schwieger). This lengthening before lost consonants is an indication of the antiquity of Greek dactylic poetry (see Introduction, p. xxiv).

For Helen's gratitude for the kindness of Priam, cp. XXIV 770, ἑκυρὸς δὲ πατὴρ ὣς ἤπιος αἰεί ('my father-in-law was always kind, like a father').

173. ὥς: exclamatory.

ἀδεῖν: ἀνδάνω.

175. παῖδα: Menelaos and Helen had had one child, Hermione.

τηλυγέτην: The adjective is obviously used of particularly loved children; its origin is quite obscure; the two most probable suggestions are 'last-born' and 'of a tender age'.

ὁμηλικίην: collective noun, my companions.

176. τά γ' οὐκ ἐγένοντο: Plural verb with neuter plural subject is not uncommon in Homer.

τό: adverbial; lit. 'with respect to which', 'wherefore'. 'But that did not happen, which is why I waste away in tears.'

177. ἀνείρεαι ἠδὲ μεταλλᾷς: a doublet for 'ask'.

179. ἀμφότερον: adverb, 'both'.

180. ἔσκε: ἦν.

κυνώπιδος: genitive agreeing with the genitive implicit in ἐμός, 'of me'.

Helen is fairly free with self-criticism.

εἴ ποτ' ἔην γε: the phrase of one looking back to happier days; 'if it ever was true', 'unless it was all a dream'. (ἔην is third person, not first.)

183. τοι: σοι (l. 54).

δεδμήατο: ἐδέδμηντο (δαμάζω); cp. l. 134 n.

ἦ ῥα . . . δεδμήατο: as Attic ἄρα with the imperfect, 'so it is true that many young men of the Achaians have been made subject to you', i.e. 'what a vast army you command'.

184–9. The battle between the Phrygians and the Amazons by the banks of the river Sangarios, at which Priam says that he was present, has been tentatively identified with disturbances caused by the invading tribes at the time of the break-up of the Hittite empire in the twelfth century. If so, this is one of the historical memories of the Mycenaean age which has survived into the *Iliad*. The Amazons are mentioned also in VI 186, as a people against whom Bellerophontes was required to fight.

185. αἰολοπώλους: 'with swift horses'.

187. ἐστρατόωντο: cp. l. 43 n. In this case the verb is in -οω, but seems to have followed the analogy of verbs in -αω.

188. ἐλέχθην: 'was counted', 'took my place'.

189. ἀντιάνειραι: 'women with the strength of men'.

192 ff. Notice the splendid description of the powerful, stocky Odysseus. It is like a portrait from life.

192. ἄγε: This, the imperative of ἄγω, is used as an exclamation, 'come now'.

193. κεφαλῇ: 'in height' (l. 168).

196. κτίλος ὥς: 'like a ram'; explained in the following two lines.

199. ἐκγεγαυῖα: from ἐκγέγαα, intransitive active perfect of ἐκγίγνομαι.

Διὸς ἐκγεγαυῖα: Helen, daughter of Leda, had both a real father (Zeus) and a putative father (Tyndareus).

201. κραναῆς περ ἐούσης: surprising though it is that such a hero should come from so rugged a place.

205. ἤλυθε: ἦλθε.

206. ἀγγελίης: Occasionally in the Iliad ἀγγελίης is more easily taken as a masculine noun meaning 'a messenger' than as the genitive of the feminine noun ἀγγελίη, and similarly ἀγγελίην as accusative masculine, rather than accusative feminine. This probably arose accidentally from such a phrase as ἀγγελίην ἐλθόντα (XI 140), meaning 'going on an embassy', but appearing to mean 'going as an ambassador'. In this way the epic dialect created by misunderstanding a previously non-existent noun. The other examples are IV 384, XI 140, XIII 252, XV 640. Trans. 'came to make representations about you'.

208. φυήν: 'physical appearance'.

209. ἀγρομένοισιν: participle of the strong aorist middle of ἀγείρω, 'in the assembly'.

210. στάντων: 'of them, standing'; almost a genitive absolute.

ὑπείρεχεν: for ὑπερεῖχεν, with the second syllable lengthened for metrical reasons. The verb is intransitive here.

εὐρέας ὤμους: accusative of respect.

211. ἄμφω ἑζομένω: nominative, but left in the air; for, by a change of construction, the subject of the sentence turns out not to be both of

the men (ἄμφω) but one of them (Odysseus). This is ungrammatical, but easily understood.

212. ὕφαινον: an obvious metaphor.

214. λιγέως: 'clearly'.

215. ἦ καὶ γένει ὕστερος ἦεν: 'and indeed he was a younger man'. Odysseus was not young; in fact he is described by Antilochos in XXIII 790 as belonging to a previous generation.

γένει: 'in birth'.

216–23. In this description of Odysseus as an orator, we again receive the impression of a portrait from life.

216. ὅτε ... ἀναίξειεν: 'when (on various occasions) he rose to speak'. Indefinite. Also ὅτε ... εἴη (l. 221).

217–19. 'He would stand, and look down with his eyes fixed on the ground, and he did not move his staff backwards or forwards, but held it still, like a man who did not know how to use it.'

From this description one can deduce the accepted technique of the public speaker in Homer's day.

217. στάσκεν, ἴδεσκε, 219. ἔχεσκεν: Tenses in -σκον, formed from either the present or aorist of the verb, are very common in Homer, as *frequentatives*; 'he would stand', etc.

ὑπαί: adverb, = ὑπό.

220. ζάκοτον: 'surly', 'ill-mannered'.

αὔτως: 'simply'.

221. εἴη: ἵημι.

222. The comparison lies in the slow inevitability and cumulative effect of falling snow.

225. Αἴαντα: the Telamonian, naturally (cp. I 138 n.).

235. καί τε: καί.

236–44. Helen cannot see her brothers Kastor and Polydeukes among the Greeks; she does not know they are already dead (l. 243).

239. ἐσπέσθην: aorist dual (ἕπομαι).

240. δεύρω: δεῦρο.

243–4. There is great pathos in the poet's comment on Helen's ignorance of her brothers' death. The *Iliad* poet does not show any knowledge of the myth that one of the two brothers was immortal, as son of Zeus.

243. φυσίζοος: It might seem strange that Homer should apply the epithet 'life-giving' to the earth at the moment when it is being described as the covering of the dead. Ruskin, indeed, the nineteenth-century critic, credited the poet with a particular poetical intention in so doing – the earth that receives the dead body is also the giver of life to all. Present-day scholars are much more likely to consider φυσίζοος a *stock epithet* (l. 37 n.), so that φυσίζοος αἶα means little, if anything, more than 'the earth'.

245. θεῶν . . . ὅρκια: 'sacrificial offerings to the gods.'

250. ὄρσεο: from ὄρνυμι; an isolated form of an imperative middle created as if from a *sigmatic second aorist* (cp. l. 262). Chantraine (I 417) considers it a metrically inspired variant of the strong aorist imperative ὄρσο. Cp. the active sigmatic imperatives οἴσετε and ἄξετε (ll. 103, 105).

252. ἵν' ὅρκια πιστὰ τάμητε: cp. l. 73 n.

253–5 = 136–8, with modifications.

256–8 = 73–5, with modifications.

255. κε . . . ἔποιτο: more hypothetical than the future κε . . . κεκλήσῃ of l. 138.

257. ναίοιμεν: The optative is taken over from l. 74, but here would have to be rather a potential than a wish.

νέονται: If this is correct (and ought not to be νέωνται, jussive subjunctive), it is present indicative with future meaning.

261. ἄν: the preposition ἀνά, shortened by *apocope*. (the cutting-off of the last syllable). So also πάρ for παρά in l. 262, and ἄν for ἀνά again in l. 268.

κατὰ δ' ἡνία τεῖνεν ὀπίσσω: 'and pulled back on the reins'.

262. πάρ: παρά (cp. l. 261 n.).

βήσετο: This is one of the examples of the *sigmatic second aorist*, i.e. the σ is added to the stem to form the aorist, as in the usual first aorist, but the endings are those of the second aorist (cp. ὄρσεο, l. 250). This is a middle aorist of βαίνω.

263. πεδίονδε: The suffix -δε shows motion towards.

ἔχον: 'directed', 'drove'.

265. ἐξ ἵππων: 'from the chariot', the regular meaning of ἵπποι in Homer.

268. ἄν: ἀνά (cp. l. 261 n.); i.e. ἀνώρνυτο (understanding ὄρνυτο from the previous line).

269. κρητῆρι: It was very rare in the ancient world to drink wine neat; it was usually diluted with water, and that was the purpose of the 'mixing-bowl'.

272. ἄωρτο: pluperfect passive of ἀείρω; 'hung'.

273–4. The distribution of hairs from the heads of the sacrificial lambs to each of the leaders on both sides involves them all symbolically in the oath.

κεφαλέων: genitive plural, for κεφαλάων, by Ionic metathesis of vowels (see Introduction p. xiii).

276. Ἴδηθεν: 'from Ida', the mountain of the Troad. Zeus, as weather-god, was regularly associated with mountain tops.

κύδιστε: superlative formed from the noun κῦδος.

278–9. 'Those beneath the ground who punish dead men (καμόντας) who are guilty of a false oath.' These lines (repeated XIX 259–60) show the beginning of a belief in divine retribution for wrongdoing, still limited to cases of perjury (because in that particular offence the credit of the gods is directly involved). By the time of the *Odyssey* (XIV 83–4) the gods may show disapproval of the wicked deeds of men; in the *Iliad*, however, the gods please themselves, taking sides in human disputes irrespective of the merits of the case.

279. τίννυσθον: dual; if this is right, then the reference must be to Hades and Persephone. In XIX 259, the underground avengers are the Erinyes.

283. νεώμεθα: like an imperative, 'we are to return'.

285. Τρῶας . . . ἀποδοῦναι: infinitive for imperative; so also ἀποτινέμεν in the next line.

286. τιμήν: 'compensation'.

287. πέληται: 'shall be known'.

288–9. εἰ . . . οὐκ ἐθέλωσιν: The negative οὐ (not μή) is perfectly correct even in the εἰ clause, because οὐκ ἐθέλειν makes a single concept, 'to be unwilling'.

290. αὐτάρ: marking the beginning of the apodosis, as δέ often does.

291. ἧος: ἕως.

κιχείω: subjunctive as if from a verb in -μι (*κίχημι), which provides tenses serving as the aorist system of κιχάνω, 'find'.

292. ἦ: 'he spoke'; past tense of ἠμί, which survived in Attic (particularly Plato) in the common phrases ἦ δ' ὅς, ἦν δ' ἐγώ.

στομάχους: 'throats', not 'stomachs'.

294. θυμοῦ: 'life'.

295. ἀφυσσόμενοι: presumably by the agency of the heralds; the subject, however, is the chiefs themselves.

296. ἔκχεον: on the ground, as a libation to the gods.

αἰειγενέτῃσι: from αἰειγενέτης, first-declension masculine.

299–301. The symbolic equation of the pouring-out of the wine with the spilling of the brains of anyone who breaks the truce finds a close parallel in the form of words used by the Roman priest at the making of a treaty, as quoted by Livy, I 24: *si prior defexit populus Romanus publico consilio dolo malo, tum tu ille Diespiter populum Romanum sic ferito ut ego hunc porcum hic hodie feriam* ('if the Roman people by public decision and with evil intention is the first to break this treaty, then do you, Jupiter on whom I have called, smite the Roman people in the same way as I here today shall smite this pig').

299. ὑπὲρ ὅρκια: 'beyond', and so 'contrary to' their oaths.

πημήνειαν: 'begin hostilities'; optative under the influence of the optative in the main clause.

300. σφι: dative, third-person pronoun.

301. δαμεῖεν: 'may (their wives) be subject to'.

302. Κρονίων: 'son of Kronos'; as well as the common Greek patronymic in -ιδης, Homer also uses forms in -ιος (adjectival) and -ιων, as here.

303. μετά . . . ἔειπε: *tmesis*.

304. κέκλυτε: cp. l. 86.

306. ὁρᾶσθαι: middle with active meaning; cp. ἰδέσθαι (= ἰδεῖν), l. 130.

309. θανάτοιο τέλος: lit. 'the conclusion, consisting in death'; so simply 'death'.

310. ἦ: cp. l. 292 n.

311–12 = 261–2, with modifications.

315. χῶρον διεμέτρεον: 'measured out the space' (for the single combat).

316. κλήρους: probably marked pebbles, as in VII 175, οἱ δὲ κλῆρον ἐσημήναντο ἔκαστος ('each of them marked his own lot').

317. ὁππότερος: indirect question, 'to see which of them . . .'.
ἀφείη: ἀφίημι; optative representing what would be a deliberative subjunctive in primary sequence.

318. ἠρήσαντο: ἀράομαι.

320 = 276.

321. 'whichever of the two brought about these troubles (i.e. this war) between the two peoples'.

322. δός: 'grant that'.
δῦναι εἴσω: 'enter within'.

328. ἐδύσετο: sigmatic second aorist; cp. l. 262 n.
τεύχεα καλά: Note the long first syllable of καλός, which had originally been καλϜός; so also at the beginning of l. 331.

330–8. One of four full-scale descriptions of the arming of a hero in the *Iliad*. The others are Agamemnon in XI 17–43, Patroklos in XVI 131–9, and Achilleus in XIX 369–91. The description follows the same order each time (greaves, breastplate, sword, shield, helmet, spear), and only differs in special detail (as l. 333 here) or ornamental expansion for greater effect. The basic phrases are clearly traditional.

330. κνημῖδας: cp. l 156 n.
πρῶτα: adverbial, 'first of all'.

331. ἐπισφυρίοις: ornamental ankle-clasps fitted to the greaves.
ἀραρυίας: The perfect of ἀραρίσκω is ἄρηρα (cp. l. 338), but in a small class of verbs the feminine of the perfect participle shortens the second vowel; cp. (θάλλω) τέθηλα, but τεθᾰλυῖα.

333. It is not explained why Paris did not wear his own breastplate. But we remember that he was light-armed when he first stepped out between the two armies (l. 17).
ἥρμοσε: intransitive, 'fitted'.

334–5. Two straps go over the shoulders – the sword belt and the shield strap.
ἀργυρόηλον: 'with rivets of silver' (for attaching the blade to the handle).

337. The regular description of the helmet, 'with a horse-tail plume; and terribly nodded the crest above',

338. παλάμηφιν: The suffix -φι seems in the earliest time to have been an instrumental or locative case-ending; but its use had been greatly widened in the epic dialect. Here παλάμηφι would not be distinguishable from the dative παλάμῃσι.

ἀρήρει: pluperfect of ἀραρίσκω; cp. l. 331 n.

339. ὣς δ' αὔτως: ὡσαύτως δέ.

342. δεινόν: internal accusative with δερκόμενοι, 'looking grim'.

344–5. στήτην, σείοντε, κοτέοντε: duals.

347. πάντοσ' ἐίσην: lit. 'equal in all directions'; 'symmetrical', 'round'.

348. οὐδ' ἔρρηξεν χαλκός: 'nor did the bronze (spearhead) break (the shield)'.

οἱ refers to the χαλκός.

349. ὄρνυτο χαλκῷ: He had been crouching in a defensive position; now he 'rose up with the spear'.

350. ἐπευξάμενος: aorist, 'having first prayed'.

351. ἄνα: vocative of ἄναξ.
ὅ: ὅς, 'who'. Also l. 354.
ἔοργε: ἔρδω.

353. ἐρρίγῃσι: perfect subjunctive; for the ending, cp. l. 62.

'In order that even among later generations a man may be afraid to do evil to his host, who has shown him hospitality.'

355. ἀμπεπαλών: reduplicated aorist of ἀναπάλλω.

357. διά: The only acceptable explanation of the lengthening of the first syllable is the metrical stress.

358. ἠρήρειστο: ἐρείδω, 'forced its way'.

360. A repeated line, 'but he leant aside and escaped black death'. It is a physical impossibility to lean aside successfully after the spear has gone through the breastplate. The original context of this formulaic line presumably had a lighter-armed soldier, without the θώρηξ of l. 358.

362. ἀνασχόμενος: 'raising his arm'.

κόρυθος φάλον: The meaning of φάλος is obscure. Opinion is divided between a 'horn' on the front of the helmet, and the 'crest-holder' running from front to back.

363. διατρυφέν: διαθρύπτω, 'shattered', i.e. the sword.

366. ἐφάμην: 'I thought', 'expected'.
τείσασθαι: aorist tense; 'that I had got my revenge'.
κακότητος: causal genitive.

367. ἄγη: for ἐάγη, ἄγνυμι.

368. ἤιχθη: ἀίσσω.
παλάμηφιν: here standing for the genitive; cp. l. 338 n.

369. κόρυθος λάβεν: 'seized him by his helmet'.

370. 'and, having twisted him round, was trying to drag him into the Greek army'.

371. ἄγχε: 'was throttling him'.
πολύκεστος: 'with much stitching'.
ἱμάς: 'chinstrap'.
ἀπαλήν: 'soft', 'tender', like a woman's.

372. 'which was tight under his chin as a strap (ὀχεύς) for his helmet'.
τέτατο: τείνω.

373. ἤρατο (κεν): 'he would have won for himself', ἄρνυμαι.

374. Aphrodite, goddess of love and patron of Paris and Helen, now intervenes to save Paris from imminent death.

375. ἶφι: 'by force', instrumental case of the noun (F)ἴς (Latin vis).
κταμένοιο: strong aorist middle participle from κτείνω, with passive meaning.
ἶφι κταμένοιο: 'slaughtered'.

376. κεινή = κενή, κενεή, 'empty'.

379. κατακτάμεναι: κατακτεῖναι.

381. ἠέρι: 'mist'.

382. κὰδ δ' εἶσε: καθεῖσε δέ; 'she set him down'.
κηώεντι: probably 'fragrant with incense'.

383. 'She herself went to call (future participle) Helen.'
    The strangely frightening scene between Aphrodite and Helen, and the following exchange between Helen and Paris, show great psychological understanding.

384. ἅλις: 'in large numbers'.

386. ἐικυῖα: from ἐικώς, participle of ἔοικα.

387. εἰροκόμῳ and 388. ἤσκειν εἴρια καλά: The longest household task in those days was the making of wool by spinning.

ναιεταώσῃ: agreeing with οἱ.

388. ἤσκειν: It is most unusual for the ν-movable to be added to the third-person singular of the imperfect of the contracted verb; uncontracted ἤσκεεν would be perfectly proper.

μιν: the old woman. Helen is the subject of φιλέεσκε.

389. Take τῇ with ἐεισαμένη, μιν with προσεφώνεε.

391. κεῖνος ὅ γε: 'there he is'.

δινωτοῖσι: 'well turned' i.e. smoothly rounded by the carpenter.

Aphrodite, who is simultaneously in this scene the force of sexual attraction and a strongly characterised goddess, attempts to interest Helen in her husband Paris.

394. νέον: adverb, 'just'.

395. θυμὸν ὄρινε: 'aroused her indignation'.

399. δαιμονίη: 'This word, always found in the vocative, seems to mean properly one who is under the influence of a δαίμων or unfavourable divine intelligence; that is, one whose actions are either unaccountable or ill-omened' (Leaf). It is used by a person remonstrating with another; trans. 'What do you want?'

ταῦτα: internal accusative with ἠπεροπεύειν; trans. 'in this way'.

400. πῃ: 'somewhere'.

προτέρω = πρόσω, 'further'.

πολίων: genitive, depending on προτέρω πῃ.

402. μερόπων: an epithet whose meaning was almost certainly lost even for Homer; it is used only in formulas with ἄνθρωποι (except II 285, μερόπεσσι βροτοῖσιν).

403–5. οὕνεκα . . . τοὔνεκα: relative . . . correlative.

406. ἀπόεικε κελεύθου: 'leave the path'. This is the reading of Aristarchus, the Alexandrian editor; the MSS. have ἀπόειπε κελεύθους, 'renounce the ways', which would probably be generally preferred if it were not for Aristarchus' authority.

407. ὑποστρέψειας: intransitive, 'return (to Olympos)'. Optative of a wish that is almost a command; cp. ναίοιτε (l. 74).

408. ἑ: 'him'.

409. εἰς ὅ: 'until'.

ποιήσεται: for ποιήσηται; aorist subjunctive with short vowel, as is normal in Homer. Also μητίσομαι (l. 416).

410. νεμεσσητόν: cp. l. 156 n.

411. πορσανέουσα: future; of the wife, 'to share (his bed)'.

414. σχετλίη: 'self-willed creature'.
μή: 'for fear that'.
χωσαμένη: χώομαι.
μεθείω: aorist subjunctive, μεθίημι.

416. μητίσομαι: cp. l. 409 n.

417. κακὸν οἶτον ὄληαι (= ὄλῃ): 'die an evil death'.

419. κατασχομένη: 'covering her face'.

422. ἀμφίπολοι: cp. l. 143.

425. ἀντία: adverb, 'opposite'.
   Aphrodite is stage-managing the scene; it is not surprising therefore that she places a chair for Helen.

426. αἰγιόχοιο: The *aigis* is a supernatural weapon of the gods, carried by Zeus, but used from time to time by Athene and Apollo. It is normally defensive, like a shield (the popular etymology suggested a goat-skin), but can be used offensively, because when shaken in the face of the enemy it strikes terror in their hearts.

427. ἠνίπαπε: ἐνίπτω.

430. εὔχεο: second-person imperfect; 'you used to say'.

432–6. All this, of course, is heavily sarcastic.

436. δαμήῃς: aorist subjunctive passive.
   Take ὑπό with αὐτοῦ, and δουρί as an instrumental dative with δαμήῃς.

438. με . . . θυμόν: both objects of ἔνιπτε; they represent 'the whole and the part' – 'me and my courage'.

440. πάρα . . . εἰσί: πάρεισι.

441. ἄγε: 'come'; cp. l. 192 n.
   φιλότητι: the normal word for 'love-making', common in the end-of-line formula φιλότητι καὶ εὐνῇ (l. 445).
   τραπείομεν: first-person plural, aorist passive subjunctive. Modern commentators, following the scholia, derive it, not from τρέπομαι,

'turn', but from τέρπομαι, 'enjoy', i.e. ἐτράπην for ἐτάρπην, by metathesis of consonants as is found in κραδίη for καρδία (l. 60) and frequently. 'Let us go to bed and find pleasure in love.'

445. Κραναῇ: The particular island referred to is uncertain; κραναός means 'rocky'.

ἐμίγην φιλότητι καὶ εὐνῇ: cp. φιλότητι (l. 441 n.).

447. λέχοσδε: 'to the bed'.

448. τρητοῖσι: an epithet of beds, meaning that they have their wood-work pierced with holes for the straps of the bedding.

450. ἐσαθρήσειεν: εἰσαθρέω, 'catch sight of'.

453. A compressed statement – they did not hide him, and they would not if they saw him; trans. 'they certainly were not going to hide him from friendship, if anyone saw him'.

454. ἴσον: adverb, 'equally'; governs the dative κηρί.

459. ἀποτινέμεν: infinitive for imperative.

460 = 287.

461. The Achaians, naturally, applauded Agamemnon's speech; the Trojan reaction is not stated.

BOOK IV

The Breaking of the Truce;
Agamemnon's Review;
the Beginning of the Battle

1. οἱ δὲ θεοί: 'But they, the gods'; what was the definite article in later Greek was still primarily a demonstrative pronoun in Homer; see ll. 3 and 9.

πάρ: the preposition παρά, shortened by *apocope* (the cutting-off of the last syllable).

Ζηνί: dative of Ζεύς.

ἠγορόωντο: This, from the verb ἀγοράομαι, would if uncontracted be ἠγοράοντο, if contracted ἠγορῶντο. By a peculiarity of Homeric Greek (caused no doubt by the opposed pressures of contraction of vowels and the requirements of the metre), the contracted form has suffered a sort of expansion or distension. This, technically called *diektasis*, is found particularly with verbs in -αω. So also εἰσορόωντες in l. 4.

2. χρυσέῳ: The choice of adjective has more to do with the splendour of the house of Zeus than with its building materials.

μετά: with dative, 'among'.

σφισί: third-person pronoun, 'them'.

Ἥβη: goddess of youth, and handmaid of the gods.

3. νέκταρ: the wine of the gods.

ἐῳνοχόει: a form with double augment (from οἰνοχοεῖν).

τοί: 'they'; an alternative form of the nominative plural οἱ; cp. l. 1 n.

4. δειδέχατο: from δείδεγμαι, a perfect form with present meaning, related to δείκνυμι; 'they pledged'. δειδέχατο is third-person plural of the pluperfect middle, for ἐδειδεκ-ντο. Notice the two following features: (*a*) the omission of the augment is very frequent in Homer; (*b*) the ν of the third-person plural has been vocalised as an α, such a collocation of consonants as -κντ- being quite impossible.

εἰσορόωντες: i.e. εἰσοράοντες; cp. l. 1 n.

5. Κρονίδης: 'son of Kronos', i.e. Zeus.

ἐρεθίζεμεν: an alternative form for the present infinitive, ἐρεθίζειν.

Ἥρην: Hera, wife of Zeus and, with Athene, chief supporter of the Greeks. The second η in her name is an example of the most obvious Ionic feature of the Homeric dialect – η for α even after ε, ι, ρ.

6. κερτομίοις: 'riling', 'annoying'.

ἐπέεσσι: Attic ἔπεσι.

παραβλήδην: 'with ulterior motive', 'with intent to deceive'. This refers particularly to ll. 17–19. Zeus does not in fact intend peace between the Greeks and the Trojans; he means to provoke Hera and Athene to do something about it.

7. θεάων: partitive genitive with δοιαί. Notice the normal genitive plural of the -α declension in Homer, in -αων (cp. Latin -arum).

8. The epithets for Hera and Athene are found only here and in the same line, v 908; both appear to be geographically derived. Hera was especially the goddess of Argos; Athene had a sanctuary at the small town of Alalkomenai in Boiotia (Pausanias IX 33.5).

9. ταί: cp. τοί (l. 3).

εἰσορόωσαι = εἰσοράουσαι (l. 1 n.).

10. τέρπεσθον: third-person dual.

τῷ δέ: 'the other one', i.e. Paris, whose rescue by Aphrodite at the end of the single combat with Menelaos was described in book III.

αὖτε: 'on the other hand'.

11. παρμέμβλωκε: from παραβλώσκω; apocope of the preposition; cp. πάρ (l. 1 n.).

αὐτοῦ: with ἀμύνει, 'from him'.

12. ὀιόμενον: 'expecting'.

θανέεσθαι: future infinitive, θανεῖσθαι. Uncontracted forms are common in Homer.

13. νίκη μέν: understand ἐστί, 'the victory belongs to'; the word μέν implies that nevertheless matters are not yet settled.

14. φραζώμεθα: jussive subjunctive, 'let us consider'.

15–16. ἤ . . . ἦ: 'whether . . . or'.

ῥα: Homeric verse uses all three forms ἄρα, ἄρ, and the enclitic ῥα, merely as required by the metre. The particle has a mild inferential force.

16. ὄρσομεν: for ὄρσωμεν, aorist subjunctive with short vowel, as is normal in Homer.

18. The optative οἰκέοιτο is a potential, but not far removed from a wish. 'The city of Priam *may* still be dwelt in.' So also ἄγοιτο in the next line. Zeus is not in fact seriously intending this outcome (cp. l. 6 n.).

Πριάμοιο: The genitive singular of -ος declension nouns and adjectives may be in -οιο as well as -ου.

19. Ἀργείην: Helen did not come from the town of Argos but from Sparta. However, Homer can use 'Argos' for the whole Peloponnese, and the title 'Argives' for all the Greeks.

ἄγοιτο: 'may take away with him'.

20. ὥς: Accented in this way, or with the circumflex ὧς, this word is an adverb = οὕτως, 'so'. The conjunction ὡς is unaccented, except when it follows its noun in a simile, e.g. λύκοι ὥς, 'like wolves' (l. 471).

ἔφατο: imperfect middle of φημί; there is no distinction of meaning from the active.

ἐπέμυξαν: 'muttered' (said μύ μῦ); an onomatopoeic word.

Ἀθηναίη τε καὶ Ἥρη: in apposition to αἱ.

21. ἥσθην, μεδέσθην: duals.

22. ἀκέων: normally an indeclinable adjective or adverb, although it has the look of a participle and is sometimes so declined.

23. μιν: the epic form of νιν, accusative third-person pronoun, 'her'.

24. ἔχαδε: from χανδάνω; 'had room for', 'contained'.

προσηύδα: imperfect of προσαυδάω.

25. τόν: demonstrative, 'this' (l. 1 n.).

ἔειπες: later contracted to εἶπες.

26 ff. Hera's argument is that it is unreasonable that the war should end without the destruction of Troy, after all her efforts.

27. ἱδρῶ: for ἱδρῶα, accusative of ἱδρώς.

καμέτην (κάμνω): 'grew weary'; dual, as referring to a two-horse chariot.

28. κακά: accusative in apposition to the sentence, in this case describing the effect of Hera λαὸν ἀγειρούσῃ.

τοῖο: 'of him', 'his'; cp. ll. 1 n. and 18 n.

29. τοι: the same as the enclitic σοι, the unstressed dative of σύ.

30. μέγ᾽ ὀχθήσας: Zeus, having succeeded in provoking Hera, is exaggeratedly angry himself – a very human reaction.

νεφεληγερέτα: nominative.

31. δαιμονίη: 'This word, always found in the vocative, seems to mean properly one who is under the influence of a δαίμων or unfavourable divine intelligence; that is, one whose actions are either unaccountable or ill-omened' (Leaf). It is used by a person remonstrating with another. Trans. 'What do you mean?'

νυ: the same as the enclitic νυν.

32. τόσσα = τοσαῦτα.

ὅ τε: accusative neuter of the relative ὅς τε; adverbial, 'with respect to the fact that', 'in that'. It is not distinguishable in meaning from ὅτι, which, however, is never elided. The τε in ὅ τε has a slight implication of habitual, general, behaviour.

35. βεβρώθοις: optative of a perfect from βιβρώσκω. An extreme expression of hatred.

36. κεν: κε (κεν) is the alternative form of the modal particle ἄν, and is used in the same way. Here the condition follows the normal rules of later Greek.

39. A much repeated line.

τοι: cp. l. 29 n.

βάλλεο: imperative middle, still uncontracted; Attic βάλλου.

σῇσιν = σαῖς.

40. ὁππότε κεν = ὁπότ᾽ ἄν.

μεμαώς: 'eager', a participle from the shorter stem of the perfect μέμονα.

41. ὅθι: 'where'.

τοι: cp. l. 29 n.

ἀνέρες = ἄνδρες.

ἐγγεγάασι: perfect of ἐγγίγνομαι.

42. διατρίβειν, ἐᾶσαι: infinitives for imperatives.

43. δῶκα: the augment is omitted; cp. δειδέχατο (l. 4).

ἑκὼν ἀέκοντί γε θυμῷ: 'of my own free will, but regretfully'.

44. αἵ: the relative, picked up by τάων (l. 46).

ἠελίῳ = ἡλίῳ.

45. ναιετάουσι: intransitive, 'are inhabited'.

πόληες = πόλεις.

46. περὶ κῆρι: Two explanations are offered: either περί (adverb), 'exceedingly', κῆρι (locative), 'in my heart'; or περὶ (preposition) κῆρι, 'around my heart', and so 'with my whole heart'. The former is preferred.

τιέσκετο: Tenses in -σκον (here passive -σκομην), formed from either the present or aorist of the verb, are very common in Homer, as *frequentatives*; 'used to be honoured'.

ἱρή: ἱερά.

47. ἐυμμελίω: genitive of the first-declension masculine ἐυμμελίης, 'of the fine ash spear'. The final vowel is parallel to the common first-declension masculine genitive endings -αο (l. 228) and -εω (l. 75).

48. ἐδεύετο: i.e. ἐδέετο, ἐδεῖτο (δέομαι).

ἐίσης = ἴσης; 'equal for all', 'abundant'.

49. 'Of libation and the fat of burnt offering; for this is the honour which we have received as our divine right (λαγχάνω).'

50. βοῶπις: It is generally agreed that this title of Hera derives from a time when she was worshipped in animal shape, as a cow (cp. γλαυκῶπις Ἀθήνη, l. 439). Nevertheless it has now come to be simply another epithet meaning 'beautiful', and can be applied even to human women (III 144); nor can it be denied that cows have lovely eyes.

The speech that follows shows the utter ruthlessness and selfishness of the goddess; she will willingly allow Zeus to destroy her three favourite cities in Greece at any time in the future, if he will support her wish to destroy Troy now. Many commentators see here an allusion to the destruction of the Mycenaean palaces by the Dorian invaders in the period after the Trojan War.

52. εὐρυάγυια: 'wide-wayed'; the epithet elsewhere describes Troy.

53. διαπέρσαι: infinitive for imperative.

περὶ κῆρι: see l. 46 n.

54. πρόσθ' ἵσταμαι: 'stand in front of', 'defend'.

55. φθονέω, εἰῶ (ἐάω): probably present subjunctives, of an assumed situation; 'If I *should* refuse.'

56. ἀνύω: present with future meaning; 'I am likely to achieve nothing'.

ἐπεὶ ἦ: 'since undoubtedly'.

ἐσσί: second person of εἰμί.

57. θέμεναι = θεῖναι (τίθημι).

59. πρεσβυτάτην: From meaning 'oldest' the word has come to mean 'most honoured'.

τέκετο: Both active and middle of this verb are used indiscriminately of both mother and father.

ἀγκυλομήτης: It is not known how Kronos, the father of Zeus, earned the epithet 'crooked-thinking', unless it was on account of his practice of swallowing his children.

60. ἀμφότερον: adverbial, 'in both respects'.

62. ὑποείξομεν: subjunctive with short vowel; cp. ὄρσομεν (l. 16).

63. ἐπί... ἔψονται: ἐφέψονται; the elements which later constituted a compound verb are still separable in Homer, with the preposition able to stand by itself as an adverb. The phenomenon is called *tmesis* (from τέμνω, 'cut'). In practice one may treat this as if a verb has been divided into its two parts, although the true situation is that the two parts have not yet coalesced.

64. θᾶσσον: This, the comparative adverb of ταχύς, is sometimes as here used with the simple sense of the positive, 'quickly'.

ἐπιτεῖλαι: infinitive for imperative.

65. 'Αχαιῶν: Notice that there are three names used by the poet indistinguishably for the Greeks – Achaians ('Αχαιοί), Argives ('Αργεῖοι) and Danaans (Δαναοί).

66. ὥς κε ... ἄρξωσι: 'how they may begin', 'that they may begin'.

67. ὑπὲρ ὅρκια: 'beyond' and so 'contrary to' their oaths.

68. ὥς: cp. l. 20 n.

69. ἔπεα πτερόεντα: 'winged words', in that they fly from mouth to ear; an ancient poetic phrase. Notice the two objects of προσηύδα.

73. πάρος μεμαυῖαν (μέμονα): 'already eager'.

75. οἷον: the same as ὥς, but grammatically in agreement with ἀστέρα.

ἧκε (ἵημι): a *gnomic aorist*, i.e. the aorist found in proverbial or general statements, of things which happen now and always have happened.

ἀγκυλομήτεω: a form of the genitive of first-declension masculines; cp. l. 228 n.

Athene descended to earth from heaven, and what the people saw looked like a shooting star; this is a little different from the usual simile, which merely describes one thing in terms of its likeness to another thing.

77. τοῦ δέ τε: The enclitic particle τε often accompanies a proverbial or general statement in Homer, and so occurs frequently in similes. It is not to be translated.

ἀπό ... ἵενται: *tmesis* (l. 63), for ἀφίενται.

79. κάδ: *apocope* (l. 1), with the final consonant of κάτ assimilated to the first sound of the following word: κατέθορε.

80. ἐυκνήμιδας: Greaves were shin-guards, worn particularly as a protection against stones and arrows.

84. ἀνθρώπων depends on ταμίης πολέμοιο.

86. κατεδύσετο: This is one of the examples of the *sigmatic second aorist*, i.e. the σ is added to the stem to form the aorist, as in the usual first aorist, but the endings are those of the second aorist.

87. Antenor was the most important Trojan outside the royal family.

88 ff. The entry in the Trojan Catalogue in II 824–7 contains several details that are repeated in these lines:

Οἳ δὲ Ζέλειαν ἔναιον ὑπαὶ πόδα νείατον Ἴδης,
ἀφνειοί, πίνοντες ὕδωρ μέλαν Αἰσήποιο,
Τρῶες, τῶν αὖτ' ἦρχε Λυκάονος ἀγλαὸς υἱός,
Πάνδαρος, ᾧ καὶ τόξον Ἀπόλλων αὐτὸς ἔδωκεν.

91. οἱ: dative of the third-person pronoun, 'who followed *him*'.

93. πίθοιο: The optative here, without ἄν, seems to be midway between a potential and a wish. Most editors print with a question-mark at the end of the line, which makes it a little easier.

94. τλαίης κεν (and 95. κε ... ἄροιο): These optatives with κε(ν) are as it were the apodosis of the wish expressed in l. 93. 'So might you take the decision to, etc.'

ἐπιπροέμεν: aorist infinitive of ἐπιπροίημι.

95. Τρώεσσι: 'at the hands of the Trojans', 'in the sight of the Trojans'; we would have expected a genitive rather than a dative.

ἄροιο: second aorist optative of ἄρνυμαι.

97. πάμπρωτα: adverb.

τοῦ ... παρ: 'from him'.

98. αἰ: the Aeolic form of εἰ.

100. ἄγε: 'come'. The imperative of ἄγω is used in this way, as an exclamation.

101. Λυκηγενέι: "This and similar epithets of Apollo suggested to the Greeks at least two ideas, *Lykia* and *wolves*. To these, etymologists

have added a third, *light*; Apollo being the sun-god" (Bayfield). The modern view is to give up the derivation from 'light', and treat Apollo as in origin a wolf-god (perhaps the god of shepherds); but one should not disregard his certain connections with Anatolia and Lykia. Pandaros is said to come from Lykia (e.g. v 105), though this has to be a different Lykia (near Troy) from the home of Sarpedon and Glaukos far to the south. Note also the name of Pandaros' father, Lykaon.

103. οἴκαδε: 'home'; the suffix -δε indicates motion towards.

νοστήσας: agreeing with the subject (understood from εὔχεο) of ῥέξειν.

104. ἄφρονι: Pandaros' action is not one which the poet expects us to approve. He has a free choice whether to agree to the suggestion put to him, and the fact that it is a god who tries to influence him is no excuse. He suffers an almost automatic punishment by being killed in the next book.

105–26. This is the most complete description of a bow and a bow-shot in the *Iliad*. It is fully discussed by Miss Lorimer in *Homer and the Monuments*, pp. 290–5. The information about the making of the bow in ll. 106–11 is more poetical than real; but the shot itself is described clearly and accurately in ll. 122–5. (For the shape of the bow, see Frank H. Stubbings in *A Companion to Homer*, p. 519.)

105. ἐσύλα: 'detached' the bow, which was carried strapped to its quiver (so Miss Lorimer, op. cit., p. 292).

αἰγός: i.e. made from the horns of a wild goat.

106 ff. The fact stated here, that Pandaros provided himself with the goat-horns, and got a human craftsman to make his bow, has seemed to some to clash with the statement of II 827 (quoted at l. 88 n. above), that Apollo himself had given Pandaros his bow. The two, however, are not necessarily inconsistent; to say that Apollo himself gave him his bow need not mean more than that he was a very successful archer.

109. ἐκκαιδεκάδωρα: 'sixteen palms in length'; a palm is the breadth of four fingers – about 3 in. The length of these horns was therefore about 4 ft.

110. ἤραρε (ἀραρίσκω): 'fitted together', i.e. with a metal clasp in the middle.

111. κορώνην: the 'tip' of the bow, over which the loop of the string was slipped when the bow was strung.

112–13. Three successive actions are described in reverse order. First he bent the bow back (ἀγκλίνας = ἀνακλίνας through *apocope* of the preposition), then he strung it, then he laid it carefully on the ground (ποτί = πρός). This meaning of ἀγκλίνας is explained by Lorimer, op. cit., p. 291 (see ll. 105–26 n., above).

113. σχέθον: a form of the aorist of ἔχω.

115. βλῆσθαι: an aorist infinitive, passive in meaning; cp. βλήμενος (l. 211), βλῆτο (l. 518).

116. σύλα: 'took off'; cp. l. 105 n.

117. μελαινέων: for μελαινάων, by Ionic metathesis of vowels (see Introduction, p. xiii).

ἕρμα: This word, which elsewhere in Homer means either a 'support' for a ship drawn up on the beach, a 'protection' for the city, or an 'ear-ring', has not been satisfactorily explained here. Ameis–Hentze connect it with ὁρμή (as ἕρμα, 'ear-ring', is with ὅρμος), and thus provide a possible sense – the 'starting point', 'origin' of pains.

119–21 = 101–3, with the verb changed to the third person.

122. γλυφίδας: These are thought to have been grooves in the side of the arrow, for the archer to hold.

123. σίδηρον: the metal tip of the arrow. Although iron was in common use in Homer's own day, the epic tradition is nevertheless very consistent in keeping bronze as the metal for weapons, as it had been in the Mycenaean age. A common epithet of arrows and spears is in fact χαλκήρης – 'bronze-tipped'. This is the *only* example of the naming of iron for the point of an arrow or spear.

124. κυκλοτερές: to be taken predicatively with ἔτεινε.

125. ἆλτο: aorist of ἅλλομαι.

126. ἐπιπτέσθαι: ἐπιπέτομαι.

127. σέθεν: σοῦ, genitive of the second-person pronoun.

It has been noticed that two particular characters in the *Iliad* are commonly addressed in the second person by the poet – Menelaos and Patroklos. Although metrical utility no doubt plays a part in this, there is also a strong impression that the poet is sympathetic to these figures, who are alike in being amiable and a little unheroic.

λελάθοντο: *reduplicated aorist*, an old tense-formation of which numerous examples are found in Homer.

128. ἀγελείη: 'she who brings in the booty'; it should not be forgotten that Athene is a fighting goddess.

Athene is in fact stage-managing this scene, first persuading Pandaros to shoot, then taking her stance in front of Menelaos to see that he is not hurt. Finally, in v 290, it is Athene who sees to it that Pandaros pays a particularly unpleasant penalty at the point of Diomedes' spear.

130. τόσον μέν: 'to a certain extent', but not completely, as is seen by the δέ clause in l. 132. The limitation implied in τόσον μέν has nothing to do with the simile beginning ὡς ὅτε, which relates simply to the action ἔεργεν ἀπὸ χροός.

ἔεργεν: Attic εἶργεν. The first ε is not the augment, but a *prothetic* vowel (as in θέλω, ἐθέλω); cp. the subjunctive ἐέργῃ (l. 131).

131. μυῖαν: a biting or stinging fly – a good parallel to the arrow.

λέξεται: aorist subjunctive with short vowel; cp. l. 16.

132. αὖτε: 'instead'.

132–3. ζωστήρ is a broad belt, clasped at the front. θώρηξ, 'breast-plate', was of leather in early times, but of metal in the later armoury. Here the adjective διπλόος (l. 133) suits a leather jerkin better, i.e. the two sides overlap where it is held together in the middle.

134. ἀρηρότι (ἀραρίσκω): intransitive in this form.

135. διά: The only acceptable explanation of the lengthening of the first syllable is the metrical stress.

ἐλήλατο (ἐλαύνω) and 136. ἠρήρειστο (ἐρείδω): pluperfects.

137. μίτρης: not unlike a metal kilt, defending the lower part of the body.

138. ἥ οἱ πλεῖστον ἔρυτο: 'which most kept off (the arrow) from him'; 'which was his biggest defence'.

εἴσατο: This aorist, probably formed from ἵεμαι, is used as if a part of εἶμι (Chantraine, I 412).

141–5. In a decidedly exotic simile, Menelaos' skin discoloured by blood is likened to ivory stained with a purple dye.

141. τε: cp. l. 77 n.

142. Μῃονὶς ἠὲ Κάειρα: a woman of Meionia or Karia, two non-Greek areas of south-west Asia Minor.

ἔμμεναι: εἶναι.

143. θαλάμῳ: 'store-chamber'.

ἠρήσαντο (ἀράομαι): a gnomic aorist; cp. l. 75 n.

145. ἀμφότερον: adverbial; cp. l. 60.

146. μιάνθην: an exceptional variant on μίανθεν, the alternative shorter form for ἐμιάνθησαν (cp. βάν for ἔβησαν, l. 209).

151. νεῦρον: the cord binding the arrow-head to the shaft.

154. χειρός: 'by the hand'.

Agamemnon's affectionate care for his brother is one of the more amiable features of his character.

155. φίλε: For the metrically lengthened first syllable, cp. διά (l. 135).

θάνατον: accusative in apposition to ὅρκι' ἔταμνον.

ἔταμνον: The throats of the sacrificial victims were *cut* at the making of a truce; so, by a metaphor, ὅρκια τάμνειν means 'to make a solemn truce'.

156. οἶον προστήσας: 'having put you forward alone'.

157. ὡς: 'seeing that'.

159. ἐπέπιθμεν: pluperfect (intransitive) of πείθω.

160-2. A proverbial form of speech, shown to be so by the gnomic τε's (in l. 160 and the second word of l. 161), and the gnomic aorists (l. 75) ἐτέλεσσεν and ἀπέτεισαν.

161. ἔκ τε καὶ ὀψέ etc.: 'he will accomplish it in full, though late; and they pay with great punishment'.

164. This is a key line in the *Iliad*. Hektor repeats it, with the preceding and following lines, in VI 447-9. Both attacker and defender know that Troy is doomed.

165. ἐυμμελίω: cp. l. 47 n.

166. σφι: dative plural.

167. ἐπισσείῃσιν: The epic dialect possessed, for the three singular persons of the subjunctive, alternative endings in -ωμι, -ῃσθα, -ῃσι. These forms are regularly used to produce a weak third-foot caesura, as here.

αἰγίδα: The *aigis* is a supernatural weapon of the gods, carried by Zeus, but used from time to time by Athene and Apollo. It is normally defensive, like a shield (the popular etymology suggested a goat-skin), but can be used offensively, because when shaken in the face of the enemy it strikes terror in their hearts.

168. ἀπάτης: genitive of cause.

169. σέθεν: cp. l. 127 n.; objective genitive with ἄχος.

172. If Menelaos dies, the Greeks will have little reason to stay at Troy, as they are there to restore his wife to him.

173. κάδ: κατά, by *apocope*; *tmesis*.
εὐχωλήν: 'triumph', 'cause for boasting'.

174. Ἀργείην Ἑλένην: defining further the εὐχωλήν of the previous line.
Ἀργείην: cp. l. 19 n.
σέο: σοῦ.
πύσει: πύθω.

175. ἀτελευτήτῳ ἐπὶ ἔργῳ: 'on an errand unfulfilled'.

176. κε ... ἐρέει: ἄν with the future indicative is occasionally found even in Attic prose.

181. κεινῇσι: κεναῖς, 'empty'.

182. χάνοι: optative for a wish; 'may the wide earth gape for me'.

184. δειδίσσεο: 'frighten', present imperative middle.

185. ἐν καιρίῳ: 'in a fatal spot'; cp. Agamemnon's death cry in Aeschylus (*Ag.* 1343):

> ὤμοι, πέπληγμαι καιρίαν πληγὴν ἔσω.

πάγη: πήγνυμι.

186. εἰρύσατο: cp. l. 138 n.
ζωστήρ, 187. μίτρη: cp. notes on ll. 132 and 137.

187. ζῶμα: 'loin-cloth'.

189. αἰ γάρ: 'I pray that', a regular way of expressing a wish.

190. ἐπιμάσσεται: 'will treat'; lit. 'lay his hands on'.

191. παύσῃσι: cp. ἐπισσείῃσι (l. 167). παύω can take the accusative of the person and genitive of the thing; here understand σε.

192. ἦ: 'he spoke'; past tense of ἠμί, which survived in Attic (particularly Plato) in the common phrases ἦ δ' ὅς, ἦν δ' ἐγώ.
κήρυκα: The functions of the herald included the taking of messages, arranging of sacrifices and general assistance to the kings. The herald's person was sacrosanct – which probably explains the epithet θεῖον here.

193. ὅττι τάχιστα: ὡς τάχιστα.

Μαχάονα: Machaon and Podaleirios were the doctors in the Greek army; they were the leaders of one of the contingents from north Greece (II 729–33).

194. φῶτα: not easily translatable; φῶτα is in apposition to Μαχάονα, and Ἀσκληπιοῦ υἱόν is in apposition to it. Machaon is the man who is the son of Asklepios.

196. τόξων εὖ εἰδώς: οἶδα takes the genitive when it means 'to know *about*', 'to be skilled in'.

197. Τρώων ἢ Λυκίων: The Lykians were the most important of the Trojans' allies, and therefore stand for the allies in general. Naturally the expression refers to Sarpedon's Lykians from the south of Asia, not the so-called Lykians of Pandaros from near Troy.

κλέος, πένθος: accusatives in apposition to the sentence; cp. θάνατον (l. 155).

ἄμμι: ἡμῖν.

199. χαλκοχιτώνων: This is a common formulaic epithet of the Achaians, and must refer to defensive armour worn in the Mycenaean age. Miss Lorimer (*Homer and the Monuments*, pp. 201, 209) refers to figures on the Warrior Vase from Mykenai who seem to be wearing both *chitons* and jerkins strengthened by metal disks. Trans. 'bronze-clad'.

201–3. Cp. 90–2.

202. Τρίκης ἐξ: ἐκ Τρίκης.

204. ὄρσο: aorist middle imperative of ὄρνυμι.

205–7 = 195–7, with a change in the verb of l. 205 (if we read ἴδῃς with the Oxford text).

209. βάν: ἔβησαν; cp. l. 146 n.

211. βλήμενος: an aorist participle, passive in meaning; cp. l. 115. ἀγηγέρατο: Attic ἀγηγερμένοι ἦσαν (ἀγείρω); cp. l. 4 n.

212. κυκλόσε: 'in a circle'.

ὁ δ' ἐν μέσσοισι, etc.: It is more likely that ὁ is Machaon than that it is Menelaos; in that case παρίστατο means, as often (cp. l. 233), 'came up and stood', and the δέ is the fairly common *apodotic* δέ, marking the beginning of the main sentence.

213. ἀρηρότος: cp. l. 134 n.

214. ἄγεν: ἐάγησαν (ἄγνυμι). πάλιν is to be taken with ἄγεν.

217. ὅθι: 'where'.

218. ἐκμυζήσας: The description of the doctor 'sucking out' the blood from the arrow wound supported Gilbert Murray in his view that the Homeric poems show the effect of occasional expurgation of more barbarous practices. The use of poison on arrow-heads is not specifically mentioned in the *Iliad* (although it is in the *Odyssey*); but Murray argued, from this scene and certain of the epithets applied to arrows, that poisoned arrows had been part of the tradition behind Homer (*Rise of the Greek Epic*, 4th ed., pp. 129 f.).

219. οἱ πατρί: a double dative, but to be translated 'to *his* father'; the father of Machaon was Asklepios (l. 194).

Χείρων: the wise centaur, who lived on Mount Pelion and taught the most eminent of the heroic youth of Greece – Asklepios, Iason and Achilleus.

220. βοὴν ἀγαθόν: 'good at the war-cry'; βοήν is the common Greek accusative of respect, most regularly used with reference to parts of the body. βοή, if not a part of the body, is at least a bodily function.

The heroes shouted in battle, to encourage their own men and frighten the enemy; cp. βοὴ δ' ἄσβεστος ὀρώρει, 'unceasing shouts arose' (XI 500). To be 'good at the war-cry' was therefore a heroic quality. Menelaos, who shares this epithet particularly with Diomedes, does not shout very much in the *Iliad* (only XVII 248, where he shouts for help); the choice of heroic epithet is as much decided by the metrical value of his name as by any particular application to himself.

221. δέ: *apodotic*; cp. l. 212 n.

ἐπί ... ἤλυθον: ἐπῆλθον.

222. κατά ... ἔδυν: κατέδυσαν.

χάρμης: 'will to fight', 'fighting spirit'.

223–421. The Epipolesis, or Review, of Agamemnon. This section has a function parallel to that of the Teichoskopia in book III in that it introduces us to, or makes us better acquainted with, the chief leaders of the Greeks. Agamemnon, with the conventional responsibility of a general before the battle, distributes praise and blame; he praises those (Idomeneus, the Aiantes, Nestor) who are actively preparing to fight; he blames those (Menestheus, Odysseus, Diomedes) who appear to be holding back, whether intentionally or not.

228. Πειραΐδαο: 'son of Peiraios'; the old form of the genitive of -α

declension masculine nouns was in -ao. This sometimes becomes -εω (l. 75), by Ionic metathesis of vowels (see Introduction, p. xiii).

229. παρισχέμεν: 'to hold *them* near'.

230. πολέας διά: διὰ πολλούς, 'through the crowd'.

235. ἐπὶ ψευδέσσι: from the adjective ψευδής; 'in the case of liars'.

236. ὑπὲρ ὅρκια: 'contrary to their oaths'; cp. l. 67.

δηλήσαντο: intransitive; in l. 67, however, δηλήσασθαι has an object.

237. ἤτοι: otherwise written ἦ τοι. This points the first half of the antithesis between the Trojans themselves and their families; αὖτε points the second half (cp. l. 10). The two particles have here a function similar to μέν and δέ.

242. ἰόμωροι: a word of uncertain meaning. The apparent parallel with ἐγχεσίμωροι (e.g. II 692) has led many to accept the interpretation 'archers', which certainly can be a term of abuse (Diomedes scornfully calls Paris τοξότα in XI 385) for those who keep safely out of the thick of the battle. On the other hand ἰός, 'an arrow', has a long ι while this word begins with a short ι. the modern view therefore inclines to a combination with the rare word ἰά, 'voice', and suggests the interpretation 'braggarts'.

ἐλεγχέες: from the adjective ἐλεγχής.

οὔ νυ σέβεσθε: 'are you not ashamed?'

243. τίφθ': i.e. τίπτε = τί ποτε.

ἔστητε: aorist, but equivalent to a perfect; also l. 246.

τεθηπότες: 'amazed'; of this verb only the perfect τέθηπα and the aorist ἔταφον are found.

ἠΰτε: 'just like'.

244. ἐπεὶ οὖν: This is a particular Homeric use of οὖν, in a subordinate clause with ἐπεί or ὡς, stressing the completion of an action.

πεδίοιο: genitive of the ground covered, a sort of partitive genitive.

248. εἰρύαται: εἴρυνται, perfect; cp. l. 4 n.

249. Κρονίων: 'son of Kronos'; as well as the common Greek patronymic in -ιδης, Homer also uses forms in -ιος (adjectival) and -ιων, as here.

253. The verb for the Ἰδομενεύς clause has to be understood from ὤτρυνε φάλαγγας in the next line.

συὶ εἴκελος ἀλκήν: 'like a wild boar *in courage*'; ἀλκήν is accusative of respect (l. 220).

F

256. μειλιχίοισιν: understand ἔπεσιν.

257. περί: adverb, 'particularly', 'outstandingly'; cp. l. 46.

258. ἠμέν . . . ἠδέ: 'both . . . and'.

259. γερούσιον οἶνον: the special wine drunk at council meetings.

260. κέρωνται: explained as the subjunctive of a form κέραμαι (cp. δύναμαι) alternative to κεράω (= κεράννυμι).

261. κάρη κομόωντες: κάρη is a neuter noun, here accusative of respect with κομόωντες; the phrase is taken to mean 'with hair growing over the whole head', as opposed to tribes such as the Thrakes, who are described (l. 533) as ἀκρόκομοι, i.e. 'with top-knots'. Trans. 'long-haired'.

262. δαιτρόν: an obscure word, which occurs only here. It is not even clear whether it is an adverb or a noun. However, the meaning is clear enough – that the other Greek leaders may be given a limited amount of wine only at Agamemnon's table, but Idomeneus' glass is always filled.

   δέ: apodotic; cp. l. 212 n.

263. ἀνώγοι: If this optative is correct (and most editors correct it to ἀνώγῃ, subjunctive), then Agamemnon's mind suddenly switches while he is speaking from what regularly happens to what has been the practice in the past.

264. ὄρσευ: i.e. ὄρσεο, from ὄρνυμι; an isolated form of an imperative middle created as if from a sigmatic second aorist (cp. l. 86). Chantraine (I 417) considers it a metrically inspired variant of the strong aorist imperative ὄρσο (l. 204).

268. κάρη κομόωντας: cp. l. 261 n.

269. σύν . . . ἔχευαν: tmesis.

271. Cp. l. 236 n.

272. κῆρ: accusative of respect; 'at heart'.

273. Αἰάντεσσι: the two heroes named Aias, the son of Telamon from Salamis and the son of Oileus, leader of the Lokrians. Although their names are the same, their contingents are elsewhere described by Homer as quite separate, and indeed the Lokrians are described (XIII 713–18) as light-armed troops, not wearing the bronze armour of the rest of the Greeks. Here, however, the picture is different; the Aiantes are treated as if they were twins (note the duals in ll. 274 and

285 ff.) and as acting as a pair in the preparation for fighting, as they do also in the actual fighting of book XIII. It is not unlikely that the very ancient figure of Aias has, through the effect of different local legends, inspired a double for himself, and the pair of Aiantes really go back to a single figure. (An alternative theory has it that 'Aiantes' really means the Telamonian Aias and his brother Teukros; see Page, *History and the Homeric Iliad*, pp. 235 ff.)

274. νέφος πεζῶν: This metaphor gives rise to the following simile.

275. εἶδεν: gnomic aorist (l. 75); also ῥίγησεν, ἤλασε (l. 279).

276. The zephyr, which we think of as the gentle west wind, is a storm wind in the *Iliad*. It has been pointed out that this suits the viewpoint of somebody living in Asia Minor, Homer's probable place of origin.

277. μελάντερον ἠύτε πίσσα: a difficult phrase. In all its other appearances in Homer (e.g. l. 243), ἠύτε introduces a comparison and means 'just as', 'like'; here, if we treat μελάντερον as a true comparative, ἠύτε has to equal ἤ, 'than'; but if we allow another force to μελάντερον ('dark rather than light'), then ἠύτε can have its normal meaning. Trans. 'black as pitch'.

282. πεφρικυῖαι: 'bristling' (φρίσσω).

285 ff. For the duals, see l. 273 n.

286. σφῶι: accusative dual of the second-person pronoun.

287. ἶφι: 'by force', instrumental case of the noun (ϝ)ἴς (Latin *vis*).

290. τῶ: 'then', 'in that case'.

294. οὕς: pronominal adjective, 'his'; cp. σφούς (l. 302), ὧν (l. 306).

295. Pelagon and the others were Nestor's subordinate commanders.

297 ff. The traditional descriptions of fighting that lie behind the *Iliad* have in general forgotten how chariots were used in battle. In the *Iliad*, the leaders are driven to and round the battlefield in chariots, but only rarely fight from them. When a fight is imminent, they usually leap down to the ground from their chariot, which the driver then keeps at hand in case of need. Nestor's tactical advice here, for chariot fighting in formation, may indeed show a more accurate memory of how chariots were used in practice in the Mycenaean age. As he says (l. 308), this is how earlier generations won their battles.

297. ὄχεσφι = ὄχοις; for the old instrumental ending -φι, which came to be used freely as a genitive or dative, cp. ἶφι (l. 287), ἠνορέηφι (l. 303).

298. πολέας: πολλούς.

299. ἔμεν: εἶναι.

ἔλασσεν: ἐλαύνω.

300. οὐκ ἐθέλων: 'unwilling'; the two words go closely together.

302. ἐχέμεν: 'hold back'.

303. Most unusually, the narrative slips without warning into direct speech.

306. ἀπὸ ὧν (cp. l. 294) ὀχέων: 'from his position in his chariot', i.e. while staying in line.

ἵκηται: 'can reach'.

307. ἔγχει ὀρεξάσθω: 'let him *reach out* with his spear', i.e. he should thrust with his spear, not throw it.

πολὺ φέρτερον (understand ἐστί): 'it is much better'.

308. πόλεας: πόλεις, 'cities'.

313. εἴθε: with the optative, expressing a wish.

φίλοισιν: 'your'; φίλος with parts of the body, possessions or close relatives is approximately the same as the personal pronoun.

314. τοι (twice): see l. 39 n.

315. ὄφελεν: 'ought'; in English we use the present tense of the auxiliary verb 'ought', and put the dependent infinitive into the past.

316. ἔχειν: understand γῆρας.

317. Γερήνιος ἱππότα Νέστωρ: an ancient formula.

Γερήνιος: a word whose origin is quite uncertain. Ancient commentators referred it to a place Gerenia or Gerenon in Messenia, where Nestor was said to have been brought up.

ἱππότα: first-declension nominative masculine; cp. νεφεληγερέτα (l. 30); 'driver of chariots'; a heroic title, not particularly applicable to Nestor in the *Iliad*.

318. ἐθέλοιμι: This must be potential – 'I could wish'.

319. Ἐρευθαλίωνα: Nestor gives a long and interesting description of Ereuthalion and the single combat here referred to in VII 136–56.

κατέκταν: 'I killed'.

321. ἔα: ἦν.

324. ἐμεῖο: ἐμοῦ.

325. γεγάασι: from the active-form perfect γέγαα, alternative to γέγονα, from γίγνομαι.

327. Πετεῶο: genitive of Πετεώς.

Menestheus, the leader of the Athenians, is a surprisingly unimportant figure in the *Iliad*. He has no particular connection elsewhere with Odysseus.

329. ὅ: 'he', that is, Odysseus.

330. πάρ ... ἀμφί: adverbs, 'beside and around him'. The Kephallenians were Odysseus' people (II 631).

331. The troops of Menestheus and Odysseus had not yet heard that the fighting was starting again. Odysseus, however, should have known, as he was one of the marshals (III 314) of the single combat between Paris and Menelaos, the infringement of which by Pandaros was causing the renewal of the fighting. There is here, as elsewhere in the *Iliad*, a slight ambiguity about the behaviour of Odysseus, whose prudence is dwelt on lovingly by the poet. To the other more simple heroes, such as Agamemnon, Achilleus and (in the later tradition) Aias, Odysseus' cleverness inspired suspicion and some dislike (see l. 339).

332. νέον: adverb.

334. ὁππότε ... ὁρμήσειε: a kind of indirect question after μένοντες, 'waiting for the time when, etc.'.

335. Τρώων: 'against the Trojans'.

339. See l. 331 n. above. Agamemnon would not speak to any other of the major heroes like this, not even to Achilleus during his quarrel in book I.

κεκασμένε: καίνυμαι.

341. σφῶϊν: dative of the dual of the second-person pronoun; 'for you two'.

ἐόντας: accusative, in spite of the dative σφῶϊν, because the participle's main syntactical relationship is as subject of the infinitive ἑστάμεν.

342. ἑστάμεν: ἑστάναι (ἑστηκέναι).

343. πρώτω, ἀκουάζεσθον, and 346. ἐθέλητον: duals.

δαιτὸς ἀκουάζεσθον ἐμεῖο: Both genitives go with the verb; 'you hear from me of a feast'.

345. φίλα (ἐστί): 'it is pleasant for you'.

ἔδμεναι: ἔδειν (ἐσθίειν).

346. ὄφρα: 'so long as'.

347. χ᾽ ὀρόῳτε: κεν ὀρῷτε (l. 1 n.).

348. μαχοίατο: μάχοιντο (l. 4 n.).

349. ὑπόδρα ἰδών: 'frowning'.

Odysseus cannot allow Agamemnon's remarks to go unanswered. His intelligence does not mean that he lacks the heroic sense of honour.

350. 'What sort of a word has escaped the *fence* of your teeth?' – a traditional phrase, commoner in the *Odyssey* than the *Iliad*.

351. μεθιέμεν: μεθιέναι (ἵημι).

It is better to put the question mark at μεθιέμεν, and treat the ὁππότε clause as beginning the next sentence.

352. ἐγείρομεν: for ἐγείρωμεν aorist subjunctive (l. 16 n.).

353. A sneering remark, suggesting that Agamemnon may not be up with the front-line troops himself when the time comes.

ὄψεαι: Attic ὄψει.
ἐθέλῃσθα: ἐθέλῃς.
μεμήλῃ: perfect subjunctive of μέλω.

354. Τηλεμάχοιο πατέρα: Odysseus is the only person in the *Iliad* who describes himself (here and II 260) in this way, in relation to his loved ones at home. Strong family attachment is one of the facets of this many-sided character, as may be seen in the *Odyssey*.

357. χωομένοιο: genitive with γιγνώσκειν, with the meaning 'know *about* something'; cp. πολέμων ἐῢ εἰδώς (l. 310).

λάζετο: ἐλάμβανε.

360. φίλοισιν: cp. l. 313 n.

361. ἤπια: 'kindly', i.e. favourable to Agamemnon and the Greeks.

362. ἀρεσσόμεθα: future, 'we will make good'; Hektor uses this same expression (in VI 526) when he wishes to speak more kindly to Paris.

363. θεῖεν: optative for a wish.

365. Diomedes, the leader of the troops from Argos and the northeast Peloponnese, was the son of Tydeus, who had originally come from Calydon in Aitolia, north of the Corinthian gulf. Sthenelos (l. 367), Diomedes' friend, second-in-command, and charioteer, was the son of Kapaneus. Tydeus and Kapaneus, the two fathers, had been two of the seven south Greek heroes who spearpointed the attack on Thebes in the generation before the Trojan War. In the lines that follow here, we get a reference to the preliminaries of that war of the

Seven against Thebes which was the main event in the *Theban* (as opposed to the *Trojan*) cycle of legends (see Introduction, p. xv).

366. The line simply means 'standing in his chariot'.

367. Καπανήιος υἱός: 'Kapaneus' son'; Καπανήιος is simply an adjective formed from Καπανεύς. The adjective formed from the father's name is often found alone as a patronymic, e.g. Τελαμώνιος Αἴας (l. 473).

370–400. Agamemnon's speech takes the form of a mythological example aimed at goading Diomedes to fight. It is composed in the common 'ring-form': (1) Why are you skulking? (2) Tydeus used not to skulk. (3) Here is a story to show how *he* behaved. (4) Such was Tydeus. (5) His son is inferior to him.

371. ὀπιπεύεις: 'eye'.

πολέμοιο γεφύρας: This phrase, which occurs five times in the *Iliad*, clearly refers to open spaces in the battlefield, whether it is the lanes between the different contingents in one's own army, or the space in the middle between the two armies.

374. πονεύμενον (Ionic for πονούμενον): 'at work', i.e. fighting.

375. περί: 'beyond', 'superior to'.

377. Polyneikes, son of Oidipous, had a claim to be king of Thebes after his father's death, but (as is familiar from Attic tragedy) his brother Eteokles (l. 386) refused him. The two expatriates Polyneikes and Tydeus married daughters of Adrastos king of Argos, and collected an army from the Peloponnese to attack Thebes. The lines that follow here (up to l. 381) are a sort of mythological attempt at explaining why the leading city of Mykenai had nothing to do with the expedition; the true explanation of course is that these are different cycles of legend.

ἀγείρων: 'trying to collect'.

380. ἐπήνεον ὡς ἐκέλευον: 'they (the Mykenaians) approved their (the visitors') request'.

381. ἔτρεψε: 'dissuaded'.

382. πρὸ ὁδοῦ: πρό is an adverb, and ὁδοῦ depends on it; 'a distance forward on their road'.

383. Ἀσωπόν: a river south of Thebes.

384. ἀγγελίην: Occasionally in the *Iliad* ἀγγελίης is more easily taken as a masculine nominative noun meaning 'a messenger' than as the

genitive of the feminine noun ἀγγελίη, and similarly ἀγγελίην as
accusative masculine, rather than accusative feminine. This probably
arose accidentally from such a phrase as ἀγγελίην ἐλθόντα (XI 140),
meaning 'going on an embassy', but appearing to mean 'going as an
ambassador'. In this way the epic dialect created by misunderstanding
a previously non-existent noun. The other examples are III 206, XI 140,
XIII 252, XV 640. Trans. 'the Achaians sent Tydeus as an ambassador'.

ἐπί . . . στεῖλαν: tmesis.

This story of the embassy of Tydeus to Thebes is referred to again,
in V 803–8 and X 285–90.

385. Καδμείωνας and 388. Καδμείοισιν: Kadmeans, the old name for
the people of Thebes, Kadmos having been the founder of the city.

386. βίης Ἐτεοκληείης: 'of the might of Eteokles' – a periphrasis for
Ἐτεοκλῆος.

387. ἱππηλάτα: nominative; cp. ll. 30, 317.

388. τάρβει: imperfect tense, as is shown by the accent.

389. πάντα: 'all the events'.

390. Those who have the qualities to win success are seen thereby to
be the favourites of Athene. This was true of Tydeus, Diomedes and
Odysseus.

392. πυκινόν: 'strong', lit. 'crowded'.

εἷσαν: ἵζω.

394–5. The murderous and bloody names, particularly of the second
assassin and his father, show a not very usual kind of almost comic
invention. One may compare the carpenter Harmonides in V 59, and
the seer Polyidos in XIII 663.

398. Tydeus was persuaded by divine signs to send Maion back un-
harmed, just as, in l. 381, divine signs dissuaded the Mykenaians from
supporting the expedition. Such unspecified signs are obviously a
handy motif for the story-teller.

400. εἷο: οὗ.

χέρεια: a by-form of χερείονα, 'worse'.

401–21. Unlike Odysseus, Diomedes accepts the king's rebuke without answering back, and reproves his friend Sthenelos for doing so.
Diomedes has the qualities of the ideal junior commander – he is
respectful to authority, clear-headed, immensely capable and con-
trolled.

404. ψεύδεο: present imperative middle.

405. μέγα: adverbial; '*much* better'.

Sthenelos is referring to the expedition of the Sons of the Seven, the Epigonoi, who took and destroyed Thebes, where their fathers had failed. Sthenelos and Diomedes were of course two of the Epigonoi; another was Euryalos, son of Mekisteus, the third of the leaders of the contingent from Argus (II 565). We know next to nothing about the incidents of this second expedition.

407. ἀγαγόντε: dual, because Sthenelos is thinking of Diomedes and himself.

ἄρειον: neuter of ἀρείων, comparative; 'better', 'stronger'; we must assume that the Thebans had strengthened their defences between the two expeditions.

410. 'Therefore do not place our fathers in equal honour with us.'

412. τέττα: This word only occurs here, and is of uncertain derivation. Its meaning, however, is quite clear from the context. It is a way of addressing one's friend, as a more modern soldier at a lower level in the army might say 'mate', 'chum', 'buddy'. Trans. 'friend'.

ἧσο: from ἧμαι, but not so much 'sit' as 'stay' quiet.

417. We must understand ἅμ' ἕψεται or ἕσσεται with πένθος.

419. ἆλτο: aorist of ἅλλομαι.

420. δεινόν: adverbial.

421. ὀρνυμένου: 'as he moved'.

ὑπό . . . εἷλεν: tmesis; 'even a brave man would have felt some fear'.

422–6. A good example of the 'Homeric' simile. The point of comparison lies in ἐπασσύτερον (l. 423) (ἐπασσύτεραι, l. 427), the line after line of waves compared with the rank after rank of the Greek army. But the simile is expanded to include detail irrelevant to the Greek and Trojan armies, and becomes a description of nature. One can see how such similes can be used to provide relief from the monotony of the fighting in later scenes.

424. κορύσσεται: 'raises itself'.

426. κορυφοῦται: 'comes to a crest'.

432. τά: internal accusative with εἱμένοι (ἔννυμι).

436. ὀρώρει: pluperfect.

438. ἔσαν: ἦσαν.

439. Ares, who supports the Trojans, is a non-Greek (Thracian) god of war; Athene is the more rational goddess of Greek warfare. The personifications of the next line motivate both sides.

γλαυκῶπις: The word doubtless meant 'bright-eyed' or 'grey-eyed' to Homer, but this is not inconsistent with the possibility that it originally meant 'owl-faced', Athene having at one time been worshipped in the form of an owl; cp. βοῶπις πότνια Ἥρη (l. 50).

442. κορύσσεται: cp. l. 424.

444. ὁμοίιον: 'equally balanced', 'equal for both sides'.

447. ῥινούς: '(leather) shields'.
σὺν δέ: understand ἔβαλον again.

448. ὀμφαλοέσσαι: 'with a central boss'.

449. ἔπληντο: πελάζω.

452. χείμαρροι ποταμοί: Mountainsides in the Greek world are scarred by ravines, dry in summer, but raging torrents in the winter.
κατ' ὄρεσφι: κατ' ὀρέων.

453. μισγάγκειαν: a hollow valley, or basin.
συμβάλλετον: dual, showing that *two* rivers are imagined as coming together (naturally on account of the two armies).

454. κοίλης ἔντοσθε χαράδρης: The picture is not wholly clear, but this is probably the watercourse which receives the two torrents.

455. τηλόσε: lit. 'to a great distance'.

456. ἰαχή τε πόνος τε: 'shouting and hard effort'. Most modern editors read πόνος, which was a correction by the Alexandrian scholar Aristarchos of the traditional reading φόβος. The occurrence of the doublet ἰαχή τε φόβος τε four other times in the *Iliad* should encourage us, in the light of modern theories of *formular composition* (see Introduction, p. xvii), to reverse Aristarchus' decision and go back to φόβος here, although he was probably right that nobody was yet running away.

457–544. A concentrated description of indeterminate and bloody fighting, making a preparation for the long *aristeia* of Diomedes in books V and VI. No fewer than three of the seventy-one leaders of contingents mentioned in the two catalogues of book II are among those killed in this short passage (Elephenor, Diores and Peiroos).

457. Ἀντίλοχος: the young son of Nestor.
ἕλεν: 'killed', as often.

459. κόρυθος φάλον: The meaning of φάλος is obscure. Opinion is divided between a 'horn' on the front of the helmet, and the 'crest-holder' running from front to back.

462. 'He fell, as a tower (falls).' G. Strasburger, in an admirable dissertation entitled *Die kleinen Kämpfer der Ilias*, pp. 38–9, points out the realism of the effect of certain wounds as described in the *Iliad*. Those who fall 'like a tree' (here a tower), i.e. stiff and unconscious, have received a blow in the top part of the body; so Echepolos here in the head Simoeisios (l. 482) in the chest.

463. ποδῶν: 'by the feet'.
Elephenor is named as leader of the Abantes (the people of Euboia) in II 540.

465. λελιημένος ὄφρα: 'eager to'.

467. Ἀγήνωρ: a leading Trojan, son of Antenor (l. 87 n.).

470. ἔργον: the toil of battle; they were fighting for the body of Elephenor.

473–4. Ἀνθεμίωνος υἱόν ... Σιμοείσιον: The names seem to be poetic invention. The young man had been called after the river; his father's name suggests ἀνθεμόεις, 'flowery', a natural attribute of river banks. Cp. II 467, ἐν λειμῶνι Σκαμανδρίῳ ἀνθεμόεντι.

473. Τελαμώνιος Αἴας: see l. 367 n.

475. Σιμόεντος: Simoeis and Skamandros were the two chief rivers of the plain of Troy. So the baby was born in peace-time on the plain where now the battle rages.

477–8. οὐδέ ... ἀπέδωκε: 'nor did he repay his parents for their care of him as a child'. The Greeks felt strongly the responsibility of children to look after their parents in old age (γηροβοσκεῖν).

479. It is rather better to take ὑπό with Αἴαντος, and δουρί as an instrumental dative with δαμέντι; cp. ὑπ' αὐτοῦ δουρὶ δαμήῃς (III 436).

480. πρῶτον: with ἰόντα; 'as he came out among the foremost fighters'.

482. He fell like a tree, having been hit in the chest; cp. l. 462 n.

483. πεφύκει: The pluperfect is difficult; Hermann, followed by many editors, changed it to πεφύκῃ, perfect subjunctive.

487. The tall poplar tree lies by the bank of a river; Simoeisios, tall

and young, lies on the ground; he had been born by a river, and named after it. There is thus a strange secondary relationship in the simile, and we think back to Simoeisios as a baby.

ἀζομένη: the wood drying out.

488. Ἀνθεμίδην: son, in fact, of Anthemion (l. 473).

494. τοῦ: causal genitive; also l. 501.

ἀποκταμένοιο: aorist with passive meaning.

497. κεκάδοντο: χάζομαι.

500. Abydos was quite close to Troy, on the Hellespont. Perhaps Priam had a stud-farm there (ἵππων ὠκειάων, 'mares') and Demokoon had been in charge of it.

505. χώρησαν δ' ὑπό: ὑπεχώρησαν δέ.

508. Περγάμου ἐκκατιδών: 'looking down from the citadel of Troy'.

κέκλετο: aorist (κέλομαι).

509. μηδ' εἴκετε χάρμης: 'do not give way from the battle'.

511. ἀνασχέσθαι: 'so as to keep out'.

βαλλομένοισιν: 'when they are hit'.

514. πτόλιος: πόλεως.

515. Τριτογένεια: This ancient title of Athene was thought by a majority of ancient writers who mention it to mean 'born at lake Triton in Libya'. Modern scholars agree, apart from the particularisation of the place; they conjecture that the stem 'Trito' had to do with the sea (Triton, Amphitrite) and that Athene's birth, like that of Aphrodite, was at some very ancient time connected with the sea. The story of her birth from the head of Zeus would then be later.

516. μεθιέντα: 'slacking'.

ἴδοιτο: ἴδοι.

517. Diores, son of Amarynkeus, was leader of the Epeioi, from Elis in the north-west Peloponnese (II 622).

518. βλῆτο: aorist with passive meaning (cp. l. 115); also χύντο (l. 526).

520. Πείρως: He is called Πείροος in II 844. The trisyllabic form can stand here and in l. 525, and the change is so slight that many editors sensibly make it, for the sake of consistency with book II.

521. ἀναιδής: 'ruthless'.

522. ἄχρις: 'completely'.

ὕπτιος: 'on his back'; the opposite word, meaning 'face down', is πρηνής (l. 544).

523. κάππεσεν: κατέπεσεν.

524. περ: adds a stress to the previous word. In l. 534 it is concessive, as in later Greek.

525. οὖτα: With a short α, this is not a contracted imperfect, but a form of aorist.

527. ἀπεσσύμενον: perfect participle, in spite of the accent, meaning 'as he dashed back'.

Thoas, leader of the Aitolians, is one of the major Greek heroes.

533. ἀκρόκομοι: with a knot of hair on the top of the head, the rest of the head being shaved; cp. l. 261 n.

536. τετάσθην (τείνω): dual of the pluperfect passive.

539. κεν οὐκέτι ... ὀνόσαιτο: 'would not now criticise'.

540. ἄβλητος καὶ ἀνούτατος: βάλλω is used of missiles, i.e. stones, arrows and javelins; οὐτάω of wounds made by weapons still held in the hand – swords and thrusting spears; cp. βάλε (l. 519), οὖτα (l. 525).

541. δινεύοι, ἄγοι, ἀπερύκοι: optatives, because this is all within the hypothetical condition begun in l. 539.

542. χειρὸς ἑλοῦσα: cp. ποδῶν ἔλαβε (l. 463).

BOOK V

The Great Deeds of Diomedes

1. ἔνθ' αὖ: The effect of these two adverbs is to connect the beginning of this book with the end of book IV. There, confused and general fighting had been outlined in a concentrated passage of less then a hundred lines, and three separate sections of the narrative had begun with the word ἔνθα (IV 473, 517, 539). With the words ἔνθ' αὖ the poet turns now to the particular exploits of Diomedes. Trans. 'Next'.

Τυδείδη: Diomedes was the son of Tydeus. Patronymics are common in Homer, either with the name of the hero as here, or in place of it (e.g. l. 16).

Παλλὰς 'Αθήνη: The goddess Athene strongly supported the Greek side; her particular favourites were Diomedes and Odysseus.

2. δῶκε: aorist; the omission of the augment is very frequent in Homer; cp. δαῖε (l. 4), etc.

μετά: with the dative, 'among'.

3. 'Αργείοισι: Notice that there are three names used by the poet indistinguishably for the Greeks – Argives ('Αργεῖοι), Achaians ('Αχαιοί) and Danaans (Δαναοί).

ἰδέ: an alternative word for 'and'.

ἄροιτο: aorist optative of ἄρνυμαι.

4. δαῖε: cp. l. 2 n.

οἱ: dative of the third-person pronoun, 'to him'; so οἱ ἐκ κόρυθος = 'from his helmet'.

5. ἀστέρ(ι) ὀπωρινῷ: 'the star of the late summer', i.e. Sirius, the brightest star in the sky. The elision of the ι of the dative is rare.

ὅς τε: τε is often added to the relative in proverbial or general statements such as this. It is not to be translated. The verb of the clause (παμφαίνῃσι) is subjunctive, another common feature of general relative sentences in Homer. Both these features (the τε and the subjunctive) occur frequently in similes.

6. λαμπρόν: adverbial.

παμφαίνῃσι: The epic dialect possessed, for the three singular persons of the subjunctive, alternative endings in -ωμι, -ῃσθα, -ῃσι. These forms are regularly used to produce a weak third-foot caesura, as here.

'Ωκεανοῖο: The genitive singular of -ος declension nouns and adjectives may be in -οιο as well as -ου. The genitive here with λελουμένος is a sort of partitive genitive. The river Okeanos was thought of as running round the edge of the flat, circular earth. The star, before it rose, had been bathed in the waters of Ocean.

7. τοῖον = τοιοῦτον.
   οἵ: cp. l. 4 n.
   κρατός: genitive of κάρα.

8. ὦρσε: from ὄρνυμι.
   μιν: the epic form of νιν, accusative third-person pronoun, 'him'.
   κατὰ μέσσον: 'into the thick of the fighting'.
   ὅθι: 'where'.
   κλονέοντο: Uncontracted forms are common in Homer.

10. ἱρεύς = ἱερεύς.
    'Ηφαίστοιο: cp. l. 6 n.
    υἱέες: nominative plural of υἱός, but with third-declension ending.
    ἤστην: dual of the imperfect of εἰμί.

11. μάχης: Verbs of *knowing* often take the genitive of what one knows *about*.
    εἰδότε: dual, as are four of the five words in the next line, and two in l. 13.

12. τώ; nominative masculine dual of what later Greek knew as the definite article; it was still primarily a demonstrative pronoun in Homeric Greek; 'they'. So also τὼ μέν, ὁ δέ in the next line.
    ἀποκρινθέντε: i.e. they moved out of the line of their own army to attack Diomedes.

13. ἀφ' ἵπποιιν: 'from the chariot'; dual again, because it was a two-horse chariot.
    ὁ δ' ἀπὸ χθονός, etc.: i.e. he was on foot, and 'rose against them' from ground level.

15. ῥα: Homeric verse uses all three forms ἄρα, ἄρ and the enclitic ῥα, merely as required by the metre; the particle has a mild inferential force.
    προΐει: imperfect of προΐημι.

16. Τυδείδεω: The genitive of first-declension masculine nouns can end in -εω; cp. l. 159.

ἤλυθε = ἦλθε.

17. χαλκῷ: 'with the bronze', i.e. 'with his spear'. Although iron was in common use in Homer's own day, the epic tradition is nevertheless very consistent in keeping bronze as the metal for weapons, as it had been in the Mycenaean age.

19. ἀφ' ἵππων: 'off the chariot'; cp. l. 13 n.

20. περικαλλέα: uncontracted (see l. 8 n.); the Attic form would be περικαλλῆ.

21. οὐδ' ἔτλη: 'nor did he dare'.

περιβῆναι: 'to bestride', i.e. stand over the body to defend it. It is a regular feature of Homeric fighting that once a warrior has killed his opponent, he attempts to strip the body of its armour.

κταμένοιο: aorist middle participle with passive meaning (κτείνω).

22. οὐδὲ γὰρ οὐδέ: The first οὐδέ connects this sentence with the last (οὐδὲ γάρ being the negative of the common connection καὶ γάρ); the second οὐδέ stresses αὐτός; 'nor indeed would even he have escaped'.

κεν: κε (κεν) is the alternative form of he modal particle ἄν, and is used in the same way. Here the condition follows the normal rules of later Greek.

23. ἔρυτο: imperfect of ἔρυμαι (= ἐρύομαι).

σάωσε = ἔσωσε (σῴζω).

νυκτὶ καλύψας: From time to time a god rescues a son or a favourite from the battle, covering him in thick mist or darkness; so here Hephaistos, and later in this book Apollo (l. 345).

24. οἱ: what is called the *ethic dative* of the person concerned – in this case Hephaistos. Trans. '*his* old priest'.

ἀκαχήμενος: 'overwhelmed with grief'.

25. ἐξελάσας: aorist participle, ἐξελαύνω.

28. κτάμενον: cp. l. 21 n.

ὄχεσφι = ὄχοις; the old instrumental ending -φι came to be used freely as genitive or dative; cp. στήθεσφιν (l. 41).

29. πᾶσιν ὀρίνθη θυμός: 'the spirits of all were dismayed'.

γλαυκῶπις: The word doubtless meant 'bright-eyed' or 'grey-eyed' to Homer, but this is not inconsistent with the possibility that it originally meant 'owl-faced', Athene having once been worshipped in the form of an owl; cp. βοῶπις πότνια Ἥρη (IV 50).

30. χειρός: 'by the hand'.

ἐπέεσσι = ἔπεσι.

προσηύδα: imperfect of προσαυδάω. Athene is the goddess of Greek warfare; Ares, who supports the Trojans, is a non-Greek (Thracian) god of war.

31. Ares, like Paris, is regularly addressed with personal abuse. This line recurs in l. 455.

Ἆρες Ἆρες: This is the unique example in Homer of what seems to be a metrical trick – the immediate repetition of the same word, but with different scansion.

τειχεσιπλῆτα: vocative of a first-declension masculine.

32. οὐκ ἂν ἐάσαιμεν: 'may we not allow?', 'shall we not allow?'

33. μάρνασθαι: infinitive.

ὁπποτέροισι: indirect question – 'to discover to which side, etc.'

ὀρέξῃ: The subjunctive is not much different from a future – 'to which side Zeus *shall grant* success'.

34. νῶι: first-person dual.

χαζώμεσθα = χαζώμεθα.

The subjunctives are jussive; 'let us withdraw, etc.'. Zeus has not yet in fact given instructions to the gods to keep off the field, but Athene wants to see that Diomedes has a free hand.

36. καθεῖσεν: from καθίζω.

ἠιόεντι: perhaps 'with high banks', although the word ἠιών means the shore of the sea rather than the bank of a river.

37. ἕλε: 'killed', as often.

In the lines that follow, up to 83, individual successes of six of the Greek leaders are recorded, before we return to Diomedes. The six are Agamemnon, Idomeneus, Menelaos, Meriones (Idomeneus' second-in-command), Meges (leader of the contingent from the western islands, II 625 ff.), and Eurypylos (from north Greece, II 734 ff.).

40. πρώτῳ: This should be taken predicatively with πῆξεν, not with στρεφθέντι; i.e. he was the first to be hit, not the first to turn to flight. Agamemnon was the first (πρῶτος, l. 38) to kill his opponent; Odios was the first opponent to be killed.

ἐν ... πῆξεν: ἐνέπηξεν (ἐμπήγνυμι); the elements which later constituted a compound verb are still separable in Homer, with the preposition able to stand by itself as an adverb. The phenomenon is called *tmesis* (from τέμνω, 'cut'). In practice one may treat this as if a verb has been divided into its two parts, although the true situation is that the two parts have not yet coalesced.

The direct object of ἐνέπηξεν is δόρυ, its indirect object μεταφρένῳ. πρώτῳ στρεφθέντι refer to Odios in the dative as the recipient of the spear in his back. Trans. 'he was the first to be killed; as he turned to fly, Agamemnon drove his spear into his back'.

41. διὰ στήθεσφιν = διὰ στηθέων; cp. l. 28 n.

42. τεύχεα: 'armour'.

43. Φαῖστον: Phaistos, son of the Meionian Boros, is a rather disconcerting figure, because he has the same name as the second city of Crete, Phaistos, and here he is being killed by Idomeneus, the king of the Cretan contingent. Most likely, however, this is just a chance association of names on the part of the poet, who has to choose a large number of minor figures, to appear once only as victims of the greater heroes.

ἐνήρατο: from ἐναίρω.

44. εἰληλούθει: pluperfect of ἔρχομαι.

46. νύξε: from νύσσω.

ἐπιβησόμενον: future participle, 'as he was about to mount his chariot (ἵππων)', i.e. to get away.

47. ἤριπε: from ἐρείπω.

μιν: cp. l. 8 n.

48. ἐσύλευον: cp. l. 21 n.

49. αἵμονα: The word only appears here; it is taken to mean 'skilled in'.

θήρης: Attic θήρας; the η for α even after ε, ι, ρ is the most obvious Ionic feature of the Homeric dialect.

50. ὀξυόεντι: Two interpretations are offered by the ancient commentators – either 'sharp' (ὀξύς) or 'made of beech wood' (ὀξύη).

51. Exceptional skill at anything is likely to be described by the Homeric poet as the personal gift of a god; so, for example, it is stated in II 827 that Apollo himself gave Pandaros his bow.

52. τά τε: cp. ὅς τε (l. 5).

οὔρεσιν: 'in the mountains' (ὄρος).

53. χραῖσμε: 'helped'.

54. ἧσιν = αἷς.

ἐκέκαστο: from καίνυμαι.

55–6. μιν, μετάφρενον: Both words are the objects of οὔτασε; this is the construction of 'the whole and the part'.

56. ἔθεν = οὗ; genitive of the third-person pronoun.

57 = 41.

59. Meriones, Idomeneus' second-in-command, is very much a hero in his own right in the *Iliad* – in fact perhaps the most significant of the heroes of the second rank.

Phereklos was son of the carpenter Harmonides (which itself means 'son of the fitter'); the coincidence of name and occupation suggests that we have here the poet's invention. (Compare the would-be assassin named in IV 395 – Polyphontes son of Autophonos.) Many editors (but not the Oxford text) print Τέκτονος with a capital letter, as the *name* of Phereklos' father.

60. Ἁρμονίδεω: cp. l. 16 n.

ὅς: Phereklos.

61. Cp. l. 51 n. Athene was goddess of crafts as well as of Greek warfare.

62. ἐίσας: 'well-proportioned'.

64. θεῶν ἐκ: ἐκ θεῶν.

ᾔδη: οἶδα.

69 ff. Meges, son of Phyleus (l. 72), killed Pedaios, bastard son of Antenor. Antenor was the most important Trojan outside the royal family; his wife was Theano (l. 70), priestess of Athene.

70. πύκα: 'conscientiously'.

71. ἶσα: adverbial, 'equally'.

φίλοισι: 'her own'; φίλος with parts of the body, possessions or close relatives is approximately the same as the personal pronoun.

ᾧ: pronominal adjective, 'her'.

73. ἰνίον: the tendon at the back of the neck.

74. ἀν' ὀδόντας: 'through the teeth'.

ὑπό . . . τάμε: for ὑπέταμε, tmesis (l. 40 n.).

77. The river Skamandros was also a local god, and as such plays some part in the later *Iliad*.

78. ἐτέτυκτο: τεύχω.

θεὸς ὥς: ὥσπερ θεός.

80. Cp. l. 56.

81. ἀπὸ δ' ἔξεσε: *tmesis*.

82–3. κατ' ὄσσε ἔλλαβε: κατά . . . ἔλλαβε is an example of *tmesis*; the compound verb is taking two objects – 'the whole and the part'.

83. ἔλλαβε: ἔλαβε. The 'liquid' consonants λ, μ, ν, ρ, Ϝ, often lengthen a short vowel before them, as if they were 'rolled' in speech (see Introduction, p. xxiv). This is sometimes shown, as here, by the doubling of the consonant.

The poet has now given a general effect of Greek superiority by means of the six separate Greek victories in ll. 37–83. It is worth noticing the six concluding lines (all meaning 'he died'); they are clearly made up of stock formulas, but the impression given is of freedom and variety, not repetition:

42. δούπησεν δὲ πεσών, ἀράβησε δὲ τεύχε' ἐπ' αὐτῷ.

47. ἤριπε δ' ἐξ ὀχέων, στυγερὸς δ' ἄρα μιν σκότος εἷλε.

58. ἤριπε δὲ πρηνής, ἀράβησε δὲ τεύχε' ἐπ' αὐτῷ.

68. γνὺξ δ' ἔριπ' οἰμώξας, θάνατος δέ μιν ἀμφεκάλυψε (this was the most painful).

75. ἤριπε δ' ἐν κονίῃ, ψυχρὸν δ' ἔλε χαλκὸν ὀδοῦσιν.

83. ἔλλαβε πορφύρεος θάνατος καὶ μοῖρα κραταιή.

84. ὥς: Accented in this way (or with the circumflex ὧς), this word is an adverb = οὕτως, 'so'; the conjunction ὡς is unaccented, except when it follows its noun in a simile, e.g. θεὸς ὥς (l. 78).

85. 'You could not tell which side Diomedes was on.'

86. ἠέ (= ἤ) . . . ἦ: These particles give the alternatives in the indirect question. Trans. 'whether . . . or'.

87. ἂμ πεδίον: The preposition ἀνά has been shortened by *apocope* (the cutting-off of the last syllable) to ἄν; it has then been assimilated to the π of πεδίον.

ἐοικώς: This starts a simile, taken as often from nature, which lasts for five further lines. The word ὥς ('so') at the beginning of l. 93 is a sign of the return to the narrative.

88. ἐκέδασσε: (σ)κεδάννυμι; a *gnomic aorist*, i.e. the aorist found in proverbial or general statements, of things which happen now and always have happened.

γεφύρας: 'embankments', i.e. dykes, to hold back the river.

89. ἐεργμέναι: ἔργω; 'closely constructed'.

ἰσχανόωσιν: This, from the verb ἰσχανάω, would if uncontracted be ἰσχανάουσιν, if contracted ἰσχανῶσιν. By a peculiarity of Homeric Greek (caused no doubt by the opposed pressures of contraction of vowels and the requirements of the metre), the contracted form has suffered a sort of expansion or distension. This, technically called *diektasis*, is found particularly with verbs in -αω.

90. ἀλωάων: 'orchards'. Notice the normal genitive plural of the -α declension in Homer, in -αων (Latin -*arum*).

92. κατήριπε: gnomic aorist (l. 88).

94. πολέες: πολλοί.

περ: The enclitic particle περ has a slight intensive effect, often as here concessive, like the later καίπερ.

ἐόντες: ὄντες.

95. ὡς οὖν: This is a particular Homeric use of οὖν, in a subordinate clause with ἐπεί or ὡς, stressing the completion of an action.

Λυκάονος ἀγλαὸς υἱός: Pandaros, the archer, who treacherously broke the truce at the beginning of book IV by shooting an arrow at Menelaos.

96. ἂμ πεδίον: see l. 87 n.

99. θώρηκος γύαλον: The γύαλα were the front and back plates of the metal breastplate.

διὰ δ' ἔπτατο: διαπέτομαι.

101. τῷ δ' ἐπί: ἐπ' αὐτῷ δέ.

103. ἑ: accusative of the third-person pronoun, 'him'.

104. ἀνσχήσεσθαι: ἀνασχήσεσθαι (ἀνέχω), by *apocope* of the preposition (l. 87).

ἐτεόν: adverb, 'truly'.

105. ἄναξ Διὸς υἱός: Apollo, the god of archery and supporter of the Trojans.

Λυκίηθεν: Here and in l. 173 Pandaros is stated to come from Lykia; this, however, must be quite different from the Lykia in the south of Asia Minor from which came the allies led by Sarpedon and Glaukos, for Pandaros' home was at the foot of Mount Ida near Troy, and his people are called 'Troes' in ll. 200 and 211, as well as in the Trojan Catalogue in book II (II 826).

106. ἔφατο: imperfect middle of φημί; there is no distinction in meaning from the active.

107. Diomedes had been fighting on foot. Sthenelos, his friend, second-in-command and charioteer, would have the task of keeping the chariot as close as possible, as a safeguard against some such eventuality as this.

108. Καπανήιον υἱόν: 'Kapaneus' son'; Καπανήιος is simply an adjective formed from Καπανεύς. The adjective formed from the father's name is often found alone as a patronymic, e.g. Τελαμώνιος Αἴας, (l. 610). Another patronymic from Καπανεύς occurs in the next line, 109.

109. ὄρσο: aorist imperative middle (ὄρνυμι).

πέπον: lit. 'ripe' or 'soft' of fruit; used in Homer as a way of addressing a friend.

καταβήσεο: aorist imperative middle (καταβαίνω); this is one of the examples of the *sigmatic second aorist*, i.e. the σ is added to the stem to form the aorist, as in the usual first aorist, but the endings are those of the second aorist.

111. ἆλτο: aorist of ἄλλομαι.

112. πὰρ δὲ στάς: apocope of the preposition (l. 87); tmesis (l. 40).

διαμπερὲς ἐξέρυσ' ὤμου: 'he drew it right through the shoulder'. The arrow was so far in that it was better to pull it right through than to try to pull it back against the barbs.

113. ἀνηκόντιζε: 'shot out'.

στρεπτοῖο χιτῶνος: The significance of στρεπτοῖο has caused some uncertainty. Probably it refers to the strength of the thread of which the doublet is woven. The lack of mention of the breastplate at this point (cp. θώρηκος γύαλον, l. 99) has been used to support the view that the metal breastplate is a late insertion into the poetic tradition, and that at an earlier stage the warriors wore only linen or leather jerkins.

114. βοὴν ἀγαθός: 'good at the war-cry'; βοήν is the common Greek accusative of respect, most regularly used with reference to parts of the body. βοή, if not a part of the body, is at least a bodily function.

The heroes shouted in battle, to encourage their own men and frighten the enemy; cp. βοὴ δ' ἄσβεστος ὀρώρει, 'unceasing shouts arose' (XI 500). To be 'good at the war-cry' was therefore a heroic quality.

115. κλῦθι: aorist imperative.

μευ: μου.

αἰγιόχοιο: The *aigis* is a supernatural weapon of the gods, carried by Zeus, but used from time to time by Athene and Apollo. It is normally defensive, like a shield (the popular etymology suggested a goat-skin), but can be used offensively, because when shaken in the face of the enemy it strikes terror in their hearts.

Ἀτρυτώνη: an ancient and obscure title of Athene, supposed to mean 'the unwearied one'.

116. πατρί: Tydeus, the father of Diomedes, was one of the seven southern Greek champions who attacked Thebes in the generation before the Trojan War, as also was Kapaneus, the father of Sthenelos; Athene had particularly favoured Tydeus. Cp. ll. 800 ff.

117. φίλαι: aorist middle imperative; the first syllable is metrically lengthened here and elsewhere.

Notice the typical prayer-form of ll. 115–17. 'Hear me, o goddess; if ever you helped my father in time past, help me now.'

118. καὶ ἐς ὁρμὴν ἔγχεος ἐλθεῖν: 'and that *he* may come within spear's throw'. There is a rather violent change of subject.

119. φθάμενος: φθάνω; 'before I saw him'.

123. ἔπεα πτερόεντα: 'winged words', in that they fly from mouth to ear; an ancient poetic phrase.

124. μάχεσθαι: infinitive for imperative, as also l. 130.

125. τοι: the same as the enclitic σοι, the unstressed dative of σύ.

ἧκα: ἵημι.

126. ἔχεσκε: Tenses in -σκον, formed from either the present or aorist of the verb, are very common in Homer, as *frequentatives*; 'used to have'.

ἱππότα: nominative.

127. ἐπῆεν: ἐπῆν.

129. τῶ: adverb, 'therefore'.

αἰ: the Aeolic form of εἰ. αἴ κε = ἐάν.

132. ἔλθησι: cp. l. 6 n.

οὐτάμεν: an alternative form for the infinitive; here with the force of an imperative; cp. l. 124 n.

135. μεμαώς: 'eager', a participle from the shorter stem of the perfect μέμονα.

137. ἄγρῳ: 'in the country'.

138. αὐλῆς: the wall or fence round the sheepfolds.

140. κατὰ σταθμοὺς δύεται: i.e. the lion.

τὰ δ᾽ ἐρῆμα φοβεῖται: 'the sheep, left deserted, run in fear'. This shows Homer's normal use of what was later the definite article as a demonstrative pronoun (l. 12 n.). It is only a little awkward that these neuter plural sheep appear as feminine plural (i.e. ὄιες) in the next line.

141. αἱ μεν: the sheep.

κέχυνται: χέω.

144–65. Diomedes kills in succession four *pairs* of opponents, all except the first pair being described as brothers. The reason for them being in pairs is clearly that he was catching them in their chariots (l. 160), and the chariots were manned by two – one to hold the reins and one to fight.

147. ἐέργαθεν: an aorist from ἔργω.

148. Πολύϊδον: a good name for the son of a seer.

150. With some pathos the poet tells us that the old man did not interpret his sons' dreams before they went to Troy.

153. τηλυγέτῳ: The adjective is obviously used of particularly loved children; its origin is quite obscure; the two most probable suggestions are 'last born' (which hardly suits here, although 'late born' would) and 'of a tender age'.

156. ἀμφοτέρω: object of ἐξαίνυτο, which like other verbs of *taking away* is construed with two accusatives.

158. The relatives divided up the property when the old man died. Again (cp. l. 150) Homer understands and can express the human sadness caused by the war to the old people at home; in Virgil's *Aeneid* this aspect outweighs all others.

159. Δαρδανίδαο: The old form of the genitive of -α declension masculine nouns was in -αο. This sometimes becomes (by Ionic metathesis of vowels) -εω (l. 16). (See Introduction, p. xiii.)

161. ὡς δὲ λέων: The simile of the wild beast leaping on its prey portrays not only the killing of the victim but also the stripping of the armour (l. 164).

ἐξ . . . ἄξῃ: ἐξάγνυμι.

162. ξύλοχον κάτα: κατὰ ξύλοχον.

βοσκομενάων: cp. l. 90 n.

164. βῆσε: from βαίνω, but transitive, 'forced'.

κακῶς: with βῆσε, 'roughly'.

165. μετὰ νῆας: 'to the ships', i.e. to the Greek camp.

167. βῆ δ' ἴμεν (= ἰέναι): 'he started to go'.
ἄν: ἀνά (l. 87).

170. ἔπος τέ μιν ἀντίον ηὔδα: ηὔδα here takes two accusatives, internal and external.

171. τοι: σοι (l. 125).

174. ἄγε: 'come'. The imperative of ἄγω is used in this way, as an exclamation.
ἔφες: ἐφίημι.

175. ἔοργε: ἔρδω.

178. ἱρῶν: genitive of cause; 'because of (the omission of) a sacrifice'.
ἔπι = ἔπεστι. 'And the wrath of a god lies heavy on us.'

180. χαλκοχιτώνων: This is a common formulaic epithet of the Achaians (here applied to the Trojans), and must refer to defensive armour worn in the Mycenaean age. Miss Lorimer (*Homer and the Monuments*, pp. 201, 209) refers to figures on the Warrior Vase from Mykenai, who seem to be wearing both *chitons* and jerkins strengthened by metal disks. Trans. 'bronze-clad'.

182. αὐλώπιδί τε τρυφαλείῃ: The meaning of neither word is certain. τρυφάλεια is a kind of helmet; it probably means the same as τετράφαλος (XII 384), i.e. (perhaps) having four horns (cp. note on ἀμφίφαλος, l. 743). αὐλώπιδι may refer to the eye-holes in the visor of the helmet.

183. εἰσορόων: cp. l. 89 n.

186. εἰλυμένος: εἰλύω.

187. τούτου: usually taken as genitive of separation with ἔτραπεν, 'away from this man'; but it could also be dependent on κιχήμενον, as verbs of hitting regularly take the genitive.

κιχήμενον: in effect an aorist middle participle (κιχάνω). ἄλλῃ: 'in another direction'.

This line seems to say that when the arrow had already reached Diomedes, a god had turned it elsewhere. This is not wholly correct, because of course it did hit him, and some ancient and modern commentators have wished to delete the line, which can be removed without detriment to the sense of the passage. A reasonable defence is to say that the arrow was indeed diverted, from a fatal to a less fatal course.

189. διὰ θώρηκος γυάλοιο: cp. l. 99 n.

190. ἐφάμην: 'I thought'.
'Αιδωνῆι: a lengthened form for 'Αΐδης, Hades, god of the under-world.

191. θεός νύ τίς ἐστι κοτήεις: cp. l. 177; 'this is then an angry god'.

192. παρέασι: πάρεισι.
The thought in Pandaros' mind is that his archery has been unsuc-cessful, and therefore he should change his style and fight at close quarters from a chariot like the other leaders. Unfortunately he had left all his chariots at home. The personality of Pandaros emerges from his words and actions – that of a foolish, blustering and self-justifying man. Cp. l. 283 n.

194. πέπλοι: to keep off the dust.

195. πέπτανται: πετάννυμι.
σφιν: dative of third-person pronoun, 'them'.
ἑκάστῳ: in apposition to σφιν.

197. αἰχμητά: nominative; cp. ἱππότα (l. 126).

199. ἐμβεβαώς: ἐμβαίνω.

202. δενοίατο: δεύοιντο (= δέοιντο); by a process that is found particularly in the Ionic dialect, the ν of the third-person plural has been vocalised as an α.

203. ἀνδρῶν εἰλομένων: genitive absolute; 'when the people are cooped up together', i.e. in a siege.

205. τὰ δέ με, etc.: 'so it turns out that they were not going to be of use to me'.
ἔμελλον: plural verb, although with a neuter plural subject. This is common in Homer.

208. ἀτρεκές: adverb, 'certainly'.

209. τῶ: cp. l. 129 n.

211. φέρων χάριν: 'doing a service to'.

212. νοστήσω, ἐσόψομαι: futures; εἴ κε is occasionally found with the future indicative in Homer.

214. ἀπ' ἐμεῖο κάρη τάμοι: ἀποτάμοι κάρη μου.

215. θείην: optative, because it is subordinate to the wish (τάμοι) of l. 214.

218. πάρος δ' οὐκ ἔσσεται ἄλλως: 'there will be no change until, etc.'.

219. ἐπί: with τῷδ' ἀνδρί.

νώ: for νῶι (l. 224), the first-person dual.

221. ἐπιβήσεο: cp. καταβήσεο (l. 109).

ἴδηαι: ἴδῃ.

222. Τρώιοι ἵπποι: We hear more of these horses in ll. 265–73 and 640. They were given to Tros by Zeus. The question whether Τρώιοι means 'Trojan' or 'of Tros' is merely a matter of translation into another language; the Greek word means both.

πεδίοιο: genitive of the ground covered, a sort of partitive genitive.

224. τώ: dual, 'they'.

πόλινδε: The suffix -δε with the accusative shows motion towards.

σαώσετον: 'will bring (us) safe'.

227. ἀποβήσομαι: The manuscripts and ancient authorities are divided between ἐπιβήσομαι and ἀποβήσομαι. If the former, Aineias means he will mount the chariot as the fighter, while Pandaros takes the reins; if the latter, preferred by the editor of the Oxford text, Aineias means that he will do what is normal in the Homeric battle – step down from the chariot and fight on foot. (The heroes use their chariots primarily as transport to and from the fighting.) The recurrence of this line at XVII 480, where it is certain that ἀποβήσομαι is the correct reading, makes it more likely here too.

228. τόνδε: Diomedes.

δέδεξο: perfect imperative; 'face'.

230. τεώ: σώ (dual).

232. Pandaros, like Aineias (l. 224), has an uneasy feeling that they may be defeated by Diomedes and have to withdraw quickly by chariot.

233. μή: 'I fear that'.

ματήσετον: dual of the aorist subjunctive; forms with the short vowel (in Attic it would be ματήσητον) are normal.

240. ἐμμεμαῶτε: cp. l. 135 n.

241. Καπανήιος υἱός: cp. l. 108 n.

243. ἐμῷ κεχαρισμένε θυμῷ: a very personal form of address, 'dear to my heart'.

245. ἶνα: accusative of ἴς, 'strength'.

248. ἐκγεγάμεν: ἐκγεγονέναι.

249. μοι: the so-called ethic dative; almost = 'please'.

251. ὑπόδρα ἰδών: 'frowning'.

252. φόβονδε: 'in the direction of flight', 'suggesting flight'.
πεισέμεν: πείσειν.

253. γενναῖον: 'an inborn quality', 'a family characteristic'.
ἀλυσκάζοντι μάχεσθαι: 'to fight while keeping out of the way'.

258. ἕτερος: 'one or other'.

261. δέ: marks the apodosis, as often in Homer.

262. ἐρυκακέειν, 263. ἐπαῖξαι, 264. ἐξελάσαι: infinitives for imperatives.

ἐξ ἄντυγος: 'from the rail of the chariot'.

263. i.e. 'remember to dash for the horses of Aineias'.

264. ἐυκνήμιδας: Greaves were shin-guards, worn particularly as a
protection against stones and arrows.

265. τῆς γάρ τοι γενεῆς: As printed in the Oxford text, with a comma
at the end of l. 267, these words are a partitive genitive, picked up
again by τῆς γενεῆς in l. 268; it is rather better to print a colon at the
end of l. 267, and treat τῆς γάρ τοι γενεῆς as a substantive sentence
with εἰσί understood; 'for they are of that stock'.

ἧς: In later Greek this would be attraction of the relative into the
case of its antecedent; such attraction, however, is not found elsewhere
in Homer, and so it is better to treat it as another partitive genitive,
'of which Zeus gave (some horses) to Tros'.

Τρωί: According to xx 215 ff., the Trojan royal family's genealogy
ran:

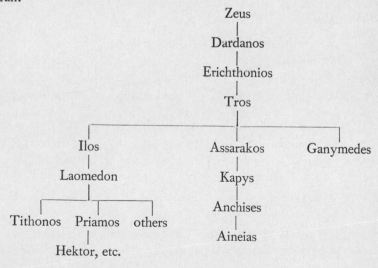

```
                        Zeus
                         |
                      Dardanos
                         |
                     Erichthonios
                         |
                        Tros
         _____|_____
        |                |                |
       Ilos          Assarakos        Ganymedes
        |                |
     Laomedon          Kapys
     ___|___             |
    |   |   |         Anchises
Tithonos Priamos others   |
        |               Aineias
    Hektor, etc.
```

περ: cp. l. 94 n.

εὐρύοπα: another masculine nominative form in -ᾰ; cp. ἱππότα (l. 126), αἰχμητά (l. 197).

266. υἷος: genitive.

ποινὴν Γανυμήδεος: 'as compensation for Ganymedes'; Ganymedes was a son of Tros, carried off to Olympos because of his beauty, to act as wine-bearer to Zeus.

268. τῆς γενεῆς: partitive genitive, 'of that stock'; cp. l. 265 n.

269. Λαομέδοντος: with λάθρῃ.

ὑποσχὼν θήλεας ἵππους: 'putting mares to the stallions', to breed from them.

270. οἱ: 'to him', i.e. Anchises.

γενέθλη: in apposition to ἕξ; 'offspring'.

273. Contrary to later practice, Homer can have κε with the optative in both parts of a hypothetical condition.

279. τύχωμι: the longer form of the subjunctive τύχω; cp. l. 6.

280. ἦ: 'he spoke'; past tense of ἠμί, which survived in Attic (particularly Plato) in the common phrases ἦ δ᾽ ὅς, ἦν δ᾽ ἐγώ.

ἀμπεπαλών: *reduplicated aorist* (ἀναπάλλω), an old tense-formation of which numerous examples are found in Homer.

283. Notice the unattractively over-confident character of Pandaros; he repeats here the premature assumption that he made in ll. 103–4. Cp. l. 192 n.

284. βέβληαι: βέβλησαι.

287. ἤμβροτες: ἁμαρτάνω.

μέν: μήν.

288. πρίν . . . πρίν: The first is the adverb, the second the conjunction; cp. πάρος . . . πρίν (ll. 218–19).

ἀποπαύσεσθαι: 'you will not stop before'.

πρὶν ἤ: expansion of πρίν; something like 'earlier than'. (πρίν itself is really an adverb, which was beginning to be used as a conjunction in the Homeric language.)

289. 'to glut with blood Ares, the shield-carrying fighter'. This is a traditional verse, occurring again twice in the *Iliad*.

290. Athene directed the spear. She had persuaded Pandaros to break the truce by treacherously shooting Menelaos (IV 93); she had

then smartly moved over to protect Menelaos from the shot (IV 129); now she supervises the punishment of Pandaros. The gods are ruthless.

291-3. The description of the wound made by the spear, although it gives an impression of accuracy and clarity, causes considerable difficulty. Pandaros is on a higher level than Diomedes, because he is still in his chariot. But the spear is described as hitting him on the bridge of the nose, passing through his mouth and coming out below his chin. The only more or less satisfactory explanation, offered by Leaf and others, is that Pandaros tried to duck to avoid the spear.

292. γλῶσσαν πρυμνήν: 'the tongue at its root'.

293. ἐξελύθη: This word must somehow mean 'came out'. (1) As an aorist passive of ἐκλύω, it can hardly have this sense ('was let out'!?). (2) More promising, although in fact unparalleled, is the suggestion that ἐξελύθη is simply ἐξέλυθε (=ἐξῆλθε, cp. l. 16), with the last syllable lengthened by metrical stress. (3) The Alexandrian scholar Zenodotus preferred to read ἐξεσύθη (from ἐκσεύω, cp. αἷμ' ἔσσευα, 'I made the blood spurt out', l. 208), and has been followed in this by some modern editors.

παρὰ νείατον ἀνθερεῶνα: 'beneath the chin'; see ll. 291-3 n.

295. οἱ: dative.

297. ἀπόρουσε: i.e. off the chariot, the horses having shied away (l. 295).

298. οἱ: trans. 'from him'.
ἐρυσαίατο: cp. l. 202 n.

299. ἀλκί: a third-declension form of the dative of ἀλκή.

300. πρόσθε: adverb, 'in front'.
οἱ: 'for him', 'to guard him', i.e. the dead body of Pandaros, to whom also the word τοῦ in the next line refers. Cp. l. 315.

πάντοσ' ἐΐσην: lit. 'equal in all directions'; 'symmetrical', 'round'.

301. κτάμεναι: infinitive.
τοῦ: cp. l. 300 n.

302. σμερδαλέα ἰάχων: It is common in Homer for a short final vowel to be lengthened in apparent hiatus before ἰάχω; the explanation is that at one time ἰάχω began with the lost consonant, the digamma (Ϝιάχω), and even a single digamma was occasionally able to lengthen a preceding short vowel (cp. ἔλλαβε, l. 83 n., and see Introduction, p. xxiv).

303. μέγα ἔργον: accusative in apposition to the sentence, 'a great feat'.

G

307. πρὸς δέ: 'and in addition'.

308. ὧσε δ' ἀπό: ἀπῶσε δέ.

311. κεν ἀπόλοιτο: In later Greek, and usually elsewhere in Homer, the aorist indicative is used for this 'past impossible' condition; but occasionally, perhaps for vividness, the optative is found; cp. οὐκ ἂν γνοίης (l. 85), and the present phrase repeated (l. 388).

313. τέκε: Homer occasionally uses τέκε in a rather confused way, with reference in the same sentence to both the birth of the child and the circumstances of its earlier conception. Exactly the same thing happens in the entry about this same Aineias in the Catalogue in book II:

II 820–1.

> Αἰνείας, τὸν ὑπ' Ἀγχίσῃ τέκε δῖ' Ἀφροδίτη,
> Ἴδης ἐν κνημοῖσι θεὰ βροτῷ εὐνηθεῖσα.

Cp. also II 513 n.

The story of Aphrodite's visit to Anchises when he was herding cattle on Mount Ida is told with much charm in the Homeric Hymn to Aphrodite.

315. πρόσθε δέ οἱ: cp. l. 300 n.

316. ἔμεν: εἶναι, 'so as to be'.

318. ἑόν: personal pronoun, 'her'; cp. ἑούς (l. 321), ὧν (l. 328).

319. συνθεσιάων: i.e. the instructions given him by Diomedes in ll. 261–4.

320. τάων ἅς: 'those which', cp. l. 12 n.; also l. 332.

323–4. καλλίτριχας ἵππους ἐξέλασε: So Diomedes got possession of the wonderful horses of Aineias; and it is these horses he uses when he wins the chariot race in the funeral games of Patroklos in book XXIII (see XXIII 291–2).

325. περί: 'beyond'.

326. ὅτι οἱ φρεσὶν ἄρτια ᾔδη: We might say 'because his mind worked in the same way as his'.

327. ἐλαυνέμεν: infinitive (l. 132); explanatory after δῶκε (l. 325).

329. μέθεπε takes here two objects; Sthenelos brought the horses up to follow Diomedes. This, as was explained in l. 107 n., was the duty of the charioteer – to keep the chariot close and available for his lord in case of emergency.

330. Κύπριν: the goddess of Kypros (Cyprus), Aphrodite.

ἐπῴχετο: imperfect; he was attacking her while she was trying to remove her son Aineias from the scene (ὑπεξέφερεν, imperfect, l. 318). These two actions of Aphrodite and Diomedes had been continuing while Sthenelos leapt in to seize the horses.

One should not fail to notice the extraordinary confidence of Diomedes in actually attacking a god; this action would cause a thrill of anxiety and excitement to the ancient audience.

331. ὅ τε: accusative neuter of the relative used adverbially, 'that'. It is not distinguishable in meaning from ὅτι, which, however, is never elided. The τε in ὅ τε has a slight implication of habitual, general behaviour (cp. l. 5 n.).

332. κάτα: preposition following its noun, and therefore with change of accent.

333. οὔτ' ἄρα: 'and she was neither'.

336. ἄκρην χεῖρα: 'the top of the hand'; that is, as is stated clearly later (ll. 339 and 458), the wrist.

μετάλμενος: μεθάλλομαι.

337. ἀντετόρησεν: (ἀντιτορέω) 'pierced'.

338. The Charites, or Graces, were responsible for charm, grace and attraction, and were therefore natural assistants of Aphrodite.

339. πρυμνὸν ὕπερ θέναρος: πρυμνόν must be used as a noun, governed by ὕπερ and with θέναρος dependent on it; 'above the blunt end of the palm', i.e. on the wrist.

340–2. That ichor, not blood, flows in the veins of the gods is stated only here. The word recurs in l. 416.

343. The last syllables of both μέγα and ἀπό are lengthened before lost consonants at the front of ἰάχυνσα and ἕο. For the former, cp. l. 302 n.; the latter was a later form of *σϜεο (cp. Latin suus). This lengthening before lost consonants is an indication of the antiquity of Greek dactylic poetry (see Introduction, p. xiii).

ἕο: οὗ.

κάββαλεν: κατέβαλεν.

344. ἐρύσατο: 'protected'.

349. ἢ οὐχ: scanned as one syllable by synizesis (see Introduction, p. xxv).

350. πωλήσεαι: Attic πωλήσει (future).

ἦ τέ σ᾽ ὀίω, etc.: 'then indeed I think that you will shudder at warfare, even if you hear of it somewhere else'.

351. πύθηαι: Attic πύθῃ (subjunctive).

352. ἀπεβήσετο: cp. l. 109 n.

353. Iris acts as the agent of the gods, as the heralds do for the kings down below. Usually it is a question of taking messages, but here she assists Aphrodite from the field, and acts as her charioteer back to Olympos.

354. χρόα καλόν: accusative of respect.

356. ἐκέκλιτο: 'his spear and chariot rested on (leant against) a bank of cloud'.

359. φίλε: The most acceptable explanation of the lengthening of the first syllable is the metrical stress.

κόμισαί με: 'look after me'.

361. ὅ με: internal and external object of οὔτασεν.

364. ἀκηχεμένη: perfect participle of ἄχνυμαι, alternative to ἀκαχημένη.

365. λάζετο: ἐλάμβανε.

366. ἐλάαν: present infinitive, of purpose.

τώ: the two horses.

370. Dione is feminine of Zeus (genitive Διός), and was an ancient wife of his, particularly connected with his worship at Dodona. She was mother of Aphrodite.

371. ἀγκάς: adverb, 'in her arms'.

374. ἐνωπῇ: 'openly'. This seems to be a playful and rather sly dig at Aphrodite, whose misdemeanours tend to take place behind closed doors.

376. οὖτα: not contracted imperfect, but a form of aorist with short α.

Aphrodite is plaintive, and feels herself unfairly treated.

382–415. Dione's speech is a good example of the use of mythological examples as a method of consolation. The three separate examples have a cumulative effect. The plan of the speech is: (1) You must endure your pain. (2) Many of us have endured pain for similar reasons. (3) Three examples. (4) Comments on the foolhardiness of mortals who cause such pain to the gods. It is interesting that the three stories given – of Ares, Hera and Hades being hurt by mortals – are to all intents and purposes unique to this passage, and not found independently elsewhere. It makes one wonder whether the stories were not altered or invented by the poet. (See, however, the note on ll. 392–7.)

382. τέτλαθι (τλάω): perfect imperative.
ἀνάσχεο (ἀνέχω): aorist imperative middle.

385. τλῆ μὲν "Αρης: Notice the rhetorical repetition of the verb: τέτλαθι (l. 382); τλῆμεν (l. 383); τλῆ μὲν "Αρης (l. 385); τλῆ δ' "Ηρη (l. 392); τλῆ δ' 'Αίδης (l. 395).

Otos and Ephialtes were young giants, who never grew to manhood, but nevertheless shook the gods on Olympos. Here they are said to have shut up Ares in a bronze jar. This seems a fairy-tale motif (cp. djinns shut up in bottles), as is the traditional theme of the stepmother who thwarts the children (l. 389).

388. For the tense of ἀπόλοιτο, cp. l. 311 n.
That a god could perish is carrying anthropomorphism rather far. Contrast l. 402, where it is stated that Hades was not καταθνητός (subject to death).

389. Eeriboia is the stepmother of the Aloadai, not of Ares.

390. Hermes was the patron of thieves, and no mean exponent of their art himself; he is therefore thematically the right person to steal Ares away. (Compare what is said about recurrent motifs in the Introduction, p. xx.)

391. ἐδάμνα: 'was weakening'.

392–7. The woundings of Hera and Hades by arrows from Herakles, like other references to Herakles in the Iliad, seem to be separate allusions to poetic versions of the Herakles legend circulating at the time of the composition of the Iliad. If an occasion is required for these particular events, it may be found in the story told in xi 690 ff. of the attack by Herakles on Nestor's home, Pylos (although the meaning of Πύλῳ in l. 397 is disputed; see note). At all events the A scholion (see III 109 n.) on XI 690 shows the decided view of the ancient commentator that the attack on Pylos was the time when Herakles fought against the gods: συνεμάχουν δὲ τῷ μὲν Νηλεῖ τρεῖς θεοί, Ποσειδῶν "Ηρα 'Αιδωνεύς, ὡς καὶ ἐν τῇ Ε φησί, τῷ δὲ 'Ηρακλεῖ δύο, 'Αθηνᾶ καὶ Ζεύς. In the case of Hera this is all the evidence; but other authorities confirm Herakles' fight with Hades at Pylos (Pindar, Ol. IX 33; Apollodorus, II 7.3; Pausanias, VI 25.2).

392. πάις Ἀμφιτρύωνος, 396 · υἱὸς Διός: Herakles was the putative son of Amphitryon, but the real son of Zeus.

396. ωὗτος: ὁ αὐτός.

397. ἐν Πύλῳ ἐν νεκύεσσι: This has been much discussed. Pylos, Nestor's home, was one of the main cities of the Peloponnese, and Herakles had campaigned against Pylos, as related by Nestor in XI 690 ff. (cp. ll. 392–7 n.). But Pylos of course means simply 'the gate', and the reference may be to the gate of hell – a significant feature, Hades himself being described elsewhere as the 'strong watcher of the gate' (πυλάρταο κρατεροῖο, XIII 415). Or the two possibilities may have been confused, and Pylos itself have been thought of as one of the gates of the underworld. 'In Pylos, among the dead men' gives a suitably vague and ghastly impression.

399. πεπαρμένος: πείρω.

400. ἠλήλατο: ἐλαύνω.

401. ἐπί ... πάσσων: tmesis.
    Παιήων: the healer; later identified with Apollo.

403–4. An outburst of expostulation against Herakles.

405. σοὶ δ' ἐπί: ἐπὶ σοὶ δέ.

406. νήπιος: Diomedes.
    τό: antecedent of ὅττι (l. 407).
    Dione makes a basic Greek point; a person who fights against the gods does not live to a peaceful old age.

408. παππάζουσιν: 'say papa'. Cp. Gray's Elegy in a Country Churchyard:

> No children run to lisp their sire's return,
> Or climb his knees the envied kiss to share.

410. τῷ: 'therefore'.

411. ἀμείνων σεῖο: 'more warlike than you'; i.e. another god.

412–15. The reference to Diomedes' mourning wife seems to be a threat, as if the poet knew later events in which the hero was punished for his sacrilege here. In fact, however, although various stories were told of Diomedes' experiences after he returned home, none of them conforms to the picture in Dione's words. We must take her as describing what *can* happen to those who attack the gods, not what *will* happen to Diomedes.

412. δήν: 'for a long time', to be taken with either or both of the verbs in the next line.

Ἀδρηστίνη: daughter of Adrestos (Adrastos).

413. ἐξ ὕπνου: with ἐγείρῃ.

416. ἀμφοτέρῃσιν: 'with both (hands)'.

ἰχῶ: accusative.

419. κερτομίοις: 'mocking"

422. τινὰ Ἀχαιιάδων: The reference is of course to Aphrodite's encouragement of Helen to go with Paris. A great part of the opposition between Hera and Athene on the one hand and Aphrodite on the other, and a strong reason for at least Hera's undying hatred of the Trojans, was the 'Judgement of Paris', when he had chosen Aphrodite as the most beautiful of the three goddesses, and she had promised him the most beautiful woman in the world as his wife. This 'Judgement of Paris' is only once specifically mentioned in the *Iliad* (XXIV 28–30), but it lies behind other situations, including the remarks of Athene here.

ἀνιεῖσα: 'arousing', 'inciting'.

423. σπέσθαι: ἕπομαι.

τούς: The later article, appearing in Homer regularly as a demonstrative, is also used as a relative, as here.

424. καρρέζουσα: καταρέζουσα; cp. l. 372.

433. αὐτὸς Ἀπόλλων: It is noticeable that whereas the other divine supporters of the Trojans in the *Iliad* (Ares, Aphrodite, Artemis) are often treated with scant respect, Apollo is always dignified and impressive.

ὑπείρεχε: ὑπερεῖχε.

436–42. 'Three times he attacked, and three times Apollo pushed him back; but when for the fourth time he rushed forward, then the god spoke, "Give way, son of Tydeus".' This thematic incident (cp. Introduction, p. xx) is used also for Patroklos at the height of his temporary success in XVI 702–9; we may well believe that it appeared in other heroic poetry, both in the fighting at Troy and elsewhere. It would be particularly suitable to Achilleus' attack on Troy in the fighting some time after the end of the *Iliad*, when he was killed by Paris and Apollo at the Skaian gate (cp. XXII 359–60).

438. ἐπέσσυτο: ἐπισσεύω.

439. δέ: apodotic, cp. l. 261.

440. φράζεο: 'think what you are doing'.
φράζεο καὶ χάζεο: Homeric verse is fond of such plays on words.

441. ἶσα φρονέειν: trans. 'to think yourself equal'.

442. χαμαί: This goes so closely with ἐρχομένων that the connective τε follows the second word.

446. νηός: Ionic for normal Greek ναός, Attic νεώς.

448. ἀδύτῳ: 'not to be entered' – the inner sanctuary which only priests would normally enter. The mention of an ἄδυτον appears in the *Iliad* only in this episode.
κύδαινον: lit. 'glorified'; 'strengthened', 'beautified', 'increased his heroic stature'.

450. τοῖος: 'like'.

452. βοείας: 'ox-hide shields'; this is the generic noun; the next line gives two types of shields in apposition.

453. λαισήϊά τε πτερόεντα: λαισήϊα are clearly smaller and lighter shields than ἀσπίδες or σάκεα. πτερόεντα is more difficult; ancient commentators thought it could just mean 'light', but that is reasonably discounted nowadays. On the other hand the modern translation 'fluttering' is unhelpful without more explanation. Most probably the λαισήϊον had a fringe, or tassels, which would wave about in the air as it was moved (so Lorimer, *Homer and the Monuments*, p. 195). Thus 'fluttering' will do as a translation.

455. Cp. l. 31 and the notes on that line.

456. οὐκ ἂν δή: 'could you not . . .?'; cp. l. 32.
ἐρύσαιο: 'draw out of', 'remove'.

458. πρῶτα: πρῶτον.

461. Τρῳάς: for Τρωίας, adjective.
οὖλος: ὀλοός, 'destructive'.

462. εἰδόμενος: 'in appearance like'; the gods rarely appear to mortals in their own shape.

465. Ἀχαιοῖς: dative of the agent.

466. ἢ εἰς: synizesis (cp. l. 349).

469. σαώσομεν: aorist subjunctive; cp. l. 233 n.

471. Sarpedon is the most important of the leaders of the Trojans' allies. His contingent is that of the true Lykians from the very south

of Asia Minor (as opposed to Pandaros' Lykians from near Troy, l. 105 n.).

473. φῆς: imperfect; 'you used to say'.

ἑξέμεν: 'that you would hold', with a reference to the name Hektor, 'the holder'.

474. Priam's numerous offspring provided large numbers of both brothers and brothers-in-law for Hektor.

477. ἔνειμεν: ἔνεσμεν, 'are in the city'.

480. 'There I left my wife and baby son.' This line has a powerful double effect: (1) It produces a personal sympathy for Sarpedon in the reader, which will be increased by his great words and actions in book XII and his death in book XVI. (2) By the mention of the wife and baby son, it prepares the way, and conditions the minds of the audience, for the scene of farewell between Hektor and his wife and baby son at the end of book VI. This 'foreshadowing' of the fate of a major character by what is said of a relatively minor character is one of the particular features of the *Iliad*'s narrative.

481. κάδ: i.e. κατέλιπον.

τά: cp. l. 423 n.

τὰ ἔλδεται ὅς κ' ἐπιδευής: probably not a specific reference to the covetousness of Sarpedon's poorer neighbours in Lykia but a general statement of the enviable nature of great possessions; 'the object of poor men's desires'.

483. τοῖον οἷον: 'the sort of possession that'.

484. The two verbs are those normally used of the carrying-off of booty – φέρειν of portable objects, and ἄγειν of living creatures such as cattle.

485. τύνη: σύ.

486. ὤρεσσι: for ὀάρεσσι, from ὄαρ, 'wife'.

487. ἁψῖσι λίνοιο πανάγρου: 'by the mesh of an all-taking line' – an untypical periphrasis for a net. ἁλόντε: Although this is the right word for the meaning required ('taken', 'captured'), it offers two unexplained difficulties – the incorrect long α demanded by the metre, and the dual number. K. Meister (*Die homerische Kunstsprache* (1921) p. 243) suggested that this might be an example of false archaism by a poet who was not familiar with the dual in his native speech.

492. ἀποθέσθαι: parallel with μέλειν (l. 490) and dependent on χρή;

'to put away from you (i.e. avoid giving opportunities for) the stern rebuke'.

497. ἔσταν: a shorter form of the third-person plural, = ἔστησαν; cp. in the next line φόβηθεν for ἐφοβήθησαν.

498. οὐδὲ φόβηθεν: 'nor did they run away'.

499–501. The simile describes the process of winnowing, that is, the separating of the wheat from the chaff by throwing it into the air, the lighter chaff being blown aside by the wind.

499. The winnowing floor (ἀλωή) is sacred; the harvesting of the ripened corn in the late summer has always played a large part in the religious side of country life; Demeter, the goddess of the corn, her hair the colour of the golden harvest (ξανθή, l. 500), herself separates the wheat from the chaff (l. 501).

501. κρίνῃ: 'separates'.

502. ἀχυρμιαί: 'heaps of chaff'; the whiteness of these is the whole point of comparison of the simile, being likened to the dust-bespattered Greek army.

503. ὕπερθε: 'from above', i.e. the dust settled down on them.
δι' αὐτῶν: 'through their ranks'.

504. ἐπέπληγον: reduplicated aorist of πλήσσω.

505. ἂψ ἐπιμισγομένων: 'as they joined battle again'.

506. νύκτα: internal object of ἀμφεκάλυψε; 'drew a veil of night over the battle'.

509. ὅς μιν ἀνώγει, etc.: This must refer to the words of Apollo in ll. 455 ff., although the reasons given there are not the same as here.

513. ἧκε: ἵημι.

514. τοί: an alternative form of the nominative plural οἱ.

517. ἀργυρότοξος: i.e. Apollo; it is not common for the epithet to stand in this way for the person.

519. τοὺς δέ: 'the others', i.e. the Greeks, further specified in the next line.
Αἴαντε δύω: the two heroes named Aias, the son of Telamon and the son of Oileus.

522–6. An extraordinary simile: the Greeks stood their ground like clouds in a windless sky. As a description this does not help very much, but the picture of peaceful nature has a definite effect, of distracting the audience momentarily from the deadly fighting on the plain.

523. νηνεμίης: genitive absolute (understand οὔσης).

524. ἀτρέμας: adverb, 'motionless'.
ὄφρα: 'while'.
εὕδῃσι: εὕδῃ; cp. l. 6.

530. αἰδεῖσθε: 'have respect for'; the heroic age is what anthropologists call a 'shame-culture'. The characters are much less concerned with what is right or wrong than with their standing in the eyes of other people, i.e. their honour.

531. πέφανται: perfect passive of the defective verb whose active aorist is ἔπεφνον.

532. ὄρνυται: 'is aroused'.

534. Αἰνείω: genitive.

538. οὐκ ἔρυτο: 'did not keep out'.
εἴσατο: This aorist, probably formed from ἵεμαι, is used as if a part of εἶμι (Chantraine, 1 412).

542. Diokles of Pherai (here Phere, l. 543) appears also in the *Odyssey*, as giving hospitality to Telemachos at the half-way stage of his journey across the Peloponnese from Nestor at Pylos to Menelaos at Sparta (*Od.* iii 488 and xv 186).

545. εὐρύ: adverbial.

546 and 547. The Oxford text gives the name of the grandfather as Ortilochos and the grandson as Orsilochos. It was a common Greek habit to call the grandson after the grandfather, and quite apart from that this variation within the family is improbable. The *Iliad* manuscripts are in general in favour of Orsilochos for both, but a few have Ortilochos in these two lines, and this is the spelling of Diokles' father's name in the *Odyssey* (in the two passages quoted in the note on l. 542, and in *Od.* xxi 16). The matter is not very important, but it would be more reasonable to print the two names alike in this passage. More worth noting, perhaps, is the fixity of detail in the epic tradition, which has preserved this minor personage, Diokles of Pherai, in both the *Iliad* and the *Odyssey*, as an apparently real historical figure.

552. τιμήν . . . ἀρνυμένω: 'striving to get compensation'; τιμή is the price that the Trojans must pay for the injury done to Menelaos.

553. τώ: 'them'.
αὖθι: 'there'.

554. οἵω τώ γε: 'such they were as'.

555. ἐτραφέτην: gnomic aorist (l. 88). This is from the active-form aorist ἔτραφον, which is used by Homer intransitively, with passive meaning.

557. ὄφρα: 'until'.

558. κατέκταθεν: κατεκτάθησαν (κατακτείνω).

564. τά: antecedent to ἵνα.

Ares was, of course, supporting the Trojans. Little touches like this line help us to know the characters better. We learn from these few words that Menelaos was no match for Aineias, and that therefore his kind-heartedness (τὼ δέ . . . ἐλέησεν, l. 561) has made him foolhardy. The next line shows that the other Greeks kept something of a watch on Menelaos in the battle, no doubt because they liked him, but also because they could not afford to lose him.

565. Antilochos was the son of Nestor, and an effective fighter among the younger and minor heroes. He saves Menelaos' life here. This incident should be remembered when one reads the competition between Menelaos and Antilochos in the chariot race in book XXIII, and the dispute which follows there. Antilochos was clearly an attractive person. In the story of the war after the end of the *Iliad*, he behaved as here, going to the rescue of his father who was cut off in the front of the fighting, and gave his own life to save his father.

566. περί: 'very much'.

567. μέγα δέ σφας ἀποσφήλειε πόνοιο: 'and greatly frustrate the point of their efforts'. If Menelaos were to be killed, the whole reason for the Greeks being at Troy (the recovery of Helen) would be invalidated.

573. νεκρούς: i.e. the two Greeks killed by Aineias in ll. 541-60, referred to also as τὼ δειλώ in the next line. The Greeks would wish to recover the bodies, to give them burial, and not let them fall into the hands of their enemies.

579. ἑσταότα: 'as he stood on the ground', not in his chariot; he is contrasted with his charioteer Mydon (ll. 581 ff.).

581. ὁ δ' ὑπέστρεφε μώνυχας ἵππους: Pylaimenes must have been standing in front of his chariot. When he was hit, the charioteer Mydon started to turn the horses for flight, but was too slow.

583. λεύκ᾽ ἐλέφαντι: This must refer to actual ivory ornamentation on the reins.

586. κύμβαχος: 'head first'.

βρεχμόν: 'top of the head'.

587. This line says that the body stood there on its head and shoulders for some time, because it happened to fall into some soft sand. It has been suggested that this provides an example of a rare physical phenomenon, a state of rigidity through shock which may accompany violent death. Even if this is so, however, the picture of the body standing on its head in this state is fantastic and unrealistic (Friedrich, *Verwundung und Tod in der Ilias*, pp. 13–16).

588. ἵππω: the horses of Mydon's own chariot, which Antilochos rapidly took as booty.

591. κεκλήγων: Aeolic form of κεκληγώς, perfect participle of κλάζω; in fact the manuscripts here read κεκληγώς, but the Oxford editor has altered it, on the grounds that the only other case of the participle found in the *Iliad* is the nominative plural, and this (four times) is κεκλήγοντες, not κεκληγότες.

593. ἔχουσα: 'bringing with her'.

Κυδοιμὸν ἀναιδέα δηιοτῆτος: Leaf translates this 'ruthless turmoil of war'.

594. ἐνώμα: A finite verb in the δέ clause balances the participle in the μέν clause; this is not uncommon.

597. ἀπάλαμνος: 'at a loss'.

πολέος πεδίοιο: genitive of the ground covered (cp. l. 222).

598. στήῃ: uncontracted form.

601. οἷον: exclamation, 'how'.

603. πάρα: πάρεστι; also l. 604.

606. μενεαινέμεν: infinitive for imperative.

ἶφι: 'by force'; instrumental case (l. 28 n.) of the noun (F)ἴς (Latin *vis*).

607. ἤλυθον: ἦλθον.

609. εἰν: ἐν.

612. Amphios son of Selagos, who lived in Paisos, is not to be confused with the Amphios who was the leader of one of the Trojan allies' contingents, the son of Merops one of whose towns was Apaisos

(II 828–31). The similarity is no doubt the result of unconscious word-association in the choice of a name for a minor figure.

ἐνί: ἐν.

623. ἀμφίβασιν: This refers to the bestriding of the dead body to defend it (cp. l. 21 n. and l. 299, ἀμφὶ δ᾽ ἄρ᾽ αὐτῷ βαῖνε). Trans. 'defence'.

628–98. The fight between Sarpedon and Tlepolemos. Interest is added to this incident by the provenance of the two opponents. Tlepolemos was the leader of a newly founded Achaian colony on the island of Rhodes (II 653–70); Sarpedon was king of the Lykians, on the mainland opposite Rhodes. Hostility between the two was natural in their homeland, and many have thought that their fight here at Troy is the result of a transfer by the *Iliad* poet from some other poem.

631. Sarpedon was a son of Zeus: Tlepolemos, as son of Herakles (l. 628), was a grandson.

633 f. Attempts at intimidation by abusive speeches before engaging in the fight are a common feature in the *Iliad*.

636. ἐπιδεύεαι: 'fall short'; from ἐπιδεύομαι, for ἐπιδέομαι.

638. ἀλλ᾽ οἷόν τινα: exclamatory; 'but what kind of a man was'. This is rather awkward; others read as one word ἀλλοῖόν τινα – 'a different kind of man'.

βίην Ἡρακληείην: 'the might of Herakles'; a periphrasis for Ἡρακλῆα. In spite of βίην, the phrase is treated here as a masculine noun (οἷον).

639. εἶναι: infinitive of the imperfect.

640. ὅς ποτε δεῦρ᾽ ἐλθών: There had been a previous Greek expedition against Troy by Herakles, long before Agamemnon's army came. Laomedon had promised Herakles the famous horses (mentioned in ll. 265 ff. of this book) as a reward if he saved his daughter Hesione from the sea-monster. But when Herakles had fulfilled his side of the bargain, Laomedon refused the reward. So Herakles had attacked and destroyed Troy.

643 κακός: 'cowardly'.

646. ὑπ᾽ ἐμοί: 'at my hands'; cp. ἐμῷ ὑπὸ δουρί (l. 653).

δμηθέντα: δάμνημι.

648. ἱρήν: ἱερήν.

651. ἀπέδωκε: 'gave what he owed'.

653. τεύξεσθαι: future middle of τεύχω, with passive meaning; 'will be achieved'.

656. ἀμαρτῇ: 'simultaneously'.

659. κατ' ὀφθαλμῶν: 'down over his eyes'.

661. βεβλήκειν: pluperfect, with ν-movable; used with aorist sense.

662. πατήρ: Zeus.

ἔτι: 'for the time'; Sarpedon is killed in book XVI.

665. ἑλκόμενον: the spear.

τὸ μέν: object of ἐπεφράσατο, clarified by ἐξερύσαι in the following line.

666. ὄφρ' ἐπιβαίη: 'so that he could stand'.

667. σπευδόντων: partitive genitive with οὔ τις.

670. τλήμονα: 'steadfast', 'brave'.

672. προτέρω: 'further'.

682. χάρη: χαίρω; aorist passive, but with the same sense as the active.

686. οὐκ ἄρ' ἔμελλον: This is the idiomatic use of ἄρα with the imperfect; 'it turns out that I was not after all destined to'. He seems to think that he is mortally wounded; cp. l. 696 n.

688. Cp. the note on l. 480.

690. λελιημένος ὄφρα: 'eager to'.

693. εἶσαν: ἵζω.

φηγῷ: This oak was near the Skaian gate of Troy; cp. VI 237. Ἕκτωρ δ' ὡς Σκαιάς τε πύλας καὶ φηγὸν ἵκανεν.

696. τὸν δὲ λίπε ψυχή: The poet is using the language of death to describe Sarpedon fainting. There is, however, no ambiguity, because he has stated clearly in l. 662 that Sarpedon is not to die now.

697. ἐμπνύνθη: 'came to himself'; the reading of the O.C.T. is that of Aristarchus; the MSS. have ἀμπνύνθη. The modern view of these words is that they are not directly derived from compounds of πνέω, although there may be an etymological connection, but are connected with such words as πινυτός ('discerning'), πεπνυμένος ('intelligent');

698. ζώγρει: imperfect 'revived'; elsewhere the verb means 'to take a prisoner alive'.

κεκαφηότα: a perfect participle, of which no other verbal part is found. It clearly means 'exhausted', and agrees with the understood object of ζώγρει, Sarpedon.

θυμόν: accusative of respect, with κεκαφηότα.

699 ff. The Greeks are obeying Diomedes' instructions (ll. 605–6) to give way before Hektor and Ares.

703. The rhetorical question is used here, as elsewhere in the *Iliad*, to enhance the significance of a particular scene, or the glory of a particular fighter.

705. ἐπί: adverb, 'in addition'.

707. αἰολομίτρην: The μίτρη was like a metal kilt, defending the lower part of the body. αἰόλος means 'glittering'.

708–10. A little corroborative detail about a minor figure.

708. ἐν Ὕλῃ: Hyle is named as one of the Boiotian towns in II 500; it has there, however, a long *v*.

μέγα πλούτοιο μεμηλώς: 'taking great care of his wealth'.

709. κεκλιμένος: 'living on the shore of', i.e. on the ground sloping down to the lake. (Kephisian lake = lake Kopais.)

οἱ: dative, 'to him'.

710. The fertility of Boiotia was an object of envy to its Athenian neighbours.

711. ὡς οὖν: cp. l. 95 n.

714. Ἀτρυτώνη: cp. l. 115 n.

715. 'Empty indeed was the promise we made to Menelaos.'

722–32. The light-weight chariot was taken to pieces for storing. These lines describe its fitting together. As this is a chariot of the gods, it has metal (often precious metal) where earthly chariots would use wood or leather, and has a larger number of spokes to its wheels, and of handrails on the car; but otherwise this is probably an accurate description.

722. Ἥβη: the goddess of youth, here acting as a servant to Hera.

ἀμφ' ὀχέεσσι: 'on both sides of the chariot'; further specified in the next line by ἄξονι ἀμφίς, 'on both sides of the axle'.

724. ἴτυς: 'rim'.

725. ἐπίσσωτρα: 'tyres'.

προσαρηρότα: 'fixed'.

726. πλῆμναι: These are the 'naves', i.e. the solid central parts of the wheels.

περίδρομοι: 'rotating'; the word is used in another sense ('running round') in l. 728.

727. δίφρος: the *car* itself of the chariot.

728. ἐντέταται: A network of plaited straps formed the front, and probably also the floor, of the car.

δοιαὶ ἄντυγες: Two rails are more impressive than one. We probably do not need to consider their relationship to each other.

729. ῥυμός: the 'pole', at the front end of which the yoke was fastened.

730. λέπαδνα: 'collars'.

732. μεμαυῖα: i.e. Hera.

736. Διὸς νεφεληγερέταο: The genitive must, by the run of the words, be dependent on χιτῶνα, however much we might prefer to take it with τεύχεσιν of the next line.

738. αἰγίδα: see l. 115 n. The aigis is in the *Iliad* like a shield, and is used not only by Zeus, but by Athene (as here) and Apollo as well.

θυσσανόεσσαν: with tassels round the edge.

739. ἣν περὶ μὲν πάντῃ: As printed in the Oxford text, with the accent on the second syllable of περί, ἥν must be the object of the verb ἐστεφάνωται (or περιεστεφάνωται by *tmesis*). Trans. 'which Fear encircles around and about on all sides'.

740. ἐν δ' Ἔρις, etc.: The personifications of this and the preceding line are perhaps to be thought of as being powers of the aigis, not as depicted on it. The Gorgon's head, however, in l. 741, is a common design on a shield, to alarm the enemy. It appears also on Agamemnon's shield, which is described in XI 32–7.

741. Γοργείη κεφαλή: 'the head of the Gorgon'; later legends said that when Perseus had killed the gorgon Medousa, whose face turned the onlooker to stone, he cut off her head and, after using it to take vengeance on his persecutor Polydektes, gave it to his protectress Athene to be placed on her shield.

δεινοῖο πελώρου: genitive agreeing with the implied genitive in Γοργείη = Γοργοῦς.

743. ἀμφίφαλον: The φάλος may have been a horn or other projection on the front of the helmet. ἀμφίφαλος would then mean 'with two horns'. But the word is obscure.

τετραφάληρον: φάλαρα were metal disks attached for greater protection to the front of the helmet; τετραφάληρον then means 'with four metal disks'.

744. 'Having upon it figures representing the foot-soldiers of a hundred cities.' The description of the shield and helmet, already of more than earthly awesomeness, ends with a detail that is hardly intelligible.

745. φλόγεα: 'bright as flame'.

749–51. The gates of heaven are formed by the clouds, and the guardians of the gates are the Ὧραι, the goddesses of the seasons. This makes general sense.

753. Κρονίωνα: the son of Kronos, Zeus; as well as the common Greek patronymic in -ιδης (e.g. l. 756), Homer uses also forms in -ιος (adjectival, cp. l. 108) and -ιων, as here.

761. ἀνέντες: 'having let loose'.

765. ἄγρει: This verb appears in the Homeric dialect only in the imperative.
μάν: μήν.
ἔπορσον: aorist imperative,
ἀγελείην: 'she who brings in the booty'; it should not be forgotten that Athene is a fighting goddess.

770. ὅσσον: accusative of extent.
ἠεροειδές: to be taken predicatively with ὅσσον; 'as far as a man sees into the misty distance'.
ἴδεν: gnomic aorist (l. 88).

773. ποταμώ: the two rivers named in the next line.

777. ἀμβροσίην: divine food for divine horses.
νέμεσθαι: 'to feed on'.

778. βάτην: dual of aorist ἔβην.
ἴθματα: accusative of respect.

781. ἔστασαν: pluperfect, with imperfect meaning; 'were standing'.
βίην Διομήδεος: cp. l. 638 n.

785. This is the only mention of Stentor in Homer; from it the power of his voice has become proverbial.

786. αὐδήσασκε: frequentative tense, of a repeated action.

787. αἰδώς: nominative used as an exclamation, 'Shame!'

εἶδος ἀγητοί: 'much admired for your physical appearance'; a scornful remark.

791. κοίλῃς ἐπὶ νηυσί: an exaggeration. This line recurs at XIII 107, where it is factually correct.

795. I.e. the wound he received in l. 98.

796. The sweat under the shield-strap was making the wound sore. The strap of the hand-grip shield would go over the right shoulder, as also would the sword-strap (Lorimer, *Homer and the Monuments*, p. 182).

797. κάμνε δὲ χεῖρα: His right arm and hand were tired, with the ache of the wound and with holding the spear.

798. ἂν δ᾽ ἴσχων: ἀνίσχων δέ.

800–13. Athene's speech takes the form of a mythological example aimed at goading Diomedes to fight on. It is composed in the common 'ring-form': (1) Tydeus' son is not as good as *he* was. (2) Here is a story showing what Tydeus was like. (3) But his son is not as good as *he* was.

The incident described was part of the preliminaries to that war of Seven against Thebes which was the main event in the *Theban* (as opposed to the *Trojan*) cycle of legends; cp. l. 116 n. (It is told more fully in IV 382–400.)

801. It is interesting that Tydeus is described as having been a small man. Pindar even makes Herakles small (*Isth.* IV 57). Odysseus (III 193–4) is not so much small as stocky.

804. Καδμείωνας and 807. Καδμείων: Kadmeans, the old name for the people of Thebes, Kadmos having been the founder of the city.

807. προκαλίζετο: 'challenged them' to athletic contests – which would not be clear if the more specific description of book IV were not available for comparison. It is worth comparing ll. 807–8 with the two very similar lines IV 389–90:

ἀλλ᾽ ὅ γ᾽ ἀεθλεύειν προκαλίζετο, πάντα δ᾽ ἐνίκα
ῥηιδίως· τοίη οἱ ἐπίρροθος ἦεν Ἀθήνη.

808. ἦα: ἦν.

812. ἀκήριον: 'without heart', 'cowardly'.

813: Οἰνεΐδαο: Tydeus' father was Oineus, king of Calydon.

817. Diomedes answers in reverse order the two alternative charges of Athene in ll. 811–12, that he is either tired or afraid.

818. σέων ἐφετμέων: i.e. the instructions Athene gave him in ll. 129–32.

ἐφετμέων: for ἐφετμάων, by Ionic metathesis of vowels (cp. l. 159 n. and Introduction, p. xiii). Also σεων. In both words there is contraction or *synizesis* of the final syllable -εων.

823. ἀλήμεναι: for ἀλῆναι, from the same verb as εἰλόμενοι (l. 782).

824. μάχην ἀνά: ἀνὰ μάχην.

826. ἐμῷ κεχαρισμένε θυμῷ: cp. l. 243 n.

827. τό γε: 'on *this* account'.

830. σχεδίην: originally an adjective, with a noun such as πληγήν understood; now used adverbially, 'at close quarters'.

831. τυκτὸν κακόν: neuter; 'a manufactured evil', i.e. 'complete'.

832. The promise seems to be invented to justify Athene's anger against Ares. Similar invention of a plausible promise or boast in a speech will be found at I 396 ff., XXI 475 ff.

834. τῶν δέ: the Argives.

λέλασται: perfect middle of λανθάνω.

835. Athene is polite enough to Diomedes, but does not waste time on Sthenelos.

836. πάλιν ἐρύσασα: 'pulling him back'; the back of the chariot was open.

842. Although the gods take part in the battle and encourage the heroes, this is the only occasion in the *Iliad* where a god personally kills one of the human fighters. The fact that it is Ares, the god of war and therefore responsible for killing in war, helps to make this acceptable. The gods often seem to act simultaneously on both the physical and the figurative level.

843. ὄχα: 'by far'; the word only occurs in the phrase ὄχ᾽ ἄριστος.

845. "Αιδος κυνέην: "Αιδος is genitive; the 'cap of darkness' which makes its wearer invisible is a folk-tale feature. In Greek it is called 'the helmet of Hades', with a clear allusion to the apparent etymology of Ἀϝίδης – 'unseen' (cp. μή μιν ἴδοι).

851. ὠρέξατο: 'lunged'; but he must have thrown the spear, not merely lunged with it, as is shown by ll. 853–4. Ares is fighting from the ground, against Diomedes in his chariot; the yoke and reins of this line are therefore those of Diomedes' chariot.

854. ὑπέκ: 'out of'.

ἐτώσιον ἀιχθῆναι: explanatory infinitive.

858. οὖτα: cp. l. 376 n.

859. ἔβραχε: 'shrieked'; the word is not normally used of sounds made by living creatures.

860. ἐπίαχον: imperfect being used like a gnomic aorist (l. 88).

864–5. It is not clear to what meteorological phenomenon the departure of Ares is compared. Most suitable would be a whirlwind or tornado, called in Greek πρηστήρ, and associated with very hot weather.

865. Take ἔξ with καύματος; 'after (or 'as a result of') burning heat'. The word-order makes it difficult to take ἐκ καύματος as dependent on the genitive absolute ὀρνυμένοιο. It is best to translate the phrases in the order in which they appear in the lines: 'Like a black (column of) air which appears out of the clouds, as a result of the heat, while a violent wind arises.'

874. χάριν φέροντες: cp. l. 211.

875. μαχόμεσθα: 'we are annoyed'; for the ending, cp. χαζώμεσθα (l. 34) and δεδμήμεσθα (l. 878).

σὺ γὰρ τέκες: This may well be a reference to Zeus having been the *sole* parent of Athene (born from his head, according to the legend); cp. αὐτὸς ἐγείναο (l. 880).

κούρην: Athene.

876. οὐλομένην: 'accursed'; this is the aorist participle middle, ὀλομένην, with the first syllable lengthened to allow it to fit into hexameter verse. The usage is exactly parallel, though on a more dignified plane, to the English slang epithet 'perishing'. Cp. οὖλος (l. 461).

878. δεδμήμεσθα: 'we are subject to'.

879. προτιβάλλεαι: προσβάλλει; 'pay attention to'.

880. αὐτὸς ἐγείναο: cp. l. 875 n.

881. ὑπερφίαλον: This, the reading of Aristarchus, is followed by the Oxford text and many other modern editions; the vulgate reading ὑπέρθυμον is more natural and should be retained.

885. ἦ τέ κε δηρόν . . . 887: Ares' alternatives are a little confused. As he was immortal, death would not have been possible; he therefore makes an artificial distinction between a long period of pain, lying

among the corpses and a total loss of strength as a result of the beating he might have received (though still remaining alive). Cp. l. 388 n.

892. μητρός τοι: 'your mother' (l. 125 n.). Ares was the son of Hera; and, as Zeus says (l. 894), it was his own mother who had asked (ll. 757 ff.) that he should be curbed.

ἐπιεικτόν: 'yielding'.

893. σπουδῇ: 'with difficulty'; Zeus sometimes finds it hard to exert his authority over his wife.

897. τευ: του, τινός.

γένευ: ἐγενου.

898. ἐνέρτερος Οὐρανιώνων: 'lower than the sons of Ouranos'; that is, the Titans, who supported Kronos son of Ouranos and were banished with him to Tartaros by Zeus. Tartaros is as far below Hades as heaven is above the earth (VIII 16). Elsewhere Οὐρανίωνες means the gods, the sons of heaven.

899. Παιήονα: cp. l. 401 n.

ἀνώγειν: pluperfect, with ν-movable.

902–3. This is an interesting simile, the clotting of blood being compared to the curdling of milk to make cheese, by the use of juice from the fig-tree as rennet.

902. ἐπειγόμενος: 'quickly'.

903. περιτρέφεται: 'coagulates'.

κυκόωντι: 'for the person stirring it'.

905. As we learn from various places in the *Odyssey*, it was the task of the unmarried daughters of the house to bathe the distinguished visitor.

ἔσσε: ἕννυμι.

906. κύδεϊ γαίων: 'glorying in his superiority'; Ares is not upset for long by the treatment he received on the battlefield.

908. The epithets for Hera and Athene are found only here and in the same line (IV 8); both appear to be geographically derived. Hera was especially the goddess of Argos; Athene had a sanctuary at the small town of Alalkomenai in Boiotia (Pausanias, IX 33.5).

BOOK VI

*Continued Fighting; Meeting
of Glaukos and Diomedes;
Hektor in Troy*

1. 'The dreadful fighting of the Trojans and the Greeks was left to itself.' This takes up the position at the end of book v; the gods had been taking a part in the battle, but Ares was wounded by Diomedes supported by Athene, and book v ended with the statement that Hera and Athene followed Ares back to Olympos. So the human fighters are now left alone.

οἰώθη: from οἰόομαι (οἶος). The augment is very commonly omitted in Homer; cp. ῥῆξε (l. 6), τέτυκτο (l. 7), πῆξε (l. 10), etc.

Ἀχαιῶν: Notice that there are three names used by the poet indistinguishably for the Greeks – Achaians (Ἀχαιοί), Argives (Ἀργεῖοι) and Danaans (Δαναοί).

2. πολλά: neuter plural used as an adverb, 'much'.

ἔνθα καὶ ἔνθα: 'backwards and forwards'.

πεδίοιο: The genitive singular of -ος declension nouns and adjectives may be in -οιο as well as -ου. The genitive here is one of the ground covered, a sort of partitive genitive, 'over the plain'.

(The scansion of this line is noteworthy. It is one of the very few examples of a weak caesura in the fourth foot (ἴθυσε / μάχη), a feature avoided in hexameter verse.)

3. ἀλλήλων ἰθυνομένων: 'as they aimed at each other'. ἰθυνομένων is genitive absolute; ἀλλήλων is the common genitive with verbs of aiming or hitting.

χαλκήρεα: Attic χαλκήρη; uncontracted forms are common in Homer.

4. These are the two main rivers of the plain of Troy – Simoeis and Skamandros (or Xanthos).

ἰδέ: an alternative word for 'and'.

ῥοάων: Notice the normal genitive plural of the -α declension in Homer, in -αων (cp. Latin -arum).

5–36. The book begins with general fighting; first there are three scenes in which the successes of three particular Greek heroes are described in some detail (ll. 5–11, Aias; ll. 12–19, Diomedes; ll. 20–8, Euryalos), and then very briefly in eight lines the killing of their opponents by seven others of the Greeks (Polypoites, Odysseus, Teukros, Antilochos, Agamemnon, Leitos, Eurypylos). One definite effect of all this is to accentuate the superiority of the Greeks, for only Trojans are killed.

5. Αἴας Τελαμώνιος: Aias is called the son of Telamon, to distinguish him from the other Aias, the son of Oileus.

Τελαμώνιος: This is simply the adjective formed from the name of his father Telamon, used as a patronymic.

ἕρκος Ἀχαιῶν: 'bulwark of the Greeks'; Aias was the great defensive fighter.

6. ῥῆξε: from ῥήγνυμι; cp. l. 1 n.

ῥῆξε φάλαγγα: 'broke the line opposite him', by killing Akamas.

φόως = φάος (Attic φῶς), 'light'. (For the form, cp. note on ἀντιόωσιν, l. 127).

7. ἐνί = ἐν.

Θρήκεσσι: Attic would be Θρᾳξί; the η and α even after ε, ι, ρ is the most obvious Ionic feature of the Homeric dialect. The dative plural ending -εσσι is Aeolic.

τέτυκτο: pluperfect passive of τεύχω, here equivalent simply to 'was'.

ὃς ἄριστος ἐνὶ Θρήκεσσι ... Ἀκάμαντα: Akamas is named as one of the two leaders of the Thracians in the Catalogue of the Trojans and their allies in book II (II 844).

8. ἠΰν: This and ἐΰς are adjectives corresponding to the adverb εὖ.

9. τόν: 'him'; what later Greek knew as the definite article is still primarily a demonstrative pronoun in Homeric Greek.

ῥα: Homeric verse uses all three forms ἄρα (l. 2), ἄρ, and the enclitic ῥα, merely as required by the metre; the particle has a mild inferential force.

πρῶτος: repeated from l. 5.

κόρυθος φάλον: The meaning of φάλος is obscure. Opinion is divided between a 'horn' on the front of the helmet, and the 'crest-holder' running from front to back.

τόν ... φάλον: two accusatives with ἔβαλε.

11. χαλκείη: Although iron was in common use in Homer's own day, the epic tradition is nevertheless very consistent in keeping bronze as

the metal for weapons, as it had been in the Mycenaean age. Cp.
χαλκήρεα (l. 3).

τόν: 'him'; cp. l. 9.

ὄσσε: a second object of κάλυψεν; 'covered his eyes'.

12. βοὴν ἀγαθός: 'good at the war-cry'; βοήν is the common Greek accusative of respect, most regularly used with reference to parts of the body. βοή, if not a part of the body, is at least a bodily function.

The heroes shouted in battle, to encourage their own men and frighten the enemy; cp. βοὴ δ' ἄσβεστος ὀρώρει, 'unceasing shouts arose' (XI 500). To be 'good at the war-cry' was therefore a heroic quality.

13. Τευθρανίδην: 'son of Teuthras'; as well as the common Greek patronymic in -ιδης, Homer also uses forms in -ιος (adjectival, l. 5 n.) and -ιων (e.g. Κρονίωνι, l. 267).

'Αρίσβη: a town on the Hellespont, not far from Troy.

14–17. The poet sometimes diversifies a list of slayers and slain by giving us some details of the home life of a minor character before he came to the war. This Axylos had been a hospitable man, and had entertained all comers who passed by his house. With some pathos the poet comments that none of his guests was there to help him when Diomedes killed him.

15. φιλέεσκεν: Tenses in -σκον, formed from either present or aorist of the verb, are very common in Homer, as *frequentatives*. 'Used to give hospitality to.'

ὁδῷ ἔπι = ἐφ' ὁδῷ.

οἰκία: neuter plural, 'house'.

16. οἱ: dative of the third-person pronoun, 'for him'.

τῶν: 'of them'; cp. l. 9 n.

ἤρκεσε (from ἀρκέω): 'kept off'.

17. πρόσθεν ὑπαντιάσας: 'facing (Diomedes) in front of him'.

ἄμφω: 'both men', explained in the next line.

ἄμφω θυμόν: ἀπηύρα (ἀπαυράω), like other verbs of depriving, takes a double accusative.

18. Καλήσιον: The name looks like 'the Inviter' (καλέω) – a suitable name for the assistant of the hospitable Axylos.

19. ἔσκεν: frequentative (cp. l. 15), for ἦν.

τώ: dual, 'they two'.

ἐδύτην: dual of the aorist of δύνω.

γαῖαν ἐδύτην: 'their *souls* went below the earth', to Hades.

20. Euryalos is the third (with Diomedes and Sthenelos) of the leaders of the contingent from Argos (II 565). He now kills two *pairs* of opponents. This is because the individual fighters (as opposed to the mass of ordinary troops) operated in pairs, one to fight and one to drive the chariot.

21. νύμφη νηΐς: 'river nymph'.

22. Both Abarbareë and Boukolion are names that suggest they have some story behind them, but they are never heard of apart from this line.

23–4. If, as must be assumed, this is the famous Laomedon, king of Troy and father of Priam, then Boukolion was Priam's illegitimate elder brother.

24. σκότιον: 'clandestine', 'in secret'.

ἑ: 'him'.

25. ὄεσσι: dative plural of ὄϊς, 'sheep'.

μίγη: 'was joined'.

φιλότητι: the normal word for love-making.

26. διδυμάονε παῖδε: dual.

27. μέν = μήν.

ὑπέλυσε: 'loosed underneath', with special reference to the knees buckling; trans. 'brought down'.

28. Μηκιστηιάδης: The commonest form of patronymic is in -ιδης, here slightly lengthened to fit the metre. Euryalos was the son of Mekisteus, one of the Seven against Thebes (l. 223).

ἀπ' ὤμων τεύχε' ἐσύλα: It is normal practice for the Homeric warrior, when he has killed his opponent, to try to strip the armour from the dead body, both on account of its material value, and because of the extra glory that thus accrues to him.

29. Polypoites was a Lapith, son of Peirithoos, and leader of one of the contingents from Thessaly (II 740).

30. Περκώσιον: from Perkote, a town not far from Troy.

31. Teukros was half-brother to the Telamonian Aias.

32. Antilochos was the young son of Nestor (l. 33).

ἐνήρατο: from ἐναίρω.

34. εὐρρείταο: The old form of the genitive of -α declension masculines was in -αο.

35. ἕλε: εἷλε, 'killed', as often.

Leitos was one of the five leaders of the Boiotian contingent, which fills such a significant place at the beginning of the Catalogue of Ships, but plays so small a part in the rest of the *Iliad* (II 494).

36. Eurypylos was the leader of another of the contingents from Thessaly (II 736).

37. Ἄδρηστον: This, though with the Ionic η, is a name famous in mythology, Adrastos; its owner here, however, is not further defined, neither by patronymic nor by place of origin.

βοὴν ἀγαθός: cp. l. 12 n.

38. ἵππω: dual, because the heroes used a two-horse chariot. More duals follow, in ἀτυζομένω, βλαφθέντε, ἄξαντε, αὐτώ, ἐβήτην.

οἱ: cp. l. 16 n.; an ethic dative, '*his* horses'.

ἀτυζομένω: 'fleeing in terror'.

πεδίοιο: 'over the plain'; genitive of ground covered, as in l. 2.

39. ἔνι: cp. l. 7; here it follows its noun.

40. ἄξαντε: from ἄγνυμι.

ἐν πρώτῳ ῥυμῷ: 'at the front of the pole', where the yoke was attached.

αὐτὼ μέν: The horses went off by themselves, leaving the chariot and their hapless master behind.

ἐβήτην: cp. ἐδύτην (l. 19).

41. ᾗ: 'in the direction that'.

περ: The enclitic particle περ adds a slight stress to the preceding word.

οἱ ἄλλοι: 'the rest of the Trojans'; the Greek victory is now more like a rout.

φοβέοντο: not contracted; cp. χαλκήρεα (l. 3).

43. κονίῃσιν = κονίαις.

πάρ: the preposition παρά, shortened by *apocope* (the cutting-off of the last syllable).

πάρ . . . ἔστη: παρέστη, 'stood beside him (οἱ)'; the elements which later constituted a compound verb are still separable in Homer, with the preposition able to stand by itself as an adverb. The phenomenon is called *tmesis* (from τέμνω, 'cut'). In practice one may treat this as if a verb has been divided into its two parts, although the true situation is that the two parts have not yet coalesced.

44. 'Ατρείδης: Both Agamemnon and Menelaos were sons of Atreus.

45. λαβὼν γούνων: 'taking hold of his knees', in the position of a suppliant. γούνων is the partitive genitive common with verbs of touching or holding.

46. 'Ατρέος: genitive of 'Ατρεύς.
ἄξια: 'suitable'.
δέξαι: aorist imperative middle.

47. ἐν ἀφνειοῦ πατρός: understand δόμῳ.

48. σιδηρός: cp. l. 11 n.; Homer consistently treats iron as a rare and valuable metal. The adjective πολύκμητος probably refers to the difficulty of working iron in those early days.

49. κεν: κε (κεν) is the alternative form of the modal particle ἄν, and is used in the same way.
τοι: the same as the enclitic σοι, the unstressed dative of σύ.
χαρίσαιτο 'would give freely'.

50. εἴ κεν ... πεπύθοιτο: Homer is more flexible in conditional sentences than the rules followed by later writers, which would require either εἰ πύθοιτο or ἐὰν πύθηται here.
πεπύθοιτο: optative of an ancient reduplicated aorist of πυνθάνομαι.
νηυσίν = ναυσίν.

51. ὧς: Accented in this way (or with the circumflex ὦς), this is an adverb, = οὕτως, 'so'; the conjunction ὡς is unaccented.
φάτο: imperfect middle of φημί; there is no distinction of meaning from the active.
ἔπειθε: imperfect, 'was beginning to persuade him'.
This incident shows the character of Menelaos, kind-hearted and rather weak.

52. μιν: the epic form of νιν, accusative third-person pronoun, 'him'.
θοάς: 'swift', a common epithet of ships, even when they are, as here, drawn up on the beach.

53. ᾧ: 'his'.
καταξέμεν: The ending is an alternative infinitive ending. The tense, however, is not future, as might appear, but aorist, this being one of the *sigmatic second aorists*, in which the σ is added to the stem to form the aorist, as in the usual first aorist, but the endings are those of the second aorist; i.e. there are parts formed as if from an aorist κατῆξον as well as κατήγαγον. So καταξέμεν = καταγαγεῖν. The infinitive is explanatory, following δώσειν.

54. θέων 'running'.

ηὔδα: imperfect of αὐδάω.

Agamemnon is not so gentle as his younger brother; in fact his actions are often brutal, as they are here. This is a recognisable characteristic of one who has the heavy responsibility of being commander-in-chief.

55. πέπον: literally 'ripe' or 'soft' of fruit; used in Homer as a familiar form of address. Here it seems something of a remonstration, 'my dear Menelaos'.

τίη: often printed τί ἤ, 'why'.

κήδεαι: Attic κήδει, second-person singular.

56. ἦ: sarcastic, 'I suppose'.

κατὰ οἶκον: 'in your own house', referring of course to Paris.

57. πρός with the genitive: 'from the side of', 'by'.

μή τις ὑπεκφύγοι: a wish, as are the following optatives φύγοι and ἐξαπολοίατο.

58. μηδέ: 'not even'.

'Not even the male child whom the mother bears in her womb.'

59. φέροι: optative by attraction from the optative in the main clause.

ὅς: demonstrative, 'he'.

60. ἐξαπολοίατο = ἐξαπόλοιντο; it is a feature of the Ionic dialect that the ν of the third-person plural is sometimes vocalised as an α. Ἰλίου depends on the ἐξ of ἐξαπολοίατο.

ἄφαντοι: 'without trace'.

61. ἔτρεψεν: 'he changed'.

62. αἴσιμα παρειπών: 'persuading him with proper advice'.

ἕθεν = οὗ, genitive of the third-person pronoun.

ὤσατο: from ὠθέω.

63. Notice that it is Agamemnon who does the killing: cp. l. 54 n.

64. οὖτα: not a contracted imperfect, but a form of aorist, with short α.

ἀνετράπετο: aorist middle of ἀνατρέπω, 'fell back face upwards'.

Ἀτρείδης: Agamemnon.

65. λάξ: with βάς.

66. Νέστωρ: Nestor, the old king of Pylos, is the natural one to give tactical advice.

Ἀργείοισιν: cp. l. 1 n.

ἐκέκλετο: reduplicated aorist (cp. πεπύθοιτο, l. 50) of κέλομαι.

μακρὸν ἀύσας: 'with a great shout'.

68–71. 'Don't waste time now collecting booty.'

68. ἐπιβαλλόμενος: 'throwing himself at'.

69. ὥς κε (ἄν) + subjunctive: a purpose clause, as often.

70. καὶ τά: 'these things also'.

71. ἄμ: apocope (l. 43) for ἀνά, with ν changed to μ before π.

συλήσετε: with two accusatives, as ἀπηύρα (l. 17).

τεθνηῶτας: perfect participle of θνήσκω.

72. ὥς: cp. l. 51 n.

73. ἔνθα κεν αὖτε: 'then the next thing would have been that the Trojans, etc.'.

74. ἀναλκείῃσι: dative plural, as κονίῃσιν (l. 43); 'by their own lack of fighting spirit'.

76. οἰωνοπόλων: 'interpreters of the flight of birds', 'prophets'.

ὄχα: 'by far'; the word only occurs in the phrase ὄχ' ἄριστος.

77. ὔμμι: ὑμῖν.

78. Τρώων καὶ Λυκίων: genitive after μάλιστα.

Λυκίων: most important of the Trojans' allies, and thus representative of them.

ἐγκέκλιται: (ἐγκλίνω), 'rests on'.

79. ἰθύν: a noun, 'enterprise'.

80. στῆτ' αὐτοῦ: 'make a stand here'.

πυλάων: cp. l. 4 n.

83. ἐποτρύνητον: subjunctive dual.

85. καί ... περ: καίπερ.

86. Ἕκτορ, ἀτὰρ σύ: It is normal in Greek for the address to a person in the vocative to be treated as external to the sentence, and thus for the connecting particle to follow it.

ἀτὰρ σύ: responds to ἡμεῖς μέν of l. 84.

πόλινδε: The suffix -δε with the accusative shows motion towards.

μετέρχεο: μετέρχου, imperative.

It may well be, and has been, objected that this is not a good time for Hektor to leave his army. The purpose of course is to motivate his visit to Troy, and in particular to give an opportunity for the scene with Andromache.

87. μητέρι σῇ καὶ ἐμῇ: Hekabe.

ἡ δέ: The instructions to Hekabe are given in direct speech.

γεραιάς: the matrons of Troy, corresponding to the male γέροντες. Our ancient sources quote a variant reading γεραίρας ('matrons of honour') here and in l. 270 (but not in ll. 287 or 296). The chief argument in its favour is that Andromache, who is not old, is by implication included among the γεραιαί in l. 379. The variant reading is supported by many modern commentators, following Schultz, *Quaestiones Epicae* (1892), p. 501, but not as yet by most editors of the text. There is no strong reason to make the change; inclusion among the γεραιαί can well be a mark of honour rather than age.

88. νηόν: Ionic for normal Greek ναόν, Attic νεών; it is accusative of the end of motion, 'to the temple'.

'Αθηναίης: The Trojans worship the same gods as the Greeks. One special function of Athene was as tutelary deity of cities (cp. ῥυσίπτολι, l. 305); it is therefore not surprising that there should be a temple of Athene on the acropolis of Troy, although the goddess is so pro-Greek in the *Iliad*.

γλαυκώπιδος: The word doubtless meant 'bright-eyed' or 'grey-eyed' to Homer, but this is not inconsistent with the possibility that it originally meant 'owl-faced', Athene having once been worshipped in the form of an owl; cp. βοῶπις πότνια "Ηρη (IV 50).

πόλει ἄκρῃ: the top of the city, the acropolis.

90. πέπλον: The offering of a robe to Athene may remind us of the procession at the Panathenaic festival at Athens, well known from the sculptures on the frieze of the Parthenon. There is no need, however, to suspect Athenian influence on this passage in Homer. Offerings of robes to Athene are known to have occurred elsewhere in the Greek world as well as at Athens.

ἠδέ: a word for 'and'.

91. οἱ . . . αὐτῇ: ἑαυτῇ, 'to herself'.

92. θεῖναι: infinitive for imperative; 'let her place'.

ἐπὶ γούνασιν: This implies a seated statue of the goddess; if so, it is the only reference in Homer to a cult image, seated or not.

93. ὑποσχέσθαι: infinitive for imperative again (ὑπισχνέομαι).

94. ἤνις (accusative plural, for ἤνιας) ἠκέστας: The adjectives are of uncertain meaning. They recur only in the two repetitions in this book, ll. 275 and 309, and ἤνις in another phrase βοῦν ἤνιν

H

εὐρυμέτωπον at x 292 and *Od.* III 382. Traditionally, they are explained as ἦνις, 'one year old', ἤκεστος, 'that has not felt the goad' (ἀ-κεντέω), 'unbroken'.

ἱερευσέμεν: future infinitive; cp. l. 53 n.

αἰ: the Aeolic form of εἰ; αἴ κε = ἐάν. Trans. 'in the hope that'.

96. ὥς κεν . . . ἀπόσχῃ: purpose; cp. l. 69 n.

Τυδέος υἱόν: Diomedes, son of Tydeus.

ἱρῆς: ἱερῆς.

99. ἐδείδιμεν: (δείδω) pluperfect.

100. θεᾶς ἐξ: ἐκ θεᾶς. Achilleus' mother was the sea-goddess Thetis.

ἔμμεναι: εἶναι.

103. ἆλτο: aorist of ἅλλομαι.

106. ἔσταν: a shorter form of the third-person plural, = ἔστησαν; cp. φάν for ἔφασαν (l. 108), ἐλέλιχθεν for ἠλελίχθησαν (l. 109).

108. φάν: cp. l. 106 n.; 'they thought'.

109. ὡς ἐλέλιχθεν: exclamatory, 'how they had turned to fight'; trans. 'seeing how'.

112. ἀνέρες: ἄνδρες.

113–15. Some difficulty has been caused by Hektor's words here, in that they do not coincide with Helenos' instructions in ll. 86–97, nor indeed with what Hektor in fact does in Troy. Instead of saying that he will ask the γεραιαί to pray to Athene, offering twelve cattle, he says he will tell 'the γέροντες and our wives' to pray to 'the gods' and promise 'hekatombs'. The difficulties are more apparent than real. Public statements are for public consumption; Hektor merely generalises what he intends to do, and chooses words which will not alarm the troops.

113. βήω: aorist subjunctive of βαίνω, Attic βῶ.

προτί: πρός.

114. ἡμετέρης: ἡμετέραις.

115. ἑκατόμβας: supposedly of 'a hundred' animal victims, but used of any large sacrifice.

117. ἀμφί: adverb; 'around him'. It was a large shield, and it covered him 'on both sides'.

μιν σφυρά: two objects of τύπτε, of 'the whole and the part'.

δέρμα: Shields were made of layers of ox-hide; here the hide which is being referred to is the part which was turned up at the edge of the shield to make a rim.

The description of Hektor's shield slung round his back and hitting his neck and ankles as he walked is one of the few memories in the *Iliad* of the old Mycenaean body-shield. Most of the heroes, and indeed Hektor himself, use a round shield; but Aias, three times 'carrying his shield like a tower' (e.g. VII 219), Hektor in our passage, and the unfortunate Periphetes in XV 645–6, reflect the older type of armament.

118. ἄντυξ ἣ πυμάτη θέεν: 'which ran as the outer rim'; ἄντυξ πυμάτη is predicative with the verb θέεν; ἥ, which really refers to δέρμα, is attracted into the gender of ἄντυξ.

ὀμφαλοέσσης: If this word means 'having a central boss', which is natural (ὀμφαλός means 'navel'), then it is more suitable as a description of the round shield than of the tall body-shield. It is likely enough that the poet is not wholly clear what he is describing.

119–236. The famous scene of chivalry between Glaukos and Diomedes, two opponents in the battle who find they have family ties of friendship, fills the time between Hektor's departure for Troy (ll. 116–18) and his arrival at the Skaian gate (l. 237).

119. Γλαῦκος: Sarpedon's friend and fellow commander of the Lykians (II 876).

120. συνίτην: dual of the imperfect of σύνειμι, came together'.

μεμαῶτε: 'eager', a participle from the shorter stem of the perfect μέμονα.

123. ἐσσί: εἶ.

124. It is idle to ask why Diomedes has not seen Glaukos before; his ignorance is necessary for the present scene.

126. ὅ τε: accusative neuter of the relative, used adverbially, 'with respect to the fact that', 'in that'. It is not distinguishable in meaning from ὅτι, which, however, is never elided. The τε in ὅ τε has a certain generalising effect which is not translatable; cp. the note on the following line.

127. δυστήνων παῖδες: 'unhappy are the parents whose sons'; a clever expression.

τε: τε is often present in proverbial or general statements. It is not to be translated.

ἀντιόωσιν: This, from the verb ἀντιάω, would if uncontracted be ἀντιάουσιν, if contracted ἀντιῶσιν. By a peculiarity of Homeric

Greek (caused no doubt by the opposed pressures of contraction of vowels and the requirements of the metre), the contracted form has suffered a sort of expansion or distension. This, technically called *diektasis*, is found particularly with verbs in -αω.

129–41. Diomedes' statement that he would not wish to fight with a god is made more forcible by a mythological example. The passage has the common 'ring-form', in five parts: (1) I would not fight with the gods. (2) Lykourgos, who did so, did not live for long. (3) This was his story. (4) He did not live for long. (5) Nor would *I* wish to fight with the gods. The story itself exemplifies a common theme, of the fatal results when a mortal presumes to challenge a god. Compare Thamyris in II 594–600, Bellerophontes in ll. 200–2 below, and Niobe in XXIV 602–9.

129. It has seemed strange to commentators that one who fought two gods in book V should say without further comment in book VI that he would not fight with the gods. A sufficient explanation is that Diomedes is here expressing a general, universally acknowledged, point of view; his particular deeds in book V are hardly relevant.

130. A mythological example regularly begins καὶ γάρ; here, as the first sentence is negative, it begins οὐδὲ γάρ. The second οὐδέ stresses Δρύαντος υἱός. Trans. 'for indeed even the son of Dryas, strong Lykourgos, was not long-lived'.

Lykourgos was a king of Thrace who tried to drive out the new Bacchic religion from his country, as Pentheus did from Thebes (see Euripides' *Bacchae*). That he chased the 'nurses' of Dionysos down from the mountain, striking them with an ox-goad, and that Dionysos himself took refuge with the goddess Thetis in the sea, is a strange and primitive tale, which seems to display a familiarity with some of the aetiological stories connected with the cult of Dionysos (W. K. C. Guthrie, *The Greeks and their Gods* (1950) pp. 161–2).

131. δήν: 'for long'.

132. μαινομένοιο: 'wild'.

τιθήνας: the nymphs of the sacred mountain Nysa, who looked after the baby Dionysos (Homeric Hymn XXVI 3).

133. Νυσήιον: understand ὄρος, the Nysaean Mount, Mount Nysa.

134. θύσθλα: probably the wands, or *thyrsi*, carried by the Bacchants.

135. βουπλῆγι: 'ox-goad'. There may be some connection with the identification in Dionysiac religion of the god and a bull.

136. δύσετο: sigmatic second aorist; cp. l. 53 n. The mention of nurses (l. 132), Dionysos' fright (l. 135), and Thetis' bosom (l. 136) all suggest that Dionysos is thought of as still a baby when he suffered this persecution.

138. τῷ μεν: Lykourgos.

ῥεῖα ζώοντες: 'living in ease', as opposed to mortal men.

ζώοντες: ζῶντες.

139. Κρόνου πάις: Zeus.

143. θᾶσσον: This, the comparative adverb of ταχύς, is used without any particular comparative sense, 'quickly'.

ὀλέθρου πείρατα: *either* 'the end, which is death' (as θανάτοιο τέλος, III 309); *or* 'the snares of death'. (The meaning of the very difficult word πείρατα is fully discussed by Merry and Riddell on *Od.* XII 51, and Leaf on *Iliad* VII 102.)

ἵκηαι: subjunctive, ἵκῃ.

145. τίη: cp. l. 55 n.

146. 'As is the generation of leaves, so are the generations of men.' This famous line inspired the elegiac comment ascribed either to the poet Simonides or to his near namesake Semonides of Amorgos:

ἓν δὲ τὸ κάλλιστον Χῖος ἔειπεν ἀνήρ·
οἵη περ φύλλων γενεή, τοίη δὲ καὶ ἀνδρῶν.

(Simonides fr. 85 Bergk[4], discussed by J. A. Davison, *From Archilochus to Pindar* (London, 1968), pp. 72–7.)

δέ: the so-called *apodotic* δέ, introducing the main sentence after a subordinate clause.

147–9. Broccia (*Struttura e Spirito*, p. 88) points out that in the lines explaining the simile the emphasis in the case of the leaves is on new birth and the springtime; but in the case of humanity the final image is of death (ἡ δ' ἀπολήγει).

147. φύλλα: This is then distributed into τὰ μέν, ἄλλα δέ.

τε: This particle demonstrates its affinity to generalising statements (l. 127 n.) by appearing twice in this line.

148. τηλεθόωσα: *diektasis*; cp. ἀντιόωσιν (l. 127).

ἔαρος δ' ἐπιγίγνεται ὥρη: What we should treat as a subordinate temporal clause appears in Homer as a separate, paratactic, main sentence.

149. φύει: Here the word must be intransitive; in the previous line it was transitive.

150. εἰ δ᾽ ἐθέλεις καὶ ταῦτα δαήμεναι: Glaukos, having pointed out the unimportance of family histories, proceeds nevertheless to tell his own family history at length. Aineias behaves in a very similar way in book xx when he is unlucky enough to meet Achilleus in the battle, recounting his family background in what certainly appears to be a nervous manner; the present line appears there as xx 213.

δαήμεναι: infinitive (for δαῆναι) from aorist ἐδάην; 'to learn'.

152. Several cities were called Ephyra. The traditional understanding of this one is that it is Corinth, and indeed both Sisyphos and Bellerophontes were later definitely heroes of Corinth. If this is the case, however, the description μυχῷ Ἄργεος ἱπποβότοιο is difficult to understand. It ought to mean 'in the innermost corner of horse-rearing Argos', whereas Corinth is at the northern extremity of Argos (whether defined as the whole Peloponnese or the domain of the king of Mykenai) and can only with difficulty be described as 'in a corner', as it lies in the key position on the road which connects the Peloponnese with north Greece.

153. Sisyphos was one of the great sinners whose punishment is described in Odysseus' visit to the underworld in book xi of the *Odyssey* (*Od.* xi 593–600). His actual offence is obscure, but his name in legend is that of the craftiest of men (κέρδιστος, as here).

ὅ: for ὅς, the later article being occasionally used as a relative.

154. Αἰολίδης: 'son of Aiolos', the ancestor of the Aiolian race.

155. Βελλεροφόντην: Glaukos now tells the story of Bellerophontes (later known as Bellerophon) from ll. 156 to 205. It has been noticed that the story is told in an *allusive* way, with many details and explanations not supplied, as if this is based on a longer and more accurate version known to the poet. The same impression is given elsewhere in the *Iliad*, where a mythological story outside the scope of the Trojan legends is told, particularly in the tale of Meleagros in book ix. Points which the poet leaves us in ignorance of are: the name of the king of Lykia (ll. 173, etc.); the name of his daughter, whom Bellerophontes married (l. 192); the divine parentage of the Chimaira (l. 180); the cause of the gods' hatred of Bellerophontes (l. 200), and of Artemis' anger against his daughter (l. 205). Moreover the winged horse Pegasos is not mentioned in this version of the story, whether through intentional omission or not (l. 179 n.).

156–9. These lines summarise in advance the results of the story up to l. 170. 160–70 then come as an explanation of a statement already made.

156. κάλλος τε καὶ ἠνορέην: These two qualities he shows in the later story.

157. Προῖτος: Proitos of Argos was king of Tiryns. Either Bellerophontes in Corinth must have come under Proitos' sovereignty, just as in the Catalogue of Ships in book II Corinth is subject to the king of Mykenai; or, as ancient mythographers told it, Bellerophontes had killed a man, and had come to Proitos to be cleansed of the blood-guilt.

159. Ἀργείων: dependent on ἐκ δήμου in the previous line.

ἐδάμασσε: It is not easy to decide whether the object of this verb is 'them' (the Argives) or 'him' (Bellerophontes). On balance, the former is preferable; the statement merely explains that Proitos was ruler over the Argives.

160. γυνή: 'wife'.

ἐπεμήνατο: (ἐπιμαίνομαι) 'was mad with love for'.

161. φιλότητι μιγήμεναι: cp. l. 25 n. μιγήμεναι = μιγῆναι; cp. δαήμεναι (l. 150).

162. ἀγαθὰ φρονέοντα: 'as his thoughts were righteous'.

164. τεθναίης: perfect optative; a wish that is like a command.

κάκτανε: for κατάκτανε, by apocope (l. 43).

165. μ': μοι, as is shown by ἐθελούσῃ; this is a rare elision.

166. οἷον ἄκουσε: exclamatory; cp. ὡς ἐλέλιχθεν (l. 109). Trans. 'at what he heard'.

168. Λυκίηνδε: This is the Lykia of Sarpedon and Glaukos, at the south-west corner of Asia Minor.

168–9. This is the only reference to writing in Homer. The recent decipherment of the Linear B tablets from Knossos and Pylos encourages one to believe that here in the Bellerophontes story there is a memory that has survived from the Mycenaean age. The position no doubt is that the poet himself was aware of the art of alphabetical writing, which the Greek world borrowed from the Phoenicians in the eighth century; but it would have been too much of an anachronism to describe such an innovation in heroic verse. Rather the vague neuter plurals σήματα λυγρά, θυμοφθόρα πολλά, reflect a dim memory, preserved in the poetic tradition, of the Mycenaean syllabic script.

170. ἠνώγειν: pluperfect, with ν-movable.

ᾧ πενθερῷ: 'his father-in-law'; the king of Lykia, then, was Anteia's father. Later sources give his name as Iobates.

172. There was a river Xanthos in Lykia as well as Troy (l. 4).

174. It was normal politeness to entertain the guest and give him food before you asked him any questions, as may be seen on various occasions in the *Odyssey*. Nine days seems somewhat exaggerated, but this is a royal court, and an important visitor.

177. φέροιτο: middle, 'brought with him'; the optative is that of a subordinate clause in historic sequence in indirect speech.

179. πρῶτον μέν: The story of Bellerophontes now becomes a common type of folk-tale. The young man is set three tasks of great difficulty and danger, and on their successful completion he is rewarded with the hand of the king's daughter in marriage, and half of the kingdom. It has often been noted that Homer says nothing about Bellerophontes' 'secret weapon', which is elsewhere an essential feature of his story, namely the winged horse Pegasos. The probable reason is not that Pegasos is a post-Homeric addition to the legend, but that Homer and Homeric poetry is realistic, and consciously avoids anything magical or supernatural in the activities of human beings.

Χίμαιραν: here the name of the composite monster described in l. 181; in that line χίμαιρα has its usual meaning, 'goat'.

ἀμαιμακέτην: a word whose etymology and meaning are both unknown; perhaps 'raging'.

180. ἀνθρώπων: with γένος.

181. This is the only example of a mythical composite animal in Homer, unless one counts the centaurs, who are not specifically described. It is worth noticing that the animal is not Greek, but from the East, where such things were commoner. The rather fuller description of Hesiod (*Theog.* 319–24), followed by representations in ancient art, shows an animal with three heads – a lion in front, a snake for a tail, and a goat's head growing from its back.

182. δεινόν: From its position in the line, this is probably an adverb, 'dreadfully'.

183. θεῶν τεράεσσι πιθήσας: 'paying attention to signs from the gods'. There is an automatic assumption that success in a difficult undertaking implies the help of the gods; cp. l. 171, θεῶν ὑπ' ἀμύμονι πομπῇ.

184. The second task is to fight the Solymi. Such evidence as there is suggests that these were the original people of the country, displaced by the Lykians when they came (Herodotos, 1 173).

185. καρτίστην: κρατίστην.
δύμεναι: δῦναι, 'entered'.

186. The third task is to fight the Amazons. This mythical race of female warriors has been held to contain a memory of the invading tribes at the time of the break-up of the Hittite empire in the twelfth century. In III 184–9, Priam says that he once fought on the side of the Phrygians by the banks of the river Sangarios 'on the day when the Amazons came'.

ἀντιανείρας: 'women with the strength of men'.

187–90. This is a typical heroic adventure, the ambush that waits to kill him on his return; the same happens to Tydeus in IV 391–8. The adventure does not fit very well with the three folklore tasks of ll. 179–86.

ὕφαινε: i.e. the king of Lykia.

189. εἶσε: ἵζω.
τοί: an alternative form of the nominative plural οἱ.

191. γίγνωσκε: i.e. the king. He recognised Bellerophontes' quality by his deeds.

θεοῦ γόνον: He is described as son of Glaukos in l. 155, but in other versions his father is Poseidon.

ἠύν: cp. l. 8 n.

192. ἥν: 'his'.

193. τιμῆς βασιληίδος: 'royal honours', as opposed to 'honour', i.e. he shared with Bellerophontes the prerogatives and material advantages of kingship.

βασιληίδος: adjective.

194. καὶ μέν: καὶ μήν.
οἱ: 'for him'.
τέμενος: (from τέμνω, which explains the use of the verb τάμον) a piece of land separated off from the common land of the tribe or people, for the private possession of a god or king; 'domain'.

195. Notice that the first syllable of καλόν (originally καλϝον) can be scanned long.

φυταλιῆς καὶ ἀρούρης: genitive dependent on τέμενος, 'consisting of, etc.'

νέμοιτο: 'cultivate'.

196. Glaukos now completes his family tree. It is

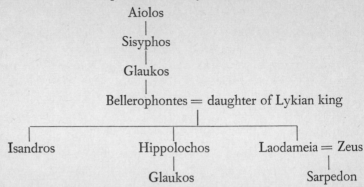

Aiolos

Sisyphos

Glaukos

Bellerophontes = daughter of Lykian king

Isandros   Hippolochos   Laodameia = Zeus

                      Glaukos   Sarpedon

198. μητίετα: nominative.

200–2. The description of the later fate of Bellerophontes clearly inter-
rupts the history of his three children. The μέν of l. 198 corresponds to
the δέ's of ll. 203 and 206. To move ll. 200–2 after l. 205, as suggested
by Leaf, does not help, as they would still interrupt the story of the
three children. Indeed there is no better position for them, because
Glaukos will wish to carry straight on to talk of himself after the
mention of his father (l. 206) as third of the children of Bellerophontes.
It seems that these three lines are an insertion by somebody, whether
the *Iliad* poet or another, who did not wish to omit the final fate of
Bellerophontes, and chose an awkward moment for it rather than none
at all.

200. καὶ κεῖνος: 'he also'; it is not easy to make sense of καί. If, as
Ameis–Hentze and others suggest, the reference is back to Lykourgos
in l. 138, then it is far-fetched, although it is true that the Lykourgos
story was told by Diomedes in this same conversation. Alternatively,
if ll. 200–2 are, as suggested above, an insertion in a previously existing
sequence about the children of Bellerophontes, the καί may have been
more intelligible in a previous setting (perhaps a catalogue of those
mythological figures who have incurred the hostility of the gods).

The poet does not explain why Bellerophontes was 'hated by all the
gods'. Fortunately Pindar, in *Olympian* XIII and *Isthmian* VII, gives us
sufficient information. Bellerophontes fell into the pattern of Lykourgos and others (ll. 129–41 n.), who through forgetfulness of their own
insignificance as human beings infringed the prerogatives of the gods,
i.e. got above themselves. In a fine allegorical image, similar to that of
Ikaros flying too high and too near the sun, Bellerophontes was said to

have tried to fly Pegasos to heaven, the home of the gods; he was un-
seated by Zeus, and wandered about alone and mad.

201. κάπ: *apocope* (l. 43) for κατά; the τ has then been assimilated to the
first letter of πεδίον.

The Aleian plain was said to have been in Kilikia, in the south of
Asia Minor. There is a sort of etymological play on words between
Ἀλήιον and ἀλᾶτο.

205. χολωσαμένη: Artemis is regularly the goddess responsible for the
sudden death of women. Why she should have been angry is not
stated; most probably because of Laodameia's presumption in having
been loved by Zeus.

ἔκτα: an aorist form from κτείνω.

208. A fine statement of the competitive heroic code. The line recurs in
XI 784, as advice to Achilleus from his father Peleus.

214. μειλιχίοισι: understand ἔπεσι.

215. νυ: a form of the enclitic νυν; ἦ ῥά νυ, 'well then'.

ξεῖνος: In those far-distant days of separate communities, in which
a stranger might be in considerable danger, some security was provided
by a system of family friendship, or (as it is called) 'guest-friendship'.
ξεῖνος (ξένος) means a stranger, but it also means a host or a guest.
The tie of having been entertained in somebody's house in a strange
land, and having exchanged gifts, was remembered into the following
generations, and even the actual gifts exchanged were recalled, as here.

216. Οἰνεύς: Oineus was king of Calydon, father of Tydeus, and thus
grandfather of Diomedes.

217. ἐρύξας: cp. κατέρυκε (l. 192).

220. ἀμφικύπελλον: 'two-handled' is the most intelligible of the
various interpretations put forward for this word.

221. μιν: the cup.

ἰών: 'when I set out for Troy'.

222–3. The point of the reference to Tydeus is no doubt to explain
why the connection with Bellerophontes is known to him through his
grandfather and not his father.

223. κάλλιπε: κατέλιπε.

Tydeus was one of the seven southern Greek champions who
attacked Thebes in the unsuccessful expedition of the Seven against
Thebes, in the generation before the Trojan War.

224. τῷ: 'therefore'.

225. τῶν: i.e. of the Lykians.

226. καὶ δι' ὁμίλου: 'even in the thick of the battle'.

227. πολλοὶ μὲν γὰρ ἐμοί: understand εἰσί.

228. κιχείω: subjunctive as if from a verb in -μι (*κίχημι), which provides tenses serving as the aorist system of κιχάνω, 'find'.

230. ἐπαμείψομεν: aorist subjunctive; the form with the short vowel is normal.

232. φωνήσαντε: dual, as are the next two verbs.
     καθ' ἵππων: 'down from the chariot'.

234-6. 'Then Zeus son of Kronos took away the wits of Glaukos, in that he exchanged armour with Tydeus' son Diomedes, giving golden armour in return for bronze, armour worth a hundred oxen in return for armour worth nine.' These lines have been much discussed. It has seemed to modern critics disconcerting that the chivalrous meeting between Glaukos and Diomedes should end with the intrusion of such materialistic considerations. But in fact the Homeric heroes are materialists, and like the accumulation of property both for its own sake and for the sake of the honour that it brings. One may compare the practice of stripping the armour from one's dead opponents; Diomedes' arrangement with Sthenelos in v 260 ff.; Odysseus' simple pleasure at collecting gifts in Scheria in the Odyssey; and Phoinix' final argument to Achilleus in IX 598 and 602. Thus to get far the better of the exchange of armour is a form of success for Diomedes.

234. φρένας ἐξέλετο: This is ἄτη, i.e. an infatuation which temporarily destroys a person's judgement, so that he behaves as he would not normally behave.

236. Notice that value is reckoned in numbers of oxen.

237-529. Hektor's visit to Troy. This famous scene derives its great effectiveness from Hektor's conversations with the three women of Troy, the non-combatants in the war – his mother Hekabe (ll. 251-85), Helen, the cause of the war (ll. 343-68), and his wife Andromache (ll. 394-502).

239. εἰρόμεναι: 'asking about'.

241. ἐφῆπτο: lit. 'had been attached to'; 'were in store for'.

243. ξεστῆς αἰθούσῃσι: 'with colonnades (or porticos) of smoothed

stone'. These colonnades were around the courtyard (αὐλή, l. 247) at one side of which was the main building of the palace.

αὐτὰρ ἐν αὐτῷ: This begins a parenthesis which goes on to l. 250. In l. 251 there then comes the main clause completing the sentence which began with ἀλλ' ὅτε δή in l. 242.

ἐν αὐτῷ: 'in the building itself'. Priam's sons had their rooms in the palace itself; his sons-in-law had quarters opposite, on the other side of the courtyard (ll. 247–50).

244. πεντήκοντα: Obviously fifty is the traditional number of the sons of Priam, an eastern king; he has twelve married daughters living with their husbands in the outbuildings of the palace, as well as some unmarried daughters, and no doubt others who live with their husbands away from Troy. Not all of these, of course, are the children of Hekabe. Twenty-two of Priam's sons and two of his sons-in-law are mentioned by name in the *Iliad*; half of them are killed in the course of the poem.

247. ἔνδοθεν αὐλῆς: see l. 243 n.

248. τέγεοι: 'roofed'.

251. ἠπιόδωρος: a charming epithet for a mother, 'loving giver'.
ἤλυθε: ἦλθε.
This line is the main sentence responding to the subordinate clause in l. 242, after the long parenthesis about the palace.

252. Λαοδίκην ἐσάγουσα (εἰσάγω): 'going in with Laodike'; Laodike was one of Priam's married daughters (III 123), and so lived in one of the θάλαμοι described in ll. 247–50.

253. ἔν τ' ἄρα οἱ φῦ χειρί: 'she held his hand tightly'; lit. 'she was *grafted* (ἐνέφυ, tmesis) into him by her hand'.

254. τίπτε: τί ποτε, 'why?'

255. δυσώνυμοι: 'evil', 'accursed'.

256. ἀνῆκεν: ἀνίημι.

256–7. ἐνθάδε is to be taken with ἐλθόντα, ἐξ ἄκρης πόλιος (= πόλεως) with ἀνασχεῖν.

258. ὄφρα κε: purpose; cp. ὥς κε (l. 69).
ἐνείκω: Attic ἐνέγκω, from φέρω.

259. σπείσῃς: σπένδω. It was the practice to put a little wine into the cup before drinking, and pour that out on the ground as a libation to the gods.

260. ὀνήσεαι: future.

πίησθα: The epic dialect possessed, for the three singular persons of the subjunctive, alternative endings in -ωμι, -ησθα, -ησι.

261. κεκμηῶτι: κάμνω.

μέγα: adverbial, with ἀέξει; 'greatly'.

262. τύνη: a strengthened form of σύ.

ἔτησι: 'kinsmen', i.e. those who have a tie of relationship more remote than the immediate family, but are of the same tribe; cp. l. 239.

264. ἄειρε: 'lift up', and so 'offer'.

265. μή: 'for fear that'.

267. Κρονίωνι: 'the son of Kronos', Zeus; cp. l. 13 n.

268. εὐχετάασθαι: for εὐχετᾶσθαι, by diektasis (l. 127).

269. ἀγελείης: 'she who brings in the booty'; it should not be forgotten that Athene is a fighting goddess.

270. γεραιάς: cp. l. 87 n.

271–8 = 90–7, with necessary changes; see the notes on the earlier lines.

280. ἔρχευ: Ionic contraction of ἔρχεο (l. 270).

Πάριν: Hektor's brother, also called Alexandros, whose carrying-off of Helen caused the war.

μετελεύσομαι: future of μετέρχομαι.

281. ἐθέλῃσι: lengthened form of the third person of the subjunctive; cp. πίησθα (l. 260 n.).

ὥς κε . . . χάνοι: The κε is difficult to explain; ὡς with the optative for a wish is quite common, but there is no obvious parallel for the particle κε. Nevertheless, it must be a wish. 'May the earth gape for him.' (The effect of κε may be similar to later Attic expressions with πῶς ἄν and the optative expressing what is in effect a wish, e.g. πῶς ἄν . . . θάνοιμι, 'How may I die?', i.e. 'I wish to die', Sophocles, Ajax 388.)

αὖθι: 'on the spot'.

Hektor views Paris with the hearty dislike of a stronger elder brother. Paris has stayed away from the battlefield ever since Aphrodite saved him from being killed by Menelaos in the single combat in book III, by spiriting him away and depositing him in his own house.

282. Ὀλύμπιος: i.e. Zeus.

284. Ἄιδος εἴσω: understand δόμον; 'within the house of Hades'.

285. φρένα: accusative of respect with ἐκλελαθέσθαι.

ἀτέρπου: 'joyless'; the form is odd (see dictionary) and the text uncertain.

ἐκλελαθέσθαι: reduplicated aorist middle.

286. ἡ δὲ μολοῦσα: Hekabe does not answer Hektor's death-wish for his younger brother.

ποτί: πρός, cp. προτί (l. 113).

287. κέκλετο: reduplicated aorist; κέλομαι.

288. κατεβήσετο: sigmatic second aorist, cp. l. 53 n. She went *down* because store-chambers were sunk into the earth.

289. οἱ: dative.

290. Σιδονίων: i.e. Phoenician. Sidon was the chief town of the Phoenicians.

τάς: i.e. the women; Paris must have carried them off, whether as a result of a successful attack on their city, or of piracy is not stated. For the article used as the relative, cp. l. 153.

291. Σιδονίηθεν: 'from Sidonia (the land of Sidon)'.

ἐπιπλώς: aorist participle from ἐπιπλέω.

292. τὴν ὁδόν: adverbial, 'on that journey'.

ἥν: similarly adverbial, 'on which'.

It appears then that Paris did not bring Helen directly to Troy, but sailed back by way of Phoenicia.

295. ἀστὴρ ὥς: ὡς ἀστήρ.

νείατος ἄλλων: It is idiomatic in Greek to use the superlative in this way, i.e. to say 'lowest of the others', where we would say 'lower than the others' or 'lowest of all'.

298–9. Antenor was the most important Trojan outside the royal family. His wife Theano, here priestess of Athene, is the daughter of Kisseus, king of Thrace. Later mythology makes Hekabe also a daughter of Kisseus, and so a sister of Theano, but in the *Iliad* Hekabe's father is called Dymas (XVI 718).

301. ὀλολυγῇ: 'with loud cries'.

305. ῥυσίπτολι: 'defender of the citadel'; cp. l. 88 n.

306. ἆξον: ἄγνυμι.

309. ἦνις ἠκέστας: cp. l. 94 n.

ἱερεύσομεν: subjunctive, cp. l. 230 n.

311. ἀνένευε: 'lifted her head', the Greek sign of refusal. This statement caused some offence to ancient critics, because they assumed it
meant that the image of the goddess in the temple moved its head.
That interpretation is not, however, necessary.

314. Paris built his own house, with the help of experts.

317. ἐγγύθι τε Πριάμοιο καὶ Ἕκτορος: It is clear from these words
that neither Paris nor Hektor lived in the palace of Priam, where there
were (l. 244) fifty rooms for Priam's sons. They had built separate
houses for themselves nearby.

319. ἑνδεκάπηχυ: Miss Lorimer (*Homer and the Monuments*, p. 261)
points out that a length of eleven cubits (about 16 ft.) is not impossible
for a thrusting-spear, but is out of the question for a throwing-spear.

320. πόρκης: a ring to hold the metal point on to the wooden shaft of
the spear.

321. ἐν θαλάμῳ: in the women's quarters of the house.
   ἕποντα: 'attending to'.

322. ἀφόωντα: 'handling'.

323. Ἀργείη: Helen did not come from Argos but from Sparta. However, Homer can use 'Argos' for at least the whole Peloponnese, and
the title 'Argives' for all the Greeks.
   μετά: 'among'.

324. ἀμφιπόλοισι: 'the servants'; the same as the δμῳαί of the previous
line.
   περικλυτὰ ἔργα: 'magnificent handiwork', i.e. spinning and weaving, the main task of the women of the household.

326. δαιμόνιε: 'This word, always found in the vocative, seems to
mean properly one who is under the influence of a δαίμων or unfavourable divine intelligence; that is, one whose actions are either
unaccountable or ill-omened' (Leaf). It is used by a person remonstrating with another; trans. 'Why do you behave like this?' The
word appears three more times before the end of this book.
   καλά: adverbial. 'It is not well that you, etc.'
   χόλον: The mention of 'anger' has caused a great deal of critical discussion; Paris has no cause to be angry with the Trojans. He has re-
mained in his own house ever since the unsuccessful result of his single
combat in book III. The probable but surprising explanation of χόλον
here is that 'anger' is thematic in this situation – of a warrior absenting

himself from the battle. Anger is Achilleus' reason, and so is it Meleagros' in Phoinix' tale in book ix (ix 565). (Compare what is said about *recurrent motifs* in the Introduction, p. xx.) So when Hektor calls to ask Paris to return to the battle, the force of the thematic repetitions common in oral poetry leads him to ascribe 'anger' to Paris when the particular situation is not one of anger.

ἔνθεο: aorist; Attic ἐνέθου.

328. σέο: σοῦ.

331. ἄνα: adverb, used as an imperative; 'up!'

333. 'Since you criticised me deservedly, and not unfairly.' αἶσα is a very ancient word, proved in fact to have been part of the 'Achaean' (see Introduction, p. xiii) dialect, meaning a 'part' or a 'portion'. The αἶσα of a man was what had been allotted to him by destiny, i.e. his fate. κατ' αἶσαν would therefore mean 'in accordance with what I am', ὑπὲρ αἶσαν 'beyond my deserts'.

It is part of the character of Paris that he shows an acceptance of his own faults which disarms criticism.

334. σύνθεο, ἄκουσον: aorist imperatives.

μευ: μου.

335. νεμέσσι: an unusual dative singular of νέμεσις, 'annoyance'.

336. ἄχει: 'depression', at losing the single combat.

339. ἐπαμείβεται: 'alternates', 'comes now to some, now to others'.

340. ἄγε: 'come'; the imperative of ἄγω is used in this way, as an exclamation.

δύω: aorist subjunctive; it is put as another main sentence without connection, instead of as a subordinate clause, just as we might say in English 'But come, wait, let me put on my armour'.

342. Hektor has had enough of Paris. Helen now tries to soothe him.

344. ἐμεῖο: ἐμοῦ.

κυνός: Helen is fairly free with self-criticism.

κακομηχάνου ὀκρυοέσσης: From this, and a few other phrases in Homer, it has been deduced that there was originally a genitive of the -ος declension in -οο, as well as the common forms in -οιο and -ου. The present two-word formula probably began as κακομηχάνοο κρυοέσσης; then, by the pressure of the normal genitive endings and the wrong division of the words, a previously non-existent adjective (ὀκρυόεις) was created.

345. ὄφελε: ὀφείλω (epic ὀφέλλω, l. 350).

348. ἀπόερσε: aorist indicative, because it is part of the past, now impossible, wish begun by ὡς ὄφελε; trans. 'where the wave *would have* swept me away'.

351. ὃς ᾔδη: 'who knew'; as with ἀπόερσε in l. 348, the past tense in the subordinate clause continues the wish of the main sentence.

νέμεσιν: Nemesis in Homer is not divine retribution, as later in Attic tragedy; it is the feeling of disapproval aroused in the onlooker by an improper action.

353. τῷ: 'therefore'.

356. Ἀλεξάνδρου ἕνεκ' ἄτης: through the blind recklessness of Alexandros'. For ἄτη, cp. l. 234 n.

357. ἐπί . . . θῆκε: tmesis.

361. ἐπέσσυται: perfect, 'is eager'.

367-8. These lines establish in advance the sense of doom and tragedy underlying the scene of farewell between Hektor and Andromache.

368. δαμόωσιν: future, for δαμῶσιν (δαμάουσιν) from δάμνημι.

370. εὖ ναιετάοντας: 'comfortable'.

373. πύργῳ ἐφεστήκει: 'was standing on the tower', the one over the Skaian gate.

374. οὐκ ἔνδον: not in the main hall of the house, the μέγαρον.

375. ἐπ' οὐδόν: 'on the threshold of the women's quarters' (the θάλαμος).

376. εἰ δ' ἄγε: εἰ is an interjection. For ἄγε, see note on l. 340; here it is used even with a plural verb. The two together mean something like 'come on now'.

378. ἐς γαλόων ἢ εἰνατέρων: understand δόμον.

γαλόῳ were husband's sisters, εἰνάτερες husband's brothers' wives, both being sisters-in-law.

379. ἐς Ἀθηναίης: understand νηόν.

381. τόν, μῦθον: two objects of προσέειπεν.

390. ἦ: 'she spoke'; past tense of ἠμί, which survived in Attic (particularly Plato) in the common phrases ἦ δ' ὅς, ἦν δ' ἐγώ.

ἀπέσσυτο: aorist, rather than pluperfect, from ἀποσεύω.

391. τὴν αὐτὴν ὁδόν: 'the same way', internal accusative with

ἀπέσσυτο. Hektor retraced his steps from his house towards the Skaian gate and the plain.

393. διεξίμεναι: διεξιέναι.

He was not then going up on to the wall or the tower to find Andromache, but proceeding straight out on to the plain (having failed to find her at home), when she, having left her position on the tower, came running to meet him.

394. πολύδωρος: In heroic society a marriage, like the entertaining of a 'guest-friend' (l. 215 n.), was the occasion of the exchange of gifts, the suitor giving gifts to the parents of the bride (XI 243, πολλὰ δ᾽ ἔδωκε), and the bride bringing gifts (a dowry) from her parents. The more important the connection, the bigger the gifts. Andromache is πολύδωρος.

396. Ἠετίων: repeated from the previous line; it has been attracted into the case of the relative which follows it. Eetion, Andromache's father, had been king of Hypoplakian Thebe; cp. ll. 414 ff.

ὑπὸ Πλάκῳ: Plakos is thought to have been a spur of Mount Ida, near Troy.

397. Κιλίκεσσι: These Kilikes are far away from Kilikia, in the very south of Asia Minor; cp. the Lykia of Pandaros in V 105, which, being near Troy, seems to have no connection at all with the far-away Lykia of Sarpedon and Glaukos.

398. ἔχετο: passive imperfect; 'was married to'.

400. νήπιον αὔτως: 'just a baby'.

403. Ἀστυάνακτα: 'lord of the city'.

406. Cp. l. 253 n.

407. δαιμόνιε: cp. l. 326 n.

410. κέρδιον: 'more profitable', 'better'.

412. ἐπίσπῃς: ἐφέπω.

413. ἄχεα: understand ἔσται.

414. Achilleus had been in command of expeditions against some of the towns around Troy. One of them was Thebe, where the father of Andromache was king. It was on that expedition and from that town that Chryseis was taken captive, she whose return to her father was the occasion for the quarrel between Achilleus and Agamemnon in book I (cp. I 366).

415. Κιλίκων: cp. l. 397 n.
εὖ ναιετάουσαν: 'well-built'.

417. ἐξενάριξε: here in its particular meaning, to strip the armour from a fallen enemy.

419. σῆμα: 'mound'.

420. νύμφαι ὀρεστιάδες: The activity of these mountain nymphs comes as something of a surprise in such a realistic story. Wilamowitz (*Die Ilias und Homer*, p. 313) deduced that the poet is describing a topographical feature known to him in his own day as 'the Grave of Eetion' – a mound with elm trees around it.

αἰγιόχοιο: The *aigis* is a supernatural weapon of the gods, carried by Zeus, but used from time to time by Athene and Apollo. It is normally defensive, like a shield (the popular etymology suggested a goat-skin), but can be used offensively, because when shaken in the face of the enemy it strikes terror in their hearts.

422. "Αιδος εἴσω: cp. l. 284 n.

424. ἐπί: 'in charge of'; the king's sons were acting as cowherds and shepherds outside the town.

425. βασίλευεν: 'was queen'.

426. ἅμ' ἄλλοισι κτεάτεσσιν: The captives in war, being now slaves, were on the same footing as the rest of the booty.

428. πατρός: Andromache's mother's father, from whose house she had long ago gone to marry Eetion, ransomed her from the Greek camp; and it was in his house, not in Thebe, that she then died.
βάλε: with an arrow.
"Αρτεμις: cp. l. 205 n. Sudden death of women was attributed to the arrows of the archer-goddess Artemis.

434. ἐστί ... ἔπλετο: The change of tense is awkward. The first describes the state of the city wall; the second how it seemed to the Greeks on the three occasions described in the next line.
ἐπίδρομον: 'assailable'.

435. τρὶς γάρ: We hear no more of the approach of the Greeks that way. Probably the whole idea is a momentary invention of the poet, to give Andromache an excuse for asking Hektor to stay near the city wall.

436. Αἴαντε δύω: cp. l. 5 n.
'Ιδομενῆα: leader of the Cretans, and one of the foremost heroes of the Greeks.

438. σφιν: dative of the third-person pronoun, 'to them'.

439. ἀνώγει: present tense, created from the perfect ἄνωγα.

442. αἰδέομαι: αἰδώς is a feeling of 'shame', in the sense of being sensitive to what other people will say. The characters of the *Iliad* are much less concerned with what is right or wrong than with their standing in the eyes of other people, i.e. their honour.

443. κακὸς ὥς: cp. ἀστὴρ ὥς (l. 295).
πολέμοιο: with νόσφιν.

444. ἄνωγεν: understand ἀλυσκάζειν.

446. ἐμὸν αὐτοῦ: αὐτοῦ agrees with the genitive implied in ἐμόν.

447–9. These famous lines are said also by Agamemnon in IV 163–5. It is significant for the tone of tragedy in the *Iliad* that even Hektor, the defender, knows that Troy is doomed.

449. ἐϋμμελίω: genitive of the first-declension masculine, ἐϋμμελίης, 'of the fine ash spear'. The -ω ending is parallel to -εω, the Ionic variation on -αο (cp. l. 34 n.).

454. χαλκοχιτώνων: This is a common formulaic epithet of the Achaians, and must refer to defensive armour worn in the Mycenaean age. Miss Lorimer (*Homer and the Monuments*, pp. 201, 209) refers to figures on the Warrior Vase from Mykenai, who seem to be wearing both *chitons* and jerkins strengthened by metal disks. Trans. 'bronze-clad'.

455. ἐλεύθερον ἦμαρ: cp. δούλιον ἦμαρ (l. 463).
ἀπούρας: aorist participle, an interesting form in which the original digamma (ἀπο-Ϝρας) has been vocalised as a *v*.

456. ἐν Ἄργει: i.e. Greece.
πρὸς ἄλλης: 'at the command of another woman, a mistress'.

457. Μεσσηΐδος ἢ Ὑπερείης: 'from the spring Messeis or Hypereia'; Hypereia was in Thessaly (II 734); Messeis either also in Thessaly (Strabo, 432) or at Therapnai near Sparta (Pausanias, III 20.1).

458. πολλά: adverbial.

459. εἴπῃσι: εἴπῃ; the subjunctive shows expectation about the future, and is less definite than the future ἐρέει (l. 462). Trans. 'will say'.

463. ἀμύνειν: explanatory infinitive, after τοιοῦδ' ἀνδρός.

464. κατακαλύπτοι: a wish.

465. σῆς τε βοῆς σοῦ θ' ἑλκηθμοῖο: 'your cries when you are taken away by force'. Hektor is thinking of the fate of the women of a

captured city, referred to by Nestor in II 356, where he speaks of the Greeks avenging the 'struggles and lamentations of Helen'.

468. πατρὸς φίλου: 'his father'; φίλος with parts of the body, possessions or close relatives is approximately the same as the personal pronoun; cp. l. 471.

ἀτυχθείς: 'dismayed', 'distressed'; but here with an object as if it was an active verb of fearing.

470. δεινόν: adverbial with νεύοντα.

474. κύσε: κυνέω.
πῆλε: πάλλω.

475. δέ: apodotic; cp. l. 146 n.

478. βίην ἀγαθόν: cp. βοὴν ἀγαθόν (l. 12).
ἶφι: 'by force'; -φι is the old instrumental case-ending (cp. l. 510 n.), here with the noun (F)ἶς (Latin vis).

479. εἴποι: a wish in the prayer.
πολλόν: (πολύ) adverbial.

480. ἐκ πολέμου ἀνιόντα: This must be describing an understood object of εἴποι, namely αὐτόν. The expression has been made awkward by the putting of the words of the onlooker into direct speech. εἴποι αὐτὸν πατρὸς ἀμείνονα εἶναι would not be so difficult.
φέροι, χαρείη: optatives continuing after εἴποι.

481. χαρείη: from the aorist ἐχάρην.

484. δακρυόεν: adverbial; 'half laughing, half crying'.

486. μοι: ethic dative, 'please'.

487. ὑπὲρ αἶσαν: 'beyond what is destined'.

488. μοῖραν δέ: μοῖραν (= αἶσαν) is stressed as the first word; 'but as for fate'.
πεφυγμένον ἔμμεναι: periphrastic perfect infinitive middle, with present sense; i.e. 'is in a state of having escaped' means 'is free from'.
ἀνδρῶν: with τινά.

489. μὲν: μήν.
τὰ πρῶτα: adverbial, 'when once he is born'.

490. τὰ σ' αὐτῆς: cp. ἐμὸν αὐτοῦ (l. 446).

493. ἐγγεγάασιν: ἐγγίγνομαι.

496. θαλερόν: 'large'.

500. γόον: 'wept for'; this strange form seems not to be from the verb γοάω, but created straight from the noun γόος.

501. ἔφαντο: 'thought'.

Hektor's household mourns him while he is still alive; and the reader gets the impression that this is the last farewell between Hektor and Andromache. In fact it is not so, for Hektor returns to Troy at VII 310, and there follows a brief truce in the latter part of book VII. From the beginning of book VIII, however, Hektor does not again return to Troy.

503 ff. The poet does not end the book on the note of family sorrow. Life must go on; the war must continue; and with a strong contrast we turn to the excited and selfish figure of Paris, who has done as he was asked, and summoned up the energy to return to the battle.

505. ποσὶ κραιπνοῖσι πεποιθώς: 'moving swiftly and confidently'.

506–11. The simile of the high-spirited horse galloping into the fields is used in exactly the same words for the return of Hektor to the battle in XV 263–8. This is a good example of the effect of formulaic composition (see Introduction, p. xvii). It is incorrect to assume that one of the passages must be an imitation of the other; the poet has simply used the same material on two occasions.

506. στατός: 'stalled', i.e. a horse that has been kept in the stable; a stallion.

ἀκοστήσας: 'fully fed with barley', and thus spirited.

507. θείη: θέω.

πεδίοιο: genitive with θείη, of the ground covered (cp. l. 2).

508. ποταμοῖο: a sort of partitive genitive; 'in the waters of the river'.

509. ἀμφί: adverb, 'on both sides'; it can also be treated as an example of tmesis with ἀΐσσονται; the effect is the same.

510. ἀγλαίηφι: The suffix -φι seems in the earliest time to have been an instrumental or locative case-ending, but its use had been greatly widened in the epic dialect. Here ἀγλαίηφι is obviously the exact equivalent of the dative case; cp. ἶφι (l. 478).

πεποιθώς: 'in the confidence of'.

511. By a vivid change of construction, the subject (ὁ δέ of l. 510) turns into the object ἑ.

νομόν: 'pasture'; note the different accent from νόμος, 'law'.

ἵππων: Virgil, in copying these lines, took these to be the females, the mares (*equarum*, *Aeneid* XI 494).

516. ὀάριζε: ὄαρος is confidential talk, as between husband and wife.

518. ἠθεῖε: 'accustomed', 'trusted'; from the same word as ἤθεα (l. 511). Trans. 'brother'.

ἐσσύμενον: (σεύω) 'in a hurry'.

519. ἐναίσιμον: adverbial.

Paris thinks only of himself, and tries by this unnecessary self-criticism to improve his brother's opinion of him.

521. τοι ... ἔργον ... μάχης: 'your efforts in the battle'. Hektor realises that Paris has been hurt by his criticisms in ll. 326 ff. and speaks more kindly. This is all very true to nature.

523. τὸ δέ: not the article with ἐμὸν κῆρ, but a neuter accusative with ἄχνυται, acting as antecedent to the ὅτε clause; 'my heart grieves *at that*'.

526. ἴομεν: subjunctive.

τὰ δέ: 'these questions', i.e. 'if I have been unfair'.

ἀρεσσόμεθα: future, 'we will make good'. Agamemnon uses this same expression in IV 362 when he wishes to take back some unfair remarks he has made to Odysseus.

528. κρητῆρα στήσασθαι ἐλεύθερον: 'to set up a mixing-bowl (for a feast) in freedom, in honour of the gods'.

529. ἐλάσαντας: accusative, in agreement with the understood subject of στήσασθαι.

Indexes

I. GREEK INDEX

(a) *Word-endings:*

-ᾰ (nominative), I 175
-ᾰ (vocative), I 159
-ᾱο (genitive), I 75
-ᾰται, -ᾰτο (for -νται, -ντο), I 239
-ᾱων (genitive), I 152
-δε, I 19
-εαι (2nd sing., pres. and fut. indic., middle/passive), I 74
-εμεν (infinitive), I 78
-εν (for -ησαν), I 57
-εο (imperative), I 214
-εω (genitive), I 1
-εων (genitive), I 273
-ηα (accusative), II 3
-ηαι (2nd sing., subj., middle/passive), I 32
-ηος (genitive), I 1
-ηοι, -ης (dative), I 26, 89
-θι, III 3
-μεναι (infinitive), I 98
-οιο (genitive), I 19
-οο (genitive), II 518
-φι, II 363

(b) *Words:*

ἀγαθός, I 131
ἀγγελίης, III 206
ἄγε, I 62
ἀδινός, II 87
αἰ, I 66
αἰγίς, I 202
αἰδώς, VI 442
αἶσα, III 59

ἀκέων, ἀκήν, IV 22, III 95
ἀμβρόσιος, II 19
ἄμμι, II 137
ἀμφιελίσσας, II 165
ἀμφικύπελλον, I 584
ἄνεῳ, II 323
ἀπούρας, I 356
ἄρ, I 8
ἀραρυῖα, III 331
ἀργυρόηλον, II 45
ἄτη, I 412

βίη Ἡρακληείη, etc., II 658
βοὴν ἀγαθός, II 408
βουλή, II 53, 405 ff.

δαιμόνιε, I 561
δέγμενος, δέχθαι, II 137
διαπρήσσω, III 14

ἑ, I 236
ἔα, IV 321
ἔασι(ν), II 125
ἔθεν, I 114
εἰ (exclamatory), I 302
εἵσας, I 306
εἴσατο ('went'), IV 138
ἑκατόμβη, I 65
ἔλε(ν), IV 457
ἔλπομαι, III 112
ἐμέθεν, II 26
ἐμεῖο, I 174
ἔμεν, IV 299
ἔμεναι, III 40

ἔμμεναι, I 117
ἐνί, I 30
ἔο, II 239
ἑός, V 318
ἔπεα πτερόεντα, I 201
ἔρδω, II 306
ἔσαν, IV 438
ἔσκε, VI 19
ἐσσί, I 176
εὔχομαι, II 82
ἔω, I 119
ἐών, II 27

ἦ ('he spoke'), I 219
ἦ μέν, I 77
ἠέριος, I 497
ἤλυθον, I 152
ἠΰς, II 653
ἠΰτε, II 87

θαλερός, III 53
θέμις, II 73
θοάς (νῆας), I 12

ἰάχω, V 302
ἵπποι, II 1
ἶφι, I 38

καὶ γάρ, II 377
κᾱλός, III 328
κάρη κομόωντες, II 11
κε (+ future indicative), I 139
κερτόμιος, V 419
κήρ, II 302
κήρυκες, I 321
κιχείω, etc., I 26
κρητήρ, I 470
κύδιστος, II 412

λιγύς, I 248

μεμαώς, I 590
μέμηλε, II 25
μέροπες, I 250

μευ, I 37
μηρία, I 40
μιν, I 29
μόρος, II 155

νέμεσις, II 223
νήπιος, II 38
νυ, I 28
νῶι, V 34

ξεῖνος, VI 215

ὄζος Ἄρηος, II 540
οἱ (dative), I 72
ὁμοίιος, IV 444
ὅρκια τάμνειν, II 124
ὅ τε (= ὅτι), I 244
οὐδὲ γὰρ οὐδέ, V 22
οὖλος, II 6
οὖν (following ἐπεί or ὡς), I 57
οὖτα, IV 525
ὀφέλλω (= ὀφείλω), I 353
ὄχ᾽ ἄριστος, I 69

πάντοσ᾽ ἐΐσην, III 347
πεδίοιο, VI 2
περ, I 131
ποτί, II 137
προτί, III 116
πυκινός, πυκνός, II 55

ῥα, I 8

σέθεν, IV 127
σεῖο, V 411
σέο, VI 328
σεῦ, II 27
σκῆπτρον, II 46
σπονδαὶ ἄκρητοι, II 341
συλάω, VI 28
σφεας, II 96
σφι(ν), III 300
σφισί, IV 2
σφωέ, I 8

σφῶι, I 336
·σφῶιν, I 257
σφωίν, I 338
σχέτλιος, III 414

ταί, III 5
τε (in proverbial or general state-
    ments), I 63
τέμενος, VI 194
τευ, II 388
τίη, VI 55
τίκτω, II 513
τοί, I 447
τοι, I 28
τῶ (adverb), II 250

ὑπόδρα ἰδών, I 148

φάλος, III 362
φάτο, ἔφατο, I 33
φίλος, IV 313

χαλκοχιτώνων, I 371
Χάριτες, V 338
χιτών, II 42
χραισμεῖν, I 28
χρύσεος, IV 2

ὦκα, III 14
Ὠκεανός, I 423
ὥς, I 33

II. ENGLISH INDEX

Accusative of respect, II 58
Achaians, I 2
Achilleus, I 54, 408
Address by the poet in second person, IV 127
Aeolic, p. xii
Agamemnon, I 31, II 478, IV 154, VI 54
Aiantes, IV 273
Antenor, III 148
Antilochos, v 565
Apocope, I 143
Apodotic δέ, I 58
Apollo
  ἑκάεργος, I 147
  ἑκατηβελέτης, I 75
  ἕκατος, I 385
  ἑκηβόλος, I 14
  Λυκηγενής, IV 101
  Σμινθεύς, I 39
Arcado-Cyprian, p. xii
Argives, I 2
Argos, III 75
Arming, III 330–8
Armour
  breastplate, III 360, IV 132, V 113
  greaves, I 17
  ζωστήρ, IV 132
  μίτρη, IV 137
  shield, II 388–9, V 796, VI 117
Arms, bow, IV 105–26
Article
  as demonstrative pronoun, I 9
  as relative, I 36

Athene, I 55, IV 128, v 290
  ἀγελείη, IV 128
  Ἀλαλκομενηΐς, IV 8
  Ἀτρυτώνη, II 157
  γλαυκῶπις, I 206
  Τριτογένεια, IV 515
Augury, II 353

Bronze, II 417

Caesura, p. xxii
Characterisation, p. xv
Chariots, IV 297
Cheiron, IV 219
Correption, p. xxv

Danaans, I 2
Diaeresis, p. xxii
Diektasis, I 31
Digamma, p. xiii
Diomedes, IV 365, 390, 401–21

Elision, p. xxv
Epigonoi, p. xvi, IV 405
Expansion denoting importance, II 455–83

Fighting, style of, III 15
Foreshadowing, v 480
Formulaic composition, pp. xvii–xxi
Free will, I 207, IV 104
Frequentative tenses, I 490

Gnomic aorist, I 218

Gods, pp. xvi–xvii
  givers of particular skills, I 72, II
    827, V 51
  present in a scene of enhanced
    awareness, II 279, 791
  punish human presumption, II
    594–600, VI 129–41, 200
  simultaneously physical and figur-
    ative, V 842

Hebe, IV 2
Hektor, VI 281, 521
Helen, III 128, 180, VI 344
  Ἀργείη, II 161
Hera, I 55, II 15, IV 50
  βοῶπις, IV 50
Hermes
  ἀργειφόντης, II 103
  διάκτορος, II 103
Hiatus, p. xxv

Imperative from future stem, III 103
Invented names, IV 394–5, V 59, VI 18
Ionic, p. xii–xiv
Iris, V 353
Iron, IV 123

Kronos ἀγκυλομήτης, II 205

Language of gods and language of
  men, I 403, II 813
Lengthening of syllable containing
  short vowel
  before liquids, V 83, 302
  before lost consonants, III 172, V
    343
  'by position', p. xxiv
Libation, I 471

Materialism, VI 234–6
Menelaos, II 405 ff., IV 127, V 564,
  VI 51
Meriones, V 59

Nestor, I 247, II 79
  Γερήνιος ἱππότα, II 336

Odysseus, I 311, II 169, 260, III 192,
  216, IV 331
  πτολίπορθος, II 278

Paris, III 59, VI 519
Patronymics
  in -ιαδης, I 1
  in -ιδης, VI 13
  in -ιος, VI 5
  in -ιων, VI 267
Perfect participle in -ων (Aeolic),
  II 222
Prayer-form, I 39–41, V 117
Prothetic vowel, II 22
Pylos, II 591–602

Reduplicated aorist, I 100
Ring-form, I 259–74, IV 370–400,
  V 800–13, VI 129–41

Sacrifice, I 458–66, II 421–32
Sarpedon, V 480
Scholia, I 343
Seven against Thebes, p. xv, II 564,
  IV 365, 377, V 116, VI 223
Sigmatic second aorist, I 428
Similes, IV 422–6, V 522–6
Stock epithets, p. xvii, III 37
Stripping the dead of their armour,
  VI 28
Subjunctives
  in -ωμι, -ησθα, -ησι, I 324
  with short vowel, I 67
Synizesis, p. xxv

Themes, recurrent motifs, etc., p.
  xx, I 402, II 356, V 390, 436–42,
  VI 326
Tmesis, I 25

Zeus, I 528–30, 551, IV 6